THE INFIDEL SEA

Travels in North Cyprus

THE INFIDEL SEA

Travels in
North Cyprus

Oliver Burch

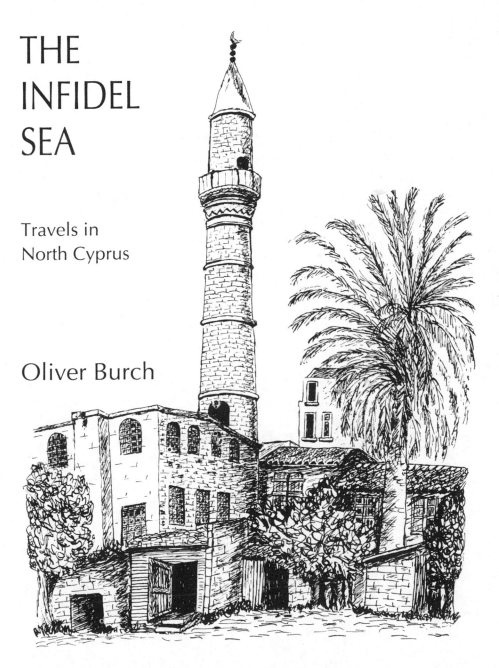

ASHFORD, BUCHAN & ENRIGHT
Southampton

Published by Ashford, Buchan & Enright
(an imprint of Martins Publishers Ltd),
1 Church Road, Shedfield, Hampshire SO3 2HW

British Library Cataloguing in Publication Data

Burch, Oliver *1951–*
    The infidel sea : travels in North Cyprus.
    1. Cyprus. Turkish-occupied region. Description & travel
    I. Title
    915.645044

    ISBN 1-85253-232-7

Printed in Great Britain by Hartnolls Ltd, Bodmin, Cornwall
Typeset in 11 on 12pt Plantin by Inforum Typesetting

CONTENTS

Map of North Cyprus   vi
Preface   vii
Acknowledgements   viii

Chapter 1   Night Flight   1
Chapter 2   Lapithos and Kormakiti   13
Chapter 3   Kyrenia, St Hilarion and the Lusignans   31
Chapter 4   Morphou and the West   53
Chapter 5   Bellapais and Kythrea   69
Chapter 6   Famagusta   83
Chapter 7   Salamis   105
Chapter 8   The Karpas Peninsula   117
Chapter 9   Maronites and Kantara   135
Chapter 10   Turkish Nicosia   153
Chapter 11   Barbarism   175
Chapter 12   The Mountains of Kyrenia   181
Chapter 13   Never Sleep Under a Fig Tree   199
Chapter 14   Sourp Magar and Antiphonitis   217
Chapter 15   The Mesaoria   223
Chapter 16   Buffavento   233
Chapter 17   Beneath the Tree of Idleness   247
Historical Chronology   255
Glossary and Abbreviations   259
Bibliography   263
Index   267

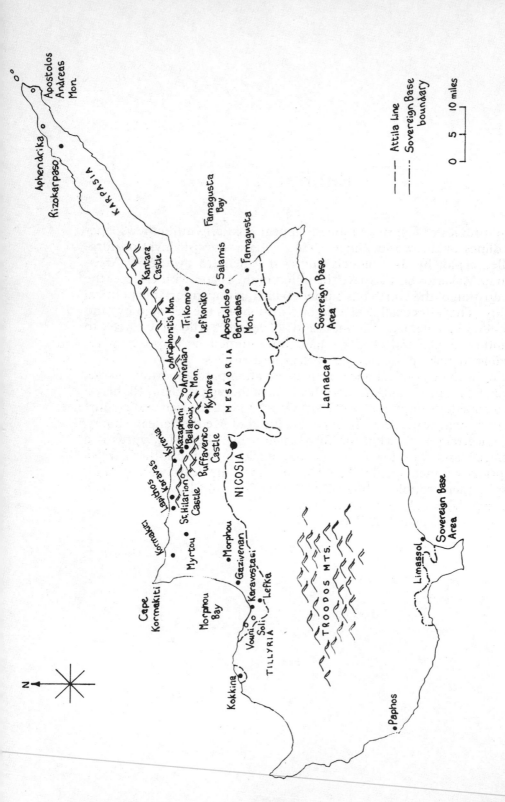

The island of Cyprus, divided by the Attila line

PREFACE

The troubles of Cyprus no longer appear regularly in the newspaper headlines of the world. Since 1974, when a Turkish invasion forestalled a plot by the colonels' junta in Athens to overthrow Archbishop Makarios and achieve the union of the island with Greece, the occupation of the North has hardened into an uncomfortable political reality. The Turks call it *taksim*, or partition. As the years go by, and talks end in stalemate, the thousands of refugees who were forced to abandon homes and property have little immediate prospect of returning to pick up the threads of their former lives.

This is not a political book. It does not attempt to apportion blame, much less suggest a solution to this long-standing problem. Rather, it is an outsider's impression of a society grounded in a rich and colourful past, living on one of the most beautiful of Mediterranean shores, yet uncertain as to what the future will bring. Turkish Cyprus is a besieged land, with few friends in the outside world, but the Turkish Cypriots we met openly shared their hopes and fears with us and, despite their troubles, showed us the warmth and hospitality which they have always bestowed on strangers.

Such is the custom in Cyprus.

Oliver Burch
April 1990

ACKNOWLEDGEMENTS

I am not the first writer to acknowledge a great debt to the scholarly Claude Delaval Cobham, one-time Commissioner of Larnaca, who in the early years of this century compiled the remarkable *Excerpta Cypria: Materials for a History of Cyprus*. This collection of extracts from the writings of 80 historians and travellers in Cyprus, translated from a dozen languages and covering more than eighteen centuries, deserves to be republished. From my point of view, the hard work had all been done.

I would also like to thank Joan my wife for her hard work with the manuscript of The Infidel Sea, and the rest of my family for their patience and support.

For Salih

CHAPTER ONE

NIGHT FLIGHT

On a wet afternoon in February we found ourselves in a departure lounge at Heathrow Airport, crowded with passengers bound for Izmir in Asia Minor. There appeared to be few tourists present, for we were surrounded by thickset, moustached men and short, head-scarfed matrons with woollen stockings who sat amidst a clutter of wicker baskets and brown paper parcels while small children with liquid black eyes rushed around the feet of their indulgent elders. The crowd had an unmistakably Mediterranean air and were it not for the language spoken, we would have taken them for Greeks waiting for an island ferry. In fact, they were almost all Cypriots who had been visiting relatives in England, and who were now returning to 'The Turkish State of North Cyprus'. Unrecognised by any other country, they, and we, were obliged to fly first to the Turkish mainland and then on to the island by Turkish Airlines.

A delay of one hour was announced, due to a technical fault with the aircraft. The middle-aged man with a weather-beaten face sitting opposite me took a string of worry beads from the pocket of his leather jacket and resignedly began to flick the little pieces of amber one by one along the string – not exactly the Greek *komboloyia* these, but the Turkish *tespi*, with 99 beads divided into three groups, one for each of the sacred names of Allah. Outside on the tarmac, two men in waterproof overalls balanced on step ladders, working on a flight deck window at the directions of one of the aircrew.

I had spent many cold hours through the winter, under the great dome of the British Library, reading the accounts of earlier travellers to Cyprus. From writers and voyagers of the ancient world, crusaders, pilgrims, Venetian and Greek monks, British empire builders, the 'Governor and Company of Merchants of England trading into the Levant Seas', to United Nations soldiers, they had all been amazed at the fertility and beauty of an island which had once been known as Makaria, the Blessed. But Cyprus, it seemed, had almost always been a place of conflict, an outpost of a series of western civilisations which met the shock of more primeval forces from the East which flowed

1

around it like a hostile sea, sometimes overwhelming the island by force of arms, more often changing the lives of its people in subtler ways. Thus the earlier Hellenic city-states were subjugated by the might of the Persian Empire, but they had already been changed by the Phoenicians and others who had come peacefully among them, bringing the worship of the Semitic lord Adon and their moon goddess Astarte. In time the Persians lost their power and the Greek and Roman empires of the West held sway, although Cyprus remained famous for its luxurious eastern customs. But in the centuries of Byzantium the tide turned again, and for generations the island was preyed upon by Arab pirates whom the Emperor in Constantinople had no power to check. Even now the word 'Saracen' in Cypriot folklore implies a force of darkness, something consummately evil. First Crusaders and later Venetians held Cyprus as the last outpost of Christendom, always threatened by the rising power of Islam. The chronicler Leontios Makhairas wrote of 'A poor island and an orphaned realm, built up on a rock in the midst of the sea and surrounded by the infidels.'

The Venetians, as had long been feared, lost their prize to the Ottoman Turks who were moving inexorably west, and the news sent a shiver of horror around Christian Europe. The Turks built minarets on to the Gothic churches of the Crusaders, brought their own settlers and introduced oriental manners and customs which remain to this day. Even the Turkish tide turned in time, and as it slowly receded the British obtained Cyprus, by a combination of opportunism and good fortune. Whether Britain retained sovereignty over Cyprus, or it was ceded to Greece, or it became independent, the Greeks of the island might reasonably have expected a future in which their land was firmly rooted in the West. But in 1974 the infidel sea betrayed them again, and in the darkness the 'treacherous sea of Kyrenia' brought a second Turkish invasion.

All of this was a very great over-simplification. Even then I knew that there were more complex forces at work in Cyprus than the simple ebb and flow of power between Asia and Europe. I had been surprised to learn that the Greek Cypriots, after harsh treatment by the Franks and Venetians, had welcomed the first Turkish invasion of 1570 with open arms. But, even as a western European, I was aware that my own psyche contained a racial memory, a legacy of those long border struggles between civilisations, cultures and religions, an almost instinctive fear of malevolent forces which come from the East. This racial memory can be found all over Europe. 'He's a Tartar,' they say in England of a man with a dangerous temper. 'There are Moors on the coast,' they say in Spain, when times are troubled.

During the Second World War, the German authorities in occupied Greece produced a propaganda poster designed to play directly on this fear. It showed two heads: one, the helmeted likeness of the goddess Athena, represented wisdom, civilisation, logic, the supposed values of the West; the other was barbarous and evil, dark-skinned and leering from under a Red Army cap. 'Three thousand years of civilisation in peril' read the caption of the poster, which was intended to discredit the ELAS guerrillas and their supposedly close connections with the Soviet Union. But the second face, plainly central Asian, with high cheekbones and slanting eyes, might as easily have been that of a Turk.

When the Turks first rode their shaggy ponies from those wild steppes and deserts beyond the Oxus, and brought their horsehair standards into the West, Europeans feared their lust for conquest, their military prowess and their cruelty in war. Later, when their empire was established, we sneered at them for their indolence and ineptitude at administration, yet at the same time we remained afraid of their cruelty. A whole series of Victorian travellers adventured into the Sultan's domains, to return and delight their readers in England with stories of Pashas of One, Two and Three Tails, outlandish and romantic dress and strange oriental courtesies. Almost without exception, they patronised and disdained the Turks who lived amidst the ruins of classical glory. Thus Spencer wrote of:

> . . . the undrained marsh, the sand-choked river, the grass-grown market place, the deserted field, the crumbling fortress, the broken arch. Stagnation, death-like stagnation has ever characterised the rule of the race of Othman.
>
> (Edmund Spencer, *Travels in European Turkey*)

There was a short period, following the heroic resistance of Osman Pasha against the Russian armies at Plevna in 1877, when a wave of admiration swept the British public for Turkey's desperate stand against the aggressor. (It was during the subsequent realignment of frontiers arranged at the Congress of Berlin that Great Britain managed to pick up the island of Cyprus). But as the nineteenth century drew to a close, Turkey was once more the 'sick man of Europe'. The news of the dreadful massacres of Armenians instigated by the paranoid Abdul Hamid, who was characterised by his own people as the Red Sultan or Abdul the Damned, only confirmed the West in its opinion that this outdated and barbaric empire must somehow be dismantled.

The Young Turks' revolution and the subsequent efforts of Kemal Ataturk to build a modern European state may have finally convinced the former subject peoples that Turkish imperialism was at an end. But could it be considered by the West to be a civilised, cultured nation? Any country so dominated by its army fulfilled few of the criteria of democracy, even when a military dictatorship was not in direct control. At the time of our visit to Turkish-occupied Cyprus, the Communist party was illegal in Turkey and much normal political activity was banned. Amnesty International reported regularly on the use of torture in Turkish police stations and prisons. Racial minorities and religious fundamentalists – any movement which could conceivably threaten the unity of Kemal's new Turkey – were brutally suppressed. All these shortcomings of modern Turkey were regularly reported in the world's press. Many British people, who would now be ashamed to confess themselves to be racially prejudiced against Negroes, for instance, would, if they troubled to think much about it, have to admit that they held a low opinion of the Turkish people. The codenaming of the invasion of Cyprus as 'Operation Attila' had done nothing to counter the doubt and mistrust of Europeans. Although I had met very few Turks, and had never visited their country, I was aware that it might not be easy to view the Turks in Cyprus objectively.

In the case of the Greeks, however, I instinctively felt I would be on familiar ground. Everything I had read indicated that the customs and lifestyle of the Greek Cypriots would correspond very closely to those of the mainland Greeks we knew and liked so well. I even understood a little of their language, although the Cypriot accent – dialect, one might say – which I had heard in London, had seemed impenetrable.

The hour passed somehow and a further delay was announced. I had no book and crowd-watching was the only possible way to kill time. There were in fact five other non-Cypriots in the lounge, all of whom we later encountered in Kyrenia: a pair of overtly homosexual men, possibly hoping that they would be more welcome in the Turkish sector than the Greek (they weren't), a middle-aged Scottish couple (he a tyre fitting bay manager and she a spiritualist), and an elderly Englishwoman with a badly fitting, conical-shaped wig, whom we gradually realised to be totally insane.

A gold-embossed portrait of Mustapha Kemal adorned the front bulkhead of the aircraft, with the quotation: 'The future is in the skies.' A cabin staff of very young stewardesses, under the command of a sulky blonde of about 35, watched us board without enthusiasm. The Englishwoman with the wig, plump and irritable, heaved herself into the seat next to us, leaned over and glared at my younger son who was occupying the window seat he had booked.

'That's my seat,' she complained. 'I specifically asked for a window seat.'

'Are you sure?' said my wife. 'Perhaps your seat is in another row. You see my little boy was so keen to sit by a window that we specially came early. Look, his boarding pass matches the seat number.'

'No, no. He's in my seat. I definitely asked them for a window seat. Nobody cares about the elderly these days. I don't see why I shouldn't have the seat I asked for just because a little boy wants it.'

'Look here,' said Joan. 'Let me see your boarding pass, this should be simple enough. Yes, there you are, this is for about eight rows further back in the cabin. Why don't you try there? It should be reserved for you.'

No such luck, for the Cypriots, whom we came to know as the kindest, most hospitable people in the world, but who never queue or do anything in an organised way, had all ignored the numbered tickets and taken the seats nearest to hand. The old lady relapsed into muttering to herself, but made no move. Then Malcolm, the diminutive occupant of the contested place, surprised her by offering her a sweet. She took it and appeared to cheer up.

'He's actually quite a nice little boy, isn't he?' she confided to Joan.

'Yes, well I've always thought so.'

Somewhere over France, with the light fading rapidly, her mood changed again.

'They're trying to kill me,' she whispered into Joan's ear.

'What!'

'Assassins! Terrorists! They're everywhere nowadays you know. They've already tried to attack us. The aeroplane was delayed because it had a bullet hole.'

As Joan struggled to take this in, the woman's glance fell on another passenger walking down the aisle.

'Are you the captain? Is there a policeman on board?'

The immaculately suited and beautifully mannered Turk was startled.

'I'm very sorry, madam, but I'm not a member of the crew. Can I be of assistance?'

'Yes, I want to speak to the captain. There's a terrorist on this aeroplane. And this woman's trying to steal my bag. I want to know if there's a policeman here.'

As we all stared at her in amazement, she jumped up, gathered up her hand luggage and began to make her way rapidly up the aisle towards the flight deck. The chief stewardess with the sour expression managed to intercept her by the portrait of Kemal. Only odd fragments of the conversation drifted back to us; she wanted a security man to watch her hand luggage while she went to the lavatory. Joan, it

5

seemed, was planning to steal it. The expression on the stewardess's face changed from merely bad-tempered to positively murderous. The second officer was called from the flight deck and a long argument ensued. Eventually the old lady disappeared into the lavatory with all her baggage around her and somehow locked herself inside. The second officer glared at the closed door, chewing his moustache. The stewardess said something in Turkish which sounded vicious to say the least.

All across Europe she was up and down with problems and complaints. The lights of Istanbul were visible below when she began to moan that she only had five pounds in hard currency with her. She hadn't brought any more lest the terrorists steal it. Would it be enough to pay for a taxi from the airport to Kyrenia?

'Probably not,' everyone answered sadistically. It now seemed quite plausible that there might be a series of desperate men following her with murder in their hearts. I would not have required much additional provocation myself. The second officer and the chief stewardess continued to hold regular conferences at the head of the aisle, occasionally throwing ferocious glances at her, looks of loathing to which she seemed quite oblivious.

A burst of clapping arose from the Turkish Cypriots as we touched down at Izmir (had something less been expected?). It seemed difficult to associate these modern concrete surroundings, almost as cold and wet as Heathrow had been, with the ancient city of Smyrna, Greek for thousands of years before the disaster of 1922. But as we huddled in our coats against the wind blowing across the harshly lit tarmac, old photographs of oily clouds of black smoke rising above sacked houses, newsreel film of refugees leaving in their thousands, and portraits of Venizelos, Lloyd George, Constantine and Kemal sprang unbidden to mind. Now Greek Smyrna is Turkish Izmir, still known for its figs, but unknown to us, for half an hour later we were continuing our journey in another aircraft to Cyprus.

A tall, somewhat overweight youth sat next to me, for we had managed to evade the dreadful old lady. He looked exactly the European's image of the 'warlike Turk', painted perhaps by Eugène Delacroix, with curling black hair and moustache, prominent nose and large flashing eyes. We had all tired of the journey and the delays by this time, but he should have been exhausted, for he had driven himself from Miami, where he was a student, to New York, flown the Atlantic and come straight on from London, almost without a break. But he had reached a state of fatigue beyond ordinary sleepiness, and wanted to talk. He taught me some useful Turkish phrases which I added to the list in my pocket book (which was later to cause so much amusement) and answered a host of questions.

His family lived in the northern sector of Nicosia, which the Turks call Lefkosa and the Greeks call Lefkosia. (Nicosia, incidentally, is a Frankish name, used by foreigners rather than native Cypriots on the whole.) He had been away for two years at university and was now coming home to undertake his National Service in the army of occupation. As a Cypriot, he would serve for two years, as opposed to the eighteen months served by a mainland Turk. I tentatively wondered if life in the Turkish army would be tough. During basic training, yes, but after that he expected to be an officer, and that, apparently, made all the difference. How many troops were stationed in North Cyprus? About 25,000. (This roughly tallied with independent estimates.) We would find the army friendly and helpful to foreigners, but should be careful about misunderstandings close to restricted areas. Two young Cypriot boys were recently shot by a sentry while swimming in a military zone.

The conversation inevitably turned to politics, Rauf Denktash, the Turkish Cypriot leader, and the possibility of a settlement. In this young man's eyes, such a solution seemed very distant indeed.

'No one in the Turkish sector is really interested in any form of reunification for Cyprus,' he stated shortly. 'As far as we are concerned the Line can stay for ever. The issues we are concerned with are the allocation of housing and land since 1974 and settlement from the mainland. A lot of Cypriots object to that.'

'Why?'

'You'll see. Some of the settlers are very primitive people. Nomads from the east, near the Iranian border. All they understand are sheep and goats. They don't fit in here.'

It became evident that he had never been in direct contact with a Greek at all. He had been twelve years of age at the time of the Turkish invasion, and during the earlier years of his childhood the two communities had lived virtually as separate armed camps. His family would have found their lives at risk, he claimed, even if their car had broken down close to a Greek area. He believed there was still some Greek population in the Karpas peninsula, the long pan-handle stretching far out to the north-east, which the Turks call Kirpasa. And there were several villages of Maronites in the Turkish sector, Greek-speaking Catholics whose ancestors came from Syria many centuries ago. But he personally had never met or held a conversation with a genuine Greek. After his military service he was assured of a good job in his father's citrus exporting business.

I craned my head to look at a sprinkling of lights as we banked over the Cyprus coast.

'There's Kyrenia,' said my neighbour. 'Now we are crossing the Five Finger mountain, Pentadactylos, and we will come down to Ercan in a few minutes.'

Ercan International Airport was a stop-gap measure: a disused Second World War field known as Tymbou, which the Turks rapidly pressed into service after 1974. It stands only a short distance from the Attila Line and was shortly afterwards superseded by a purpose-built airport on the new ring road around the north of Levkosa. Even by today's standards security was tight, and there was an armed guard around the aircraft before it had come to a halt. At this point the fearsome old lady proved that she was perhaps saner than she appeared. For the last half-hour of the flight she had been pestering the cabin staff for a wheelchair at the airport and, sure enough, it was waiting at the foot of the steps. First out of the aircraft, she sprinted down and flung herself into the chair to be wheeled rapidly over the tarmac, through passport control and customs before everyone else, and, we fervently hoped, out of our lives.

It was one o'clock in the morning, the night was cold and we were weary. The queue stretched outside the arrivals building and moved dreadfully slowly. Soldiers patrolled in pairs, their breath steaming under the glare of sodium lamps; marionette figures in shiny red and white steel helmets, carbines at the slant, their white-gaitered feet slowly pacing in step, looking left, looking right in unison. I reflected that I had never yet seen an airport which looked attractive at night and tried not to feel discouraged. There were three passport desks: two for civilians and one for soldiers returning from leave. The details of each passport were being laboriously tapped out at a terminal and compared with some central list in the computer's memory. Whom were they looking for, I wondered. Infiltrating EOKA gunmen? Deserters? The PLO? Unsympathetic journalists or writers? At last we reached the desk. Oliver and Joan Burch, two children, Malcolm and Steven, nine and ten years old. A close scrutiny of previous Greek stamps in the passports. Then the computer decided that it would accept us and the official's hand reached for the visa stamp.

'No, please don't stamp our passports.' The 'Kibris Turk' stamp subsequently debars one from entry to Greece or the Republic of Cyprus. The official shrugged, stamped separate visa forms and tucked them into the backs of the passports before pushing them across the desk to us.

'Mr Burch? Have you had a good journey? Welcome to Cyprus.' The driver was waiting as promised. In a daze we piled our luggage into a minibus and were off at breakneck speed, vaguely aware of ugly billboarding, dusty areas of wasteland and the lights of the city at a distance as we made a bewildering series of turns. Each road junction was guarded by ASIZ, the military police, their white gloves and webbing showing up brightly in the headlamp beams as they yawned their way through the long hours. Then came a sign for Girne, as Kyrenia is now know, and a warning with which we were to become all too familiar, written in Turkish, English, French and German: 'Controlled Road. No stopping, no photography. Restricted Military Area.'

There was a long climb into the Kyrenia mountains, nothing visible in the headlamps but barren limestone, before we descended towards the lights of the town, past advertisements for Scotch whisky, and into deserted streets. The main crossroads were guarded as before by military police, while lesser positions were held by plain khaki-clad troops as we turned west along the coast road through a series of small villages to reach Lapithos and our apartment. Someone had left coffee and sandwiches out for us, which we consumed gratefully before taking to our beds.

★   ★   ★   ★

I was up early the next morning and, leaving everyone else asleep, wandered out of the front door to find my bearings. It was a small group of apartments, set around a swimming pool in gardens bright with spring flowers. The apartments were of the usual Mediterranean type: two-storeyed with varnished window shutters and solar heating units on the roofs. They all seemed to be locked up and the car park was empty. On the far side of the long straight coastal road stood the solitary tower of the main hotel, the only building for some distance in either direction. Behind the hotel, the blue sea sparkled in the sunlight.

On the landward side, beyond the garden boundary, was a vineyard, overgrown with yellow flowers, and extensive groves of lemon trees rising to the scattered houses of Lapithos up the hill. The village was overshadowed by the flanks of the Kyrenia mountains, steep pinnacles of splintered grey limestone which form a 100-mile-long wall, dominating most of the north coast. A few tendrils of mist clung to the nearer crags, but the rest of the sky was clear and bright. It was six o'clock in the morning, warm enough to be wearing a short-sleeved shirt, and we had escaped the English winter. Life seemed pretty good.

Someone else was moving about. At the back of our apartment was a small patio, shaded by a trellis and overlooking the swimming pool. A bulky figure, clad in a thick woollen sweater and blue jeans tucked into heavy army boots, was up a ladder, pruning away the bougainvillaea which had run wild over our windows.

'*Selam*,' I said, surreptitiously sneaking a glance at the list of phrases I had written down. '*Cok tesekkur ederim*, thank you very much.'

'*Selam*.' The figure descended ponderously and stiffly, a large shambling man in his late fifties with a pronounced stoop, a long face and bulbous nose. His body moved slowly as he swept the prunings from the marble floor, but his eyes twinkled with goodwill. He had stuck a blue flower behind one ear.

'You speak Turkish?' he asked in English. I handed him the list for reply. We sat down in chairs by the pool while he carefully scanned the paper.

'Cigarette? Cyprus cigarette?' he asked, proferring a blue packet marked 'Caraman'.

'Where do these come form?'

'Cyprus tobacco. Kirpasa. Strong tobacco.' He inhaled and coughed. So did I.

'Some of this is not right,' he said. 'Who gave you this? I speak Turkish, English, Greek and Arab. I will be your professor. My name is Salih.'

Salih, the gardener, was the first of many friends we made amongst the Turkish Cypriots. It was a rare morning when I did not make him a cup of the thick, sweet Turkish coffee he liked and join him for a cigarette in one of the many sunny niches he favoured for his morning break. Here he would take the weight off his knees, which were nearly crippled by arthritis and years of work. When I came to know him, I found that he worked eight hours a day, six days a week, in the garden, starting at dawn and finishing at lunchtime. Then he would pedal his rusty old bicycle up the hill to work in a lemon grove for the afternoon, before returning at dusk to his house in the nearby village of Karavas. He even worked on most Sunday mornings at the lemon trees. Greeks tend to accuse the Turks of laziness – it certainly wasn't true of Salih.

True to his word, he made great efforts to teach me some Turkish, although I am afraid I made little progress. He was something of a purist and objected to odd Americanisms and slang words which had gained currency on the mainland and among the young. Although the Greeks of Cyprus speak a strongly dialectal version of their language, the Turks hold to a curiously old-fashioned and unadulterated form of their native tongue.

'Turkish is an easy language,' Salih would say. 'East to write now. Once we had Arab writing. Then, ten years to learn it. The *imams*, the *hodjas* could read and write, but no one else. Then Ataturk bring the new writing, like yours. Suddenly anyone can learn it – six months. Little children learn it.'

10

Salih did speak some Arabic, which he had picked up serving with the British army in Palestine. And he was delighted to hear that I spoke a little Greek.

'*Ti kaneis?*' he would ask in a remarkably thick accent.

'*Mia xara, efkaristo.*'

'You see, we understand each other. I come from a mixed village, near Baf, which the Greeks call Paphos. All Turkish mens learn some Greek. But Greek mens never speak Turkish.'

(When the Archduke Louis Salvator came to Cyprus in Ottoman days, he found a reversed situation. Then, Turkish being the language of the rulers, most Greeks had taken the trouble to learn it and even used the abrupt upward and backward motion of the head which Turks employ to indicate the negative.)

It pained Salih to remember his village and the farm he had lost in 1974.

'My place is Yolustu, Turkish name. Greek name, Koloni. Mixed village. Everything grows there, too much grapes, too much melons.* I had the land from my father and his father. Melons big like this. Here it is too cold; the mountains hide the sun. In Baf, too much sun. There is a river there called Ezousas. We catch big fish. No-one fishes on this coast. Not now.

'Of course I miss Yolustu. But what can we do? Makarios want to kill us, cut our throats. Now we are safe. I have three children, two sons, one daughter. One son is policeman, good job, 48 hours a week. The other is carpenter, very good pay. Now I must work for dowry to marry daughter. But all family safe.

'For years I am soldier, first for British in Palestine, 1945 to 1948. I still remember my number. [He reeled it off.] Then, later, Turkish reserve soldier, thirteen years to 1971. Now finish. No more war. In five years, finish work too. Just drink coffee.'

I took a stroll along the coast road to the west. An occasional early morning lorry loaded with lemons droned past. Beyond a small grove of pine trees, a lane led up towards the village under the mountains. Women were beginning to work on the lemon trees, leaving sacks of ripe fruit on the roadside for the lorries to collect. Little brown lizards lay basking in the sun on the stones and flicked out of sight into the lush undergrowth as I approached.

At a bend in the road, I came to a small Orthodox church built of grey stone. It was the kind of little barrel-vaulted chapel which often lies on the outskirts of a Greek village, as opposed to the large,

---

*I found it very confusing at first that both Greek and Turkish Cypriots whose English was less than perfect often used 'too much' where 'many' was really intended. I eventually concluded that it came about through literally translating the Greek *para poli.*

modern church by the central square. The graveyard was tangled with twelve years of unchecked growth, roses and briars rambling wild. The wrought-iron gate was jammed open and the door of the church itself had been pulled away. A martin flitted from the entrance as I approached to find a completely bare interior, without *iconostasis*, altar or any fittings whatever, only the droppings of sheep on the floor and the remains of a small fire someone had made in a corner.

As I pushed through the tall grass and weeds of the churchyard, I realised that every grave had been broken open and lay empty. Crooked slabs of marble lay everywhere at crazy angles, like a Byzantine painting of the Day of Resurrection. The Greek inscriptions on the tombstones were still clearly visibile when I pulled away the encroaching creepers: 'Nikolas G. Metaxas, 27.12.1966, aged 72.' 'Andreas Anastasiou, 22.11.1971, aged 50.' I wondered whether the opened graves were part of the general desecration of churches in the Turkish sector since 1974. Or had the departing Greeks hurriedly disinterred the bones of their dead to take with them to the south for reburial as the populations were exchanged? Such things, it was said, had occurred in Asia Minor in 1923. Later I found that the former was the case.

Our hire car had arrived when I returned to the apartment, not the new Ford model promised, but a battered Renault, built under licence in Turkey. The exhaust was held up with twisted pieces of wire, most of the interior fittings were broken, and when the engine was pulling hard some very odd noises came from underneath. But it had a removable glass sun roof, raised suspension and, best of all, a very solid sump guard. It was also remarkably cheap. I signed for it and came back from the car park jingling the keys to find a man in an elegant dark suit standing at the patio door. He was talking to Joan and the boys,who were breakfasting on toast with rose-petal jam.

'Good morning, sir,' he said, proferring his hand. 'My name is Mr Kemal. I am the manager of the apartments.'

'How do you do. You have a famous name.'

'Oh thank you. But I really must tell you that is quite a common name here in Cyprus. I wish to welcome you here, and if you have any problems, if there is ever anything I can do for you, please call on me at any time.'

Salih appeared at the door at that moment and handed me a bunch of flowers, before taking the boys to see the bananas he had been growing, wrapped in polythene, around the swimming pool. Suddenly we felt very welcome indeed.

CHAPTER TWO

LAPITHOS AND KORMAKITI

On the coast, a short distance to the east of Lapithos, stands the Monastery of Akhiropiitos, near a small cape of the same name and the site of the ancient city of Lambousa. The name means 'built without hands' and refers to an old legend that the monastery floated miraculously across the straits from Asia Minor where it was in danger of desecration at the hands of the infidels. It dates from the twelfth century, was altered many times over the years and is famous for its enormous seven-sided apse. We knew that it had fallen into disuse and was later taken over as a training school by the Greek National Guard.

We set out to find our way down to it, armed with the large-scale Greek map of Cyprus I had bought in London and the new Turkish map issued with the car. The first proved very accurate, but all the place names shown in the north were those in use before 1974, i.e. Greek with the exception of a few villages which had always been Turkish. The Attila Line was clearly marked and the northern sector in which we were travelling was overprinted with the legend: 'Inaccessible because of the Turkish occupation'. By contrast, the Turkish map, on a much smaller scale, showed only the new names which have been ruthlessly imposed on every Greek village and hamlet in the occupied sector. Some are recognisable (Kyrenia becoming Girne, our local village of Lapithos becoming Lapta and Karmi becoming Karaman), simply because the Turks had always had their own names for these places. Others are totally imposed, particularly in the case of all-Greek villages settled from the mainland, or by Turkish refugees from the south; thus Vouno has become Tashkent. And in some cases, Turks from the south of Cyprus brought the name of their old village with them; thus Greek Syrianokhori, the Place of the Syrians, became Yayla, an old Turkish word for a nomad's encampment, after a village in Tillyria. As might be imagined, this is extremely confusing, even for the local Turks who frequently still use the old names anyway. Salih, for example, always spoke of his house as being in Karavas, as opposed

13

to the new name of Alsancak, which has not really caught on, whatever the sign may say.

Struggling with the two maps, we turned off the main road too early and at the end of a narrow country lane found ourselves among a series of long barrack-like huts, surrounded by bare dusty earth and untidy gardens. A few ancient men and women sat out in chairs in the sunshine, while a nurse could be seen in the distance pushing a wheelchair. A faded blue notice read: 'United Nations Commission for Refugees'. It was obvious that the camp was virtually empty, a problem nearly solved, except perhaps for a few old people with nowhere to go and no family left to look after them. Our second left turn was no more successful as it led to a military camp. A gate in the barbed wire was guarded by a sentry in khaki fatigues with an American carbine held diagonally across his chest, the broad flat cheeks and expressionless face under the green helmet speaking of Anatolia rather than Cyprus. But through the wire we caught a glimpse of a domed red-tiled roof, which looked suspiciously like the Akhiropiitos Monastery.

The third side road emerged from the fields at the corner of the camp and ran along beside the wire to the sea. Here was an area of open ground and a single-storey prefabricated building of glass and steel, like a café or restaurant. There was a sentry box outside the wire and the road was guarded by another soldier, narrow-eyed and olive complexioned, watching us curiously from the top of a steep grassy bank, shuffling his feet in their long boots which laced halfway up the calf. I got out of the car and climbed up to ask for directions.

'*Gunaydin*, good morning,' I said.

'*Gunaydin*. Hey, are you Americans?'

'No, English,' I replied, considerably taken aback by the strong transatlantic accent.

'Hi, how are you. I'm English too. Anyway I was born in England – Liverpool. Then my family went to Canada.'

He struggled to push the rifle strap out of the way and shook hands.

'Are you tourists? We never see them.'

'I suppose so. Are your people still in Canada?'

'Sure. I've lived in Canada since I was two. Until I came here. I'm nineteen now. Nineteen today in fact.'

I had to ask. 'You've got a Canadian passport?'

'Sure.'

'So how come you're doing National Service with the Turkish army in Cyprus?'

He shrugged. 'Just something our people have to do. We still have family here. Only seventeen days left though.' He grinned with relief. His teeth were in a terrible state; his Canadian dentist would have a fit when he saw them.

'So how's it been?'

'Not so bad. The food's pretty dull sometimes. And the pay's terrible, just pocket money for cigarettes.'

I looked over his shoulder through the wire. There was our Byzantine monastery, surrounded by sandbags and rows of Nissen huts.

'Do you live in those?'

'Sure. Boy, will I be glad to get home.'

'I bet. We were looking for the monastery there. I suppose there's no chance of seeing inside it?'

'Sorry, I can't let you go in there. It's dangerous. There's nothing to see inside anyway. You can go on down the road to the restaurant if you like.'

'Is that a restaurant?'

'Yeah, it's real good. We all go there when we're off duty. They have pizzas, but not pizzas like we know. Turkish pizzas are kind of spicy. On Saturday nights they have a band and dancing. But best of all it's cheap. You should try it.'

'We will,' I said. 'And thanks for your help. Oh and happy birthday.'

'Sure, nice talking to you. See you tonight maybe.'

The monastery may have been unapproachable, but it seemed that the occupying army certainly was not. During our stay in North Cyprus we came into contact with many soldiers, a few of them Cypriots, but the majority Turks from the mainland who rarely spoke English. (We never found another Canadian.) They were almost invariably courteous, presumably having been carefully instructed to show every consideration to foreigners, for the authorities were desperate to re-establish tourism, which had virtually dried up after the invasion. I am speaking of the privates in this conscript army, mostly shy, polite farm boys with an average age of about eighteen. The NCOs and officers were another breed.

★ ★ ★ ★

The village of Lapta, or Lapithos in Greek, is very old, having been settled in AD 654 by people from the ancient city of Lambousa on the coast, which had become uninhabitable due to the raids of Arab pirates. At this time the population of all the coastal districts of Cyprus was fleeing inland to safety, for there was little prospect of organising a serious defence against the Saracen incursions. Byzantine Cyprus had enjoyed a remarkably peaceful period of prosperity in the fifth and sixth centuries, but the next 300 years must have been a veritable reign of terror.

When the Arabs began their Holy War to spread the faith, the sea was something unknown and fearful to a desert-dwelling race. After Muhammad's death, according to the Egyptian historian Suyuti, the Caliph Omar sent to Mu'awiyah, his general in the newly conquered land of Syria, asking for a description of the sea and the ships which rode upon it. The following reply came back to Mecca:

> Verily I saw a huge construction, upon which mounted diminutive creatures; if it is still it rends the heart, if it moves it terrifies the senses. Within it the faculties grow diminishing and calamities augmenting. Those inside it are like worms in a log. If it inclines to one side they are drowned, if it escapes they are confounded.

(Trs. C. D. Cobham, *Excerpta Cypria*)

When Omar read the letter he was horrified and wrote back to Mu'awiyah, saying: 'By Allah, I will not set a true believer upon it.'

But Muhammad had prophesied that the sea *would* be crossed and, for all the terrors caused by this appalling new element, the Arabs were soon to master it absolutely. Mu'awiyah, now Emir of Syria, brought 1,700 ships to Cyprus in 647 to sack the capital city of Constantia, and his lieutenant Abu'l Awar returned with a fleet of 500 six years later and established a garrison. This Arab force was not left on the island with any idea of conquest, but in order systematically to plunder the monasteries for valuables and the villages for slaves. The brutality and pointless destruction of this period left an indelible mark on the folklore of the island and the word 'Saracen' is still synonymous with rapacious violence.

The garrison was later withdrawn and Cyprus paid a regular tribute to keep the Arabs at bay. A formal treaty of neutrality was concluded in 689 and the Cypriots now found themselves paying tribute to both the Caliph and the Emperor of Byzantium. The treaty of neutrality was broken by the Emperor Justinian II, who attempted to resolve the problem by effectively abandoning Cyprus and forced the population to leave the island for his new city of Nea Justinianopolis on the Hellespont. The Metropolitan of Cyprus was made Bishop of Nea Justinianopolis and Metropolitan of the Hellespont, with the same autocephalous powers and privileges as were enjoyed by the Church of Cyprus. But the experiment was not a success, and most of the Cypriots of Nea Justinianopolis returned to the island during the reign of the Emperor Leontius.

The treaty of neutrality was re-established and the Arab tribute continued. 'Cyprus lived between the Greeks and the Saracens', according to Willibald, an English pilgrim who passed through the

16

island on his way to the Holy Land in 723. And the tribute proved to buy very little in the way of protection, for the Arab raids continued in 743, 747, 772 and 790. Harun-ar-Rashid attacked with a large force in 806 and captured 16,000 Cypriots, including the Archbishop and many of the clergy. These were taken away to Raqqa on the Euphrates, to be held for ransom until the treaty of neutrality had been renewed. It was the great Emperor Nicephoras Phokas, the tough general who had expelled the Arabs from Crete, who finally rid Cyprus of this curse. He sent Nikitas Chalcutzes to defend the island, and the Byzantine fleet finally defeated that of Egypt in 965.

Yet the sea remained treacherous. For most of its history the vulnerable island of Cyprus has been bedevilled by pirates and slavers. To live near the sea was to be in constant risk of attack and abduction to the slave markets of Algiers or Turkey. Thus, even today, the map reveals that except for the large walled sea ports there are few communities directly on the coast. Cypriots are traditionally not fishermen or seafarers but farmers and craftsmen, and their eyes turn inland. The last known instance of slave traffic in Cyprus occurred on this northern coast in 1910.

The name of Lapithos is even older than the village, having been one of the four administrative districts of Cyprus, each ruled by a *strategos* appointed by Alexandria during the time when the island was ruled by Ptolemy's Egypt after the division of Alexander the Great's empire. The village was built, using masonry from ancient Lambousa, on the steep slope of the mountain, plentifully watered by a *kephalovryson*, a large spring which bursts out of the limestone 1,000 feet above sea level at the head of the village. Water is the most precious commodity in this dry land and the *kephalovryson* is channelled through ancient stone aqueducts and modern concrete channels, under great plane trees whose roots suck up the water and through mysterious ravines overgrown with giant reed. The rushing sound of the waters can be heard all over the hillside, through the ruins of the mills they once drove, gurgling into the cisterns of crumbling, deserted houses with great arched rooms and carved wooden doors, trickling into the citrus groves which run down to the sea. A similar spring serves Karavas, or Alsancak, a more recent village founded from Lapithos, and the two communities have spread until they have grown together, a network of narrow lanes and water channels at different levels on the fertile slope.

In the Byzantine period, Lapithos retained some of the importance of its ancient name and that of its forerunner, the city of Lambousa, although its Orthodox bishopric was suppressed by the Catholic Lusignans in 1222. In 1307 it was recorded as the estate of Echive d'Ibelin, one of the powerful Crusader family, Counts of Jaffa, and

17

during the fifteenth century, when its great citrus groves were already renowned, it belonged to Sor de Naves, Constable of Cyprus. In Turkish times, cotton was grown and later sweet potatoes, sesame and onions. The people had a reputation for skill in pottery, wood carving and needlework. In addition, Lapithos was famous for its silk. The Turks who live there now keep no silkworms (at least I could not find anyone who still did), but later, in the Greek sector, the craft was explained to us and we were shown some of the implements used.

In the square, with its locked and barred church, of which the bell had been taken down from the campanile, we parked by the new bust of Kemal Ataturk, which nearly every village in the North proudly displays, together with the twin flags of Turkey and North Cyprus. A friendly crowd of men were chatting in the nearby shop where we bought the makings of a picnic: *haloumi* cheese, made with sheep's milk and mountain herbs, which we learned to toast over an open fire on a sharp stick, crisp bread loaves shaped like cartwheels, strong garlic sausage, oranges, wine, *raki* and bottled spring water. This last was a travellers' habit rather than a necessity, for the tap water in Cyprus is generally good, having been installed by the British in the 1950s – something for which they are sometimes remembered with gratitude.

We attempted to find our way up the hill through the labyrinth of narrow paths and beautiful old houses, many constructed of mud brick and straw, a surprisingly durable material in this dry climate when covered by stucco. Everywhere were carved wooden beams and doors, many of them decorated with the lozenge-shaped patterns which the Archduke Louis Salvator had noticed when he visited Cyprus in the nineteenth century. Windows and balconies were adorned with spiralling wrought iron, and through open doorways could be seen the huge internal arches used to support the ceilings in Turkish houses. Many were ruined or empty, for, large as these villages are, their present population does not fill them and the old houses were crumbling and decaying slowly among the bright gardens of lilies, geraniums and cyclamen.

We had hoped to locate, for future reference, a decent local restaurant, close enough to our apartment for convenience, but away from the main road. At every steep, narrow corner leading to the upper parts of Karavas, a faded arrow and sign painted on a house wall indicated a restaurant further up the hill. We followed, with the car groaning in bottom gear, under sprays of pinkish-white almond blossom hanging over the road, past faint blue slogans, still visible through whitewash and scrubbing marks – 'ENOSIS', 'EOKA' – until we emerged at the head cistern of the spring under a giant plane tree. Here someone had once run a fine restaurant in an old water mill, with a superb view over the roofs and cypress trees of the village to the lemon groves and the sea below. But the dead leaves of the plane tree had collected in drifts in the courtyard, the dust was thick on the windows and the creepers were spreading over the flagstones. It was a long time since any meals had been served here.

We left the car and continued to follow the watercourse up the hill, past a sheepfold where fierce dogs were tied to a tree, to the place where the spring emerged from a fissure in the rocks before running through a natural amphitheatre amid steep slopes covered with stunted pines. In the middle of the clearing stood a huge mound of earth, from the apex of which a thin curl of blue smoke lazily arose, the air above quivering in the heat. Nearby were the three stones which formed the charcoal burner's cooking hearth, his bedroll, knapsack and water bottle. He himself was higher up the slope, the only concession to modernity in his ancient craft being the petrol-driven chain saw with which he was trimming dead branches from the lower parts of the trees. He clambered down the slope to greet us, a slight, sunburnt young man with a thin moustache, but he spoke only Turkish and could explain little of his trade, only that he had to watch the fire for a long time. Charcoal is used everywhere in Cyprus, for cooking kebabs and in braziers to heat rooms in cold weather.

★　★　★　★

The coast road to the west of Lapithos is broad and straight, running through lemon trees and market gardens, until a crossroads is reached by another statue of Ataturk. The turn to the left leads up to the village of Vasilia, or Turkish Karsiyaka, and beyond it to a lonely track over the western end of the Kyrenia range into the Korphi Forest. This was the ancient 'Sacred Way' to Lapithos' former colony of Larnaca tis Lapithou. The turn to the right leads to Vavilas, now called Guzelyali, a tiny hamlet with a very good restaurant by the sea. The main road swings to the south, around the foothills at the end of the mountain chain, and doubles back to Nicosia in the centre of the island, first over rolling green downs and then across the flat plain of the Mesaoria. This route once terminated in the southern, Greek quarter of Nicosia, but now this is cut off by the Green Line where it bisects the city. It would, in fact, be a road leading nowhere, were it not for some suburban side roads which have been enlarged, connecting it through into Turkish Nicosia, north of the Line. At first glance, there seems no logical reason for such a well-made road to take this long course west from Kyrenia, around the mountains and back to the capital, forming two sides of a large triangle. There are only a few small villages in this district and almost all the other roads of Cyprus radiate directly out from Nicosia like the spokes of a wheel. But we came to learn that, during the inter-communal violence of the 1960s and early 1970s, this long circuitous route was the one taken morning and evening by the Greek commuters of Kyrenia on their way to and from the city. Astride the direct road between Kyrenia and Nicosia, the route we had taken on the night of our arrival, lie the Turkish strongholds of Ortakeuy and Geunyeli, both fiercely nationalistic and supporters of TMT, the Turkish underground organisation, and places any Greek would wish to avoid. Moreover the Turks were in St Hilarion Castle and dominated the mountain pass, where they had installed a roadblock.

Beyond the crossroads we passed a checkpoint, where the Military Police first stared and then, to our surprise, saluted smartly. A sentry stood at the entrance to an army camp on our left, near a sign to the 'Muslim Youth Organisation Summer Camp'. Beyond was wild open countryside and a lonely beach where we stopped the car and strolled along to the reed beds where the Paleomylos, the Old Mill river, joins the sea. The sky was fine and clear, with a warm breeze blowing, and the bare headlands stretched away towards Cape Kormakiti. We revelled in the fresh clean air and the miles of empty coast before us, until we turned back towards the car and realised uneasily from the intermittent glint of sun on binoculars that we were being watched from the ASIZ checkpoint on the main road.

A dirt road turned off the main highway and skirted the sea in the direction of Cape Kormakiti. After a mile or two, the going became very hard indeed. On steep gradients the gravel had washed away to the bedrock in deep runnels where the sump guard rasped and jarred. The track switchbacked up and down over rocky hills, constantly threatening to become impassable as the tyres struggled to find a grip. A stage was reached when we continued forward hopefully, rather than face the obstacles which lay behind us for a second time. Besides, there were no turning places. The countryside was completely deserted, the view inland being dominated by Mount Kornos, over 3,000 feet in height, the final peak of the Kyrenia range.

On a bleak stretch of moor, we came upon a shepherd with a large flock straggling across the road, a thin, ragged-looking fellow with high leather boots. He spoke only Turkish and a few words of German, but he gave us to understand that the road ahead was better than that behind. 'Asphalt,' he repeated several times. Further on we came to his village of Kayalar, which the Greeks called Orga, a squalid little hamlet obviously afflicted by great poverty, for this is barren land and the people can only live off their flocks. The village was inhabited not by Cypriots, but by settlers from the mainland of Turkey, noticeable for their archaic dress and the Asiatic cast of their features.

Women with prominent gold bangles and earrings squatted before cooking fires in the dust outside the ruinous houses. Their clothes glowed in all the bright colours of the rainbow, in contrast to the dingy greys and ochres of their suroundings.

Among these lonely hills, close to a place marked Ayios Yeoryios on the Greek map, the road descended to a little bridge at the bottom of a valley. Here the dry bed of a stream ran down to a stony beach. At its mouth stood an abrupt cone of rock surmounted by large overhanging boulders, perhaps 200 feet in height, like the sand castle of a giant child left beside the shore. I struggled up behind Steven and Malcolm, through the stems of white-flowered asphodel, until we reached the summit and could gaze down at the sea, a rich Oxford blue over the deep water before us, suddenly breaking into white foam on the rocks at our feet. By the strand, where Joan was strolling, were the ruins of two large stone buildings, fortified boathouses perhaps, with high roofs and enormous arched doorways facing the sea. There was also a little white-painted chapel which must have been in use until 1974. Although the roof was still in place, the interior had been gutted and desecrated with obscene drawings, something unusual in the East, for both Greeks and Turks are fastidious about such things. Strangely, somebody (who?) had attempted to restore the damage, and, in an attempt at reconsecration, had chalked a large cross on each wall over the erect phalluses daubed there.

A hawk arose from a juniper bush and flew off up the valley as we approached. A large lizard cocked up a crested head and then scampered away with a rhythmic switching of its long tail. We sat down by the blackened remains of some shepherd's or hunter's fire under a solitary olive tree. Empty cartridge cases were scattered over the ground. Large ivory-coloured butterflies moved over yellow gorse flowers which released a sweet, sickly perfume and there was a persistent droning of bees. Malcolm found the sloughed skin of a fair-sized snake curled up by a stone.

Liveras is now called Sadrazamkoy in Turkish, or the Town of the Grand Vizier. A remote settlement, near the end of the cape, it seemed a dead-and-alive sort of place, in spite of its grandiloquent name. As with so many villages in the Turkish sector, many houses had not been reoccupied and were slowly becoming ruined by wind and weather. A flock of goats was moving through the single street, driven by a small boy with a stick and a leather satchel. A few ragged, bare-foot children laughed and called and ran beside the car, while the women, in baggy Turkish *shalvar* trousers, tended large metal pans of smoking charcoal or the beehive-shaped clay ovens which stand in every Cypriot yard. There was a faint smell of roasting meat, combined with the sour, heavy odour of the goats. Everywhere were rusty pieces of scrap metal, peeling plaster and stained, unpainted walls. The people were friendly, though their sheepdogs were not.

We stopped beyond the village to eat our own picnic lunch on a great, flat stone, huddled against the wind which was now sweeping over the low, scrubby peninsula. Down by the lighthouse at the point we could see army lorries, radio antennae and camouflaged tents. A few personnel carriers crawled like beetles over the stony tracks.

Cape Kormakiti is the closest point of the island to Turkey, being divided from Cape Anamur in Anatolia by the 41 miles of the Caramanian Straits. Often, nothing can be seen through the haze, but in fine, clear weather the peaks of the great Taurus mountains of Lycia, snow-covered through most of the year, can be seen from various high points in the Kyrenia range. The first time I came in sight of these giants, white heads majestic above rolled banks of cloud, shining far away in the early morning sunlight, my breath was taken away.

The cape itself is now in the hands of the Turkish army, and contains nothing of great interest, although the wreck of a Turkish pirate ship which raided this coast in the fourteenth century is reputed to lie somewhere offshore. In Venetian days, detachments of Albanian mercenaries were stationed in such lonely places as this to keep a watch on the dangerours sea. 'Six hundred horsemen of Alba watch the coast' a traveller wrote, and no doubt their feared reputation did much to keep pirates from the shore. Their ruined watchtowers can still be seen in various parts of the island and, after our lunch of bread, cheese and Turkish beer, we searched unsuccessfully for one said to remain nearby. No one in the village seemed to know anything about it, and only an Englishman, they plainly thought, would be so eccentric or deranged as to walk into Liveras and ask such a question. They shook their heads politely, but there was pity in their eyes.

The shepherd of Kayalar had been quite right, for a second, paved road led back inland to the village of Kormakiti. The Turks have renamed this place Korucam, a name the inhabitants themselves never use, for they are Greek-speaking Maronites. Although Christians, they are Roman Catholic, not Orthodox, and traditionally have never allied themselves with either the Greek or Turkish cause. Thus, in theory at least, they were officially tolerated in the North after 1974, and were among the few Cypriots with the freedom to travel on either side of the Line. In practice, at the time of our journey, their communities were coming under heavy pressure in a number of ways.

The Maronites are an ancient race and their strange history goes back to the seventh century, a time of internal strife in the Roman Empire of the East. All Byzantium was then divided into two camps: that of the Monophysites who believed that Christ had a single nature, and that of the Orthodox who believed that He was both God

22

and man. This was no obscure theologians' argument, but a deep schism throughout society which threatened its very structure. At the height of the wrangling between the bishops and scholars, the Emperor Heraclius came to stay at the Monastery of St Maron, on the river Orontes in Syria. Here the monks innocently told the Emperor that in their view Christ had a dual nature, simultaneously human and divine, but that His Will was single.

At last Heraclius saw a way out of his perplexity and attempted to unite the Empire by declaring this as official policy. The monks of St Maron found themselves elevated to the status of a sect, which spread steadily through the Levant, and particularly in the mountains of North Lebanon. Later their doctrine was declared heretical and their monastery on the Orontes was sacked by Justinian II. But the Maronites thrived for centuries in their mountain strongholds, in spite of the enmity of the Caliphs of Baghdad. During the Crusades many fought with the Frankish knights, and when the Holy Land was finally lost some followed their old comrades back to Cyprus, where there was already a Maronite colony, and founded nearly 60 villages.

At that time, their presence in Cyprus must have been as strong as it is today in the Lebanon, in whose convoluted internal strife their right-wing militia has played its part. Many Cypriot Maronites still maintain connections with the Lebanese community, and children are sometimes sent there to be educated.

Some Maronites state that their people were in Cyprus even earlier, from ancient times in fact. But their folklore is full of myths and legends and extravagant claims about their Church. Their numbers have steadily declined, until in 1960 the census taken at the time of independence recorded 2,708, living in four villages. As far as we could ascertain (and reliable figures are not easy to come by in the present situation), this has now fallen to two villages in the Turkish sector, one of which is visibly dying. There are perhaps a thousand people in Kormakiti today.

On the outskirts we stopped by a very old church, long and low, with a barrel-vaulted roof. As we stood by its whitewashed walls, an elderly lady came down the road from the village, holding a few brown candles and a rosary in her hand. When we spoke to her in Greek, she started and then smiled.

'I did not expect that, my children – strangers to say *xerete*. Who are you?'

We explained, and she told us about Kormakiti with an air of sadness, rather than bitterness.

'This village . . .' She made an uncertain, balancing movement with her hand to indicate that it was poised on the brink of extinction, a very eloquent and Greek gesture. 'We have many empty houses in our village. You know that we are all Christians here? Our young people go to the Greek sector. My children are all there. In one month, I will go to visit them. Soon, perhaps, I will go for ever as so many others have done. Kormakiti . . .?' She shrugged.

'Why is it so difficult for you here?'

'We are surrounded. We are alone. What could the young do here?'

'This is the first undefiled church we have seen here,' we told her.

'I am not sure who will care for it if I leave. Let me show you. It is the Church of the Panayia, St Mary the Virgin.'

She led us into the cool dark interior, the frescos on the walls dimmed by centuries of lamp and candle smoke, the air sharp with the smell of incense.

'It is very old,' she whispered, as we stood before a statue of the Virgin, partly concealed by blue curtains. 'From the time of the Lusignans.'

We left her to pray and light her candles. As we emerged, a convoy of lorries thundered past on their way out to the cape, filled with soldiers in the black berets of the armoured regiments.

The fields around Kormakiti looked fertile and well-tilled, but the village itself was half deserted. We parked in the little square by the steps of the huge modern church of Ayios Yeoryios and looked inside, to be confronted with a magnificence of decoration, more in keeping with a large cathedral than a village church. The priest sat in a corner with a book of prayer, from which he never raised his eyes to acknowledge our presence. His dress was unfamiliar, with a strange flat-topped hat. The Maronite Church has recognised the supremacy of Rome since the time of the Crusaders, but the liturgy is still recited in Syriac.

Half a dozen middle-aged men sat in the café opposite, whiling away the afternoon with desultory conversation. It looked like any Greek coffee shop: a large concrete-floored room with dented metal tables and chairs. On the wall were a Greek calendar, a Turkish calendar and a photograph of the Turkish Cypriot leader, Rauf Denktash. They certainly were not giving anything away. Rather more prominence was given to a series of pin-ups and photographs of the entire cast of the American soap opera, *Dallas*. The radio was on: a Greek broadcast from the south.

The customers looked up with surprise when we came in, obviously uncertain as to what to make of us, but replying politely to our 'Good afternoon.' The proprietor brought us coffee and lemonade, pleased to find that we had a little Greek. Had we seen the *ekklisia*, they wanted to know, for they were obviously proud of their great church.

The Maronites were among the last people in Cyprus to keep camels, the main method of transport on the island before the motor lorry superseded them. The doorways of the khans, the old Turkish travellers' inns, were always wide and high enough for a fully laden camel to enter, and the long lines of plodding beasts were once a common sight on the roads of the Mesaoria plain. A census of 1903 gave 348 professional camel drivers, and during the Second World War there were still some thousands of camels in use. Lawrence Durrell, in his remarkable book *Bitter Lemons* described meeting a train of camels near the Bay of Morphou during the 1950s, carrying grain to Nicosia in the moonlight, a sleeping man nodding on the back of each animal. By 1965 there were only 90 animals remaining and now, as far as I could ascertain, they have all gone. I asked Mr Kemal about this one morning.

'I remember when I was a kid, I used to see them,' he told me, 'but I don't think there are any left here now. But you might still see some near Famagusta, because there are many people from Anatolia in that district.'

Later still, the Maronites had a reputation for owning mules. The mules of Cyprus are large and beautiful beasts and have been remarked upon by travellers since Richard the Lionheart's Crusaders first admired them. The British army bought up large numbers to use in the Crimea, Abyssinia, Egypt and, later, the Great War. Much to the displeasure of the British administrators, the Greeks of Cyprus sent a present of mules to Greece in 1880, together with volunteers for the war against Turkey. Archbishop Sofronios II wrote to George, King of the Hellenes:

> The Greek people of the Island charged me to send to Your Majesty by Colonel Hadji Yianni – he too a son of Cyprus – one hundred and seven mules. Be pleased to accept in the name of our nation this modest gift from our now impoverished Cyprus, with my ardent prayers for the fulfilment of her Pan-hellenic longings.

> (Colonial office original correspondence co 67/18/805, Stavros Panteli,
> *A New History of Cyprus*)

Cypriot muleteers at the evacuation of Dunkirk were obliged to destroy their prized beasts before boarding the ships. Mules are still in daily use among the Greek villages of the Troodos mountains in the south of the island, although for some reason they are much less common in the Turkish sector. Even the Maronites now seem to have resigned themselves to living with the petrol engine.

Another lorryload of soldiers was waiting, pulled off to the side of the narrow village street. Their green painted steel helmets and gun muzzles gleamed dully above the camouflaged side of the truck. We drove past them on our way back to rejoin the main road at Myrtou. This large village, now known to the Turks as Camlibel, is important because of its position at the junction of the main Nicosia road with the route which leads to the far western part of the Turkish sector. Presumably for this reason, several large army camps have been built in the area of Camlibel and its nearby satellites of Tepebasi and Karpasha, and there are ASIZ checkpoints on all the approach roads.

Myrtou, or Camlibel, is very old, and the remains of Byzantine houses can be seen from the old settlement, once known as Margi. It had been famous for its Monastery of St Pantaleimon, the seat of the Bishop of Kyrenia until 1921. But once again we found ourselves gazing at the object of our interest through a barbed-wire fence, nervous to risk photographing what had obviously become an important military installation, surrrounded by sentries. It did not, on reflection, seem surprising that an occupying army had taken over a large empty building, of little practical use to the local Muslim population. And I found out later that the Greek National Guard had been in possession of the building for some years before the invasion, for the monastery itself had ceased to function during the 1950s. The large, domed, cross-in-square church, which stands in the centre of the village, had been put to a better use, having been converted into a medical and dental centre. Here, as on all public buildings, flew the red flag of Turkey and the red and white flag of North Cyprus. Mothers, clutching children and toddlers by the hand, were chatting in a group outside the door.

Dusk was not far away as we drove out for a few miles on the road beyond Myrtou, to the low hills and scattered trees of the Karpasha Forest. As we stopped for a while on the last slope before the great central plain of the island, we saw a strange commotion in the sky to the south; a twisting, smoking column of grey dust reaching up to the clouds which had drawn overhead. There was an occasional rumble of thunder in the distance and lightning flickered around the cloud base as the whirlwind moved slowly towards us, the sinister tower sometimes dark and distinct, sometimes fading almost from sight before reforming. Finally, it veered away to the east to come under the southern flank of the Kyrenia mountains before disappearing from view. The atmosphere remained close and humid, and the sunset tinged the low clouds with a dirty, copper glow.

An extraordinary vehicle came driving up from the plain, an archaic type of bus made of curved wooded panels painted bright red and blue with a long, projecting bonnet, a high, black radiator and ramshackle mudguards. The windscreen curved like the bay window of a Victorian villa, while the rear window was a sort of ornate, Moorish arch. The tail hung far out over the rear wheels and a ladder led up to a rack which covered the entire roof. On this were tied numerous sacks, baskets of produce and several crates full of live chickens. Reminiscent of a 1920s charabanc or an old-fashioned fairground engine, it laboured slowly along, a cloud of black diesel smoke pouring out behind, while an occasional orange rind was tossed from a side window.

We found that almost every village in Cyprus has one of these buses, which are made by fitting a hand-made local body on to the chassis of a Bedford lorry, bought second-hand from England. After many years of service, or when the chassis finally cracks, they are left to rust away in odd corners as a home for livestock and poultry. The buses do not operate regular services, but are usually owned by one man, who will drive his fellow commuters into Nicosia for a fee, work at a part-time job himself during the day, perhaps on a market stall, and drive them all home again in the evening. Perhaps the villagers will decide, *en masse*, to have an evening out at the cinema, or to pay a visit to friends in another village on a Sunday; then out comes the old bus, which, in spite of the hard wooden seats, has a festival air about its gaily painted exterior guaranteed to put the party in a holiday mood.

We caught up with this bus at Camlibel, where a slight diversion of the road had ensured that all traffic from the west must pass before the door of the police station. The bus had stopped, and the identity cards of the occupants were being checked by policemen whose dark uniforms looked almost identical to the British model from which they had derived. We were waved through and on to the main road, which we followed in the dark back to Lapithos and a welcome drink before dinner.

★　★　★　★

The car park of the restaurant by the Akhiropiitos Monastery was quite deserted when we reached it; even the sentry on the perimeter of the camp had retreated up the bank to his box. The lightning of a distant storm was flickering away over the sea towards Turkey. A few lights were on in the restaurant, which looked more than ever like a greenhouse, bare and uninviting. We made our way towards the front door, where a young man came out to greet us.

'Good evening, sir, madam.'

'Good evening. Is this a public restaurant? I mean can we eat here?'

In spite of the soldier's recommendation that morning, it seemed rather unlikely.

'Certainly. Come in. Where would you like to sit?'

There were no other customers and at least 50 empty tables to

27

choose from. Our waiter pulled chairs up to one table beside the big wood-burning stove in the centre of the room. The stove was giving out a comforting heat, for the night had turned cold. About nineteen years old, thin and brown-faced with crew-cut hair, the waiter was dressed in a white pullover and neatly pressed slacks. He spoke English pretty well. The other waiters, who were involved in various odd jobs and chatting by the till at the door, were about the same age. There were one or two private soldiers, not eating but hanging about the door to the kitchen, while a sergeant with red tabs on his uniform was sitting at one of the tables working on some papers. I found him looking sharply at us, once or twice.

'You seem to be very quiet this evening,' we remarked to our waiter.

'Yes, but it's early in the week. You should come on Saturday night. Then we have a band and dancing and all the tables are full. You like Turkish pizzas? Very good, with meat and herbs in. Then *kebabs*, fried potatoes, salad? Some yoghurt?'

He brought a bottle of red Turkish wine, opened and poured it. There was a dramatic flash of sheet lightning over the sea, which lit up every object in the room for a split second, and then a long rumble of thunder. There still seemed to be something odd about this restaurant.

'You get a lot of business from the soldiers in the camp, I suppose?'

'Of course. We are all soldiers,' said the waiter.

'You are a soldier and you work here as well?'

'Yes, when I have no duty. My name is Ibrahim.'

'Don't they mind?'

'No, it's OK.'

'So who runs the restaurant?' we asked.

Ibrahim nodded at the sergeant, sitting working at his books. What an entrepreneur, I thought! How Sergeant Bilko would have loved this. But we eventually gathered, although Ibrahim was not able to explain the rationale of the scheme in detail, that this was one of three such restaurants established by the Turkish army in North Cyprus. They were run by soldiers and open to anybody, presumably in an attempt to improve public relations. Most of the soldiers involved seemed to have had hotel or restaurant experience, Ibrahim for instance having been a waiter in a large hotel near Salamis before receiving his call-up papers. But the work in the restaurant (of which they were very proud) was an extra, not a soft billet, and they had to do the usual camp duty and stand guard along with the rest.

The meal was actually very good, the meat subtly flavoured with fresh coriander and lemon, and served with *pitta* bread straight from the oven. I remembered that Dr Sibthorp, the botanist who had wandered through Cyprus in 1787, had been delighted to find coriander, that fragrant and delightful herb, growing wild on the island. As we ate, the storm drew closer, and a torrential downpour, almost a tropical monsoon, began to hammer on the roof. With this noise above our heads, added to the commotion of thunder and lightning over the sea, ordinary conversation became impossible. Somewhat to our surprise, considering that the building was almost entirely made of glass, there were no water leaks. The boys stopped eating and gazed enthralled at the elemental spectacle; white electric flashes followed one another almost continuously. Eventually the storm proved too much for the power supply; the lights gave a couple of warning flickers and then cut out all along the coast. Ibrahim, who truly was an excellent waiter, appeared in a moment with a paraffin lamp, nonchalantly lighting Joan's cigarette.

'Come and have coffee in the officers' room,' he said.

We all retreated into a smaller sanctuary, with solid walls and curtains over the windows, behind the main restaurant. There was a brick fireplace, a rather spartan leather suite and an enormous rubber plant reaching up to the ceiling. An outsize television set and an old-fashioned radiogram stood against one wall, while a brass samovar adorned an antique oak sideboard. In spite of these luxuries, it was a heavy, masculine room.

'This is where the General eats when he comes,' said Ibrahim, pulling up armchairs for everybody.

'The General?'

'Officer Commanding, North Cyprus. He comes and eats here when he's in this district.'

We felt very privileged. The atmosphere had now become informal, and as we clustered around the fire Ibrahim joined us for coffee and lit up one of my cigars. However, he could not accept a glass of wine, for serving soldiers are not permitted to drink alcohol. There was a comforting hiss from the paraffin lamp; even the sergeant's reserve melted a little and he too accepted a cigar.

Ibrahim interested us, having come with his parents from Mersin in Anatolia shortly after the occupation began. His father worked in Famagusta, the family having settled in the north part of Varosha, the Greek quarter, which was abandoned by its inhabitants in 1974 and was still largely empty. As a domiciled Cypriot, Ibrahim had two years of military service to complete, and, like every soldier we met, he knew exactly how many days he had left at any time he was asked. He was looking forward to a full-time job as a waiter again when he was released in June.

'I wanted to be in the Tanks when I joined,' he said. 'You know, the black berets. I could have learned to drive. But they said no.'

29

The boys, after the initial excitement of the storm, were falling asleep in their chairs. Ibrahim brought us a bill for the equivalent of five English pounds, the tip went into a communal pot, and the entire staff, including the cook, lined up at the door to wish us goodnight. Ibrahim brought his hurricane lamp out into the downpour to light us to our car.

Bellapais Abbey in the foothills of the Kyrenia mountains

CHAPTER THREE

KYRENIA, ST HILARION AND THE LUSIGNANS

The next morning Malcolm and Steven slept late. I took Joan to see the abandoned church on the road to Lapithos. We were not yet inured to the sight of the derelict churches in every village, the cross and bell removed if they could be safely reached, or shot up from the ground if not. Those which had been converted into mosques, easily recognisable by the loudspeakers affixed to the tower in order to spread the *muezzin*'s prayers over the village, seemed the more fortunate.

We continued through the lemon trees to the outskirts of the village, where we found a dusty little shop, a grocery and general store, run by a couple with their two teenaged daughters. We bought tubs of thick-crusted ewes' milk yoghurt, a pack of finely ground coffee and a small Turkish coffee pot. There was a pigeon loft behind the shop and we could dimly see the birds strutting about through a murky glass, behind shelves of cereal packets and bottles of wine from the mainland, which appeared to have been left undisturbed for years.

The Turks may have appropriated the prime agricultural land of Cyprus during the 1974 operation and much of the mining and quarrying, together with the main sea port of Famagusta – but the Greeks at least have the wine, for the vine-growing district around Paphos and Limassol is well south of the Attila Line. We occasionally saw tiny patches of vines, but nothing on a commercial scale. All the wine we saw on sale was from the mainland and usually of mediocre quality. But the Turks did not seem unduly interested in wine, preferring to drink coffee during the day in the cafés and reserving *raki*, the traditional, fiery spirit flavoured with anise, for serious drinking in the evening. There was a firm near Famagusta producing weak, syrupy Cyprus brandy, and the Turkish beer 'Efes' was generally available and quite reasonable, together with Danish lager. Scotch whisky was highly prized and expensive.

We collected the boys from the bungalow, where Mr Kemal was showing some kind of VIP around the complex (the new manager of the hotel, as we later discovered) and Salih was doing his best to look active. There were few signs of the vast quantities of rain which had fallen during the night, the dusty land having soaked it up like a sponge, but the sky was still somewhat overcast. We retraced our journey of the previous evening, for the site of ancient Lambousa lay by the sea, somewhere behind the soldiers' restaurant. As we parked our car, there was a friendly shout from the group of soldiers mustered on the field. It was Ibrahim, looking extremely military and impressive in uniform – I had not realised that he was a corporal. He directed us along a rough track parallel with the coast to the east.

'That is Lambousa – old place. Be careful of the firing range and assault course. Just go along the road.'

We walked along the littoral, over a stony moor, until we came across a shepherd moving his flock along the track. We asked him if he knew where Lambousa was.

'Lambousa? It is here!' he said, describing a circle with his crook. And we realised that this stony, hummocky ground, overgrown with delicate pink and white cyclamen, was all that remained of that great city, founded in the twelfth century BC by Peloponnesian Greeks from the plain of Lakonia.

Lambousa later became a Phoenician trading post and it was an important port through the Roman and Byzantine periods, where 20,000 people lived behind strong walls with a lighthouse to guide ships to its shore. It had a reputation for its fine amphorae, and a Christian bishop was established as early as AD 61. Yet as the power of Byzantium waned, Lambousa's position on the coast, once so advantageous for trade, became dangerously exposed. Even the strong walls could not keep out the Arab pirates, and when they sacked the city in 647 the inhabitants abandoned it, moving inland to found Lapithos. For centuries the Lapithians helped themselves to the stones from the old city to build their houses, occasionally finding coins and artefacts which the Arabs had overlooked, so stories of buried treasure grew up around the place. And in 1905 a treasure really was found by the nearby chapel of Ayios Evlambios, being silver plate from the early Christian era, depicting scenes from the life of David.

We wandered about the tumbled stones, listening to the waves of the grey, timeless sea beating a slow rhythm on the shore. There was little enough left now; except for a few fragments of shaped masonry and tiny pieces of potsherd, the bones of Lambousa had been picked clean. In truth, the plants were more interesting and we were trying to identify a tiny, star-shaped blue flower, growing low in a hollow, when we heard a call from above and looked up to see an NCO in charge of a group of soldiers standing on a high bank above us. He beckoned us towards him. When we reached the top of the bank, we could not understand his Turkish, but gathered that we were being politely asked to clear the area. At this point, another party of soldiers arrived from the direction of the camp, carrying a mortar, with base plate and ammunition. We left them engaged in assembling the weapon, prior to adding a few more craters to the disturbed ground of Lambousa.

★   ★   ★   ★

The road to Kyrenia was busy with trucks and cars, and with people hitching rides, stopping to talk with friends or walking to their fields. This stretch of coast was one of the prime tourist areas of the island before 1974. Tourism in the North never recovered after the war, although the authorities entertained great hopes. The hotels along the coast are now virtually empty, although a number of restaurants by the roadside are well patronised by the local population. The village of Ayios Yeoryios, now Karaoglanoglu, is a lively little place, with the traffic passing through its main street and a number of well-stocked shops which we fell into the habit of using as we came and went between Kyrenia and Lapithos.

On this day, our eye was caught by the huge modern sculpture which stands where the road runs close to the sea at Five Mile Beach. This monument marks the site of the first landing during the invasion of 1974 (or the 'peace operation of 1974' as the authorities prefer to call it in Turkish Cyprus). We found it surrounded by lush grass clustered with bright yellow ranunculus, an aggressive sheaf of concrete piles thrusting diagonally inland from the sea. On it are commemorated the names of the Turkish boys – and they were only boys – who died on that first day, while the flags of Turkey and North Cyprus flutter in the sea breeze nearby. As might be expected, there is no mention of the Greeks who died while resisting them.

★   ★   ★   ★

Ask any Englishman who knew Cyprus in the old days, and he will speak nostalgically of Kyrenia, once the favourite resort of the whole island and the home of a substantial British community. Many retired colonial officials, drifting towards home as the Empire disintegrated, came no closer than Kyrenia. In their hearts they knew full well that the England whose memory they had cherished over the years, the England of their youth, did not really exist any more. Here in Cyprus, suspended between the Africa and Asia where they had spent their working lives and the cold, modern Europe which had so little time for them, they could be content. Moreover, they lived among a people who, despite all the upheavals and atrocities which were to come, fundamentally liked the British. The Greeks liked freedom even more, but the British were slow to appreciate that. Here, where the sun shone, prices were low and the scenery was delightful, they created what seemed to be a safe little world composed of bridge parties, the amateur dramatics society, church on Sunday and walks in the mountains. Here, too, was a second British community, an entirely male one which coexisted uneasily with the first. Unwelcome in a society where overt homosexuality was still unacceptable, the 'remittance men' of Kyrenia lived in shameful exile, maintained by contributions from their embarrassed families.

In the days of the Ottoman administration, Kyrenia, Cerines, Cherimes or Ceraunium, as it was variously known, was not much of a town; a minor port crouching at the foot of its castle, which carried on a modest trade with Syria. The eighteenth-century English traveller, Pococke, reported that Kyrenia traded with Seleucia and imported rice and coffee from Egypt; there were, he thought, no more than six Christian families. John MacDonald Kinneir of the East India Company came here in 1814 and found 'not above fifteen families'. Sir Samuel Baker, who travelled in Cyprus during 1879, the first year of the British occupation, estimated that there was a population of about 600, mostly Turks, who worked in a nearby quarry. With the turn of the century the British began to settle here in numbers, and by 1974 there were 2,500 British residents, representing about half the population.

An English friend described to us the night the Turkish army arrived. She woke up to the distant rumble of tank engines in the early hours and the squeal of their tracks as they approached through the outer suburbs. Warned to pack only one suitcase and to be ready with her children for the evacuation of British passport holders, she had no idea whether her Greek Cypriot husband, who had been mobilised with the National Guard, was alive or dead. It was to be months before she had news of him. Her husband's parents, who held Cypriot passports, had to be left behind. She never saw her home or business again and still, she says, wakes sometimes in the night with the noise of those tank engines in her ears.

Some British residents stayed on, but with the looting of private property by the Turkish army their numbers dwindled until after two years there were less than 200, these either being too stubborn to leave or having nowhere else to go. Now there are signs that the little colony is beginning to grow again. There are, in all, about 5,000 people in Kyrenia today, including Turks resettled from Limassol in the Greek sector and a number from the mainland.

We stopped our car on the outskirts of town to ask directions from a sentry. He was from the mainland, with broad Mongolian features and pockmarked skin under the dull green steel of his helmet. Not surprisingly, he spoke no English, so we had recourse to the phrase book:

'*Gunaydin. Lutfen liman nerede?*'

The Turks, I noted, used the same word for harbour as the Greeks. But the rest of the words sounded barbarously from my lips and probably sounded barbarous also to the sentry, who nevertheless made gratifying signs of having understood and directed us down a side street. Here we came upon the famous Dome Hotel, which seemed to be making the best of these leaner times, and passed a line of car hire offices, including the one responsible for our own battered conveyance, which we left by the Custom House at the beginning of the quay.

Having read so much about Kyrenia and its horseshoe-shaped harbour, I was prepared now to find it modernised and overdeveloped. But in fact it was still a charming place, particularly in the early spring; a town one might even fall in love with. The ground floors of the old merchants' houses along the waterfront had been converted into restaurants and bars, but still retained their original arched windows and heavy wooden balconies, while the minaret of the town mosque stood against russet tiled roofs and a backdrop of jagged mountains. The huge bulk of the castle, built in honey-coloured stone to guard the entrance to the anchorage, faced out towards Turkey. High above the parapet, a single palm tree tossed its fronds and the twin red flags flickered like flames in the sea breeze. Below the castle wall, a little gunboat was moored, lean, grey and purposeful with the barrel of the forward armament raking upward under a canvas cover. Nearby, a large fishing caique was drawn up on the dock with most of the stern cut away, while modern yachts lay like a flock of white gulls in front of the town. In the centre of the harbour, opposite where we stood by the Custom House wall, was a crumbled stele, a pillar of obvious antiquity surrounded by water, which served as a mooring post for the hawsers of larger vessels. This was one of the original four towers of the Byzantine defences against the Arab corsairs, and great chains would once have been run from it to close the harbour mouth when danger threatened. Everything was brightly coloured and clean, glowing in the sunlight – and peaceful, for in time we discovered that the waterfront was a place of idlers and coffee drinkers where no one ever hurried, the bustle and traffic of the modern town centre being away up the hill, out of sight and hearing.

We would have plenty of opportunities to become acquainted with Kyrenia in the weeks to come, but today the castle seemed to be the obvious place to begin. Accordingly we walked around to the dock where the gunboat was moored beneath the walls. Here a guard stood at attention by the gangway and a notice warned: 'Military Area. Photography forbidden.' (Military Area, *Askeri Bolge*, were words which eventually became very familiar to us. Whenever we felt moved to take a photograph of the castle, or the very picturesque harbour, we had to be careful not to point the camera too ostentatiously at the little warship.) The rest of the crew, a cheerful bunch of lads dressed in track suits, were playing football in the dry bed of the castle moat, where a paved road wound up under the great walls. This football match went on for day after day, interrupted only about once a week when the vessel made a fast cruise along the north coast.

We climbed up a steep, stone stairway to find a little wooden cabin, where an elderly gentleman sold us tickets for a few lire and directed us across the drawbridge into an entrance tunnel running through the immense thickness of the wall. Narrow steps led down to a water gate, for it was once possible to bring ships right into the moat, perhaps even within the protection of the castle walls. Having emerged into the main courtyard with its overgrown garden, we climbed up further steps until we stood by the flags fluttering on the western wall and could look out over the town along the mountains stretching towards Cape Kormakiti.

The Achaeans, who founded a city here in the tenth century before Christ, first called this place Kerynia. To the Romans it was Corineum, and they seem to have built the first fortress, for as we walked along the broad southern wall we could look down to recently discovered Roman masonry and carved stone lions. The Byzantines enlarged it in order to secure the only harbour of any account on the whole north coast from Arab sea-raiders. This citadel was never successfully stormed by any attacker, although it was starved into surrender on several occasions. And each successive occupier thickened and enlarged the fortifications, so as to build the castle up in layers. Thus the south-west tower and the chapel by the main gate are still recognisably Byzantine, though of a later date than that turbulent period between the seventh and tenth centuries when Cyprus continually changed hands between Arabs and Greeks.

The eleventh and twelfth centuries, the 'Golden Age' of Byzantium, were a time of peace and prosperity never to be repeated in Cyprus. This was the time when the Orthodox monasteries throve, the most beautiful churches were built and many of the finest frescos were painted. Nevertheless, it was a time of apprehension too, for although the Saracens had been defeated they and a new people from the East, the Seljuk Turks, continued to menace this outpost of Christendom. Constantinople ordered the building of a chain of great fortresses around the island, of which Kyrenia is but one. And it was also a period of decline, for the power of Constantinople was weakening year by year, due not only to the incursions of the Turks into the Empire, but also, paradoxically, to pressure from western Europe. The Catholic Crusaders, the hated Franks, had proved since the Great Schism to be almost as ill-disposed to the Orthodox Church as the Muslims.

In 1184 an opportunistic governor, the Byzantine prince Isaac Comnenus, rebelled against the Empire and declared himself 'Despot of Cyprus', Constantinople being in no condition to restrain him. In time, this title seeming inadequate to him, he announced himself to be the 'Emperor of Cyprus'. After seven years he made the mistake of ill-using and insulting the party of Berengaria of Navarre, the betrothed of Richard the Lionheart, who was shipwrecked near Limassol on her way to the Third Crusade in an English ship. Shortly afterward, Richard arrived in Cyprus with a large fleet, furious at the insult to his lady's honour.

After inflicting a defeat on the self-styled Emperor's army, he married Berengaria in the Chapel of St George at Limassol. In what is believed to be the only English coronation to have taken place abroad, Berengaria became Queen of England, while Richard had himself crowned King of Cyprus. The Emperor's wife and child fled here to Kyrenia Castle, which was besieged in 1191 by Richard's fellow Crusader, Guy de Lusignan, the Frenchman who had been King of Jerusalem until Saladin recaptured it in 1187. Kyrenia surrendered without a fight, while Isaac Comnenus was induced to give himself up on condition that he was not put in irons. It was thus in specially made silver chains that he was sent off to his incarceration and death in Palestine.

Cyprus was of merely passing interest to the Lionheart, and he himself left the island for Acre almost immediately. When he ran short of funds, he offered his new kingdom to the Knights Templar for 100,000 gold bezants, on the basis of 40,000 down, the balance to follow. The Templars proposed to raise the remaining 60,000 by taxing their Cypriot subjects. This provoked such a bloody uprising that within a year they asked to return the island to Richard, who did not, however, refund the downpayment. He next sold Cyprus to his old friend and ally Guy de Lusignan, founder of a long line of Kings of Cyprus and Jerusalem, although this last was for ever to remain an empty title.

The Lusignans, that romantic, cursed breed, were great builders and their French-Gothic cathedrals are one of the wonders of the island. They also improved upon the old Byzantine fortresses, and during the thirteenth century the north and east walls were rebuilt at

Kyrenia, while a new south wall was built outside the existing one on the landward side. They made the castle into a state prison, as the British were to do more than 600 years later, and in 1310 the Prince of Galilee and other nobles who had attempted to take the throne were starved to death in the oubliettes, grim black pits which we inspected below the courtyard. In 1349 King Hugh IV locked his own sons up here, as a punishment, apparently, for attempting to travel to Europe without his permission. It was one of these two princes who was later to become the greatest Lusignan monarch, Peter I, whose fame spread throughout Europe, and whose tragic story was told by Chaucer and is woven into the folklore of Cyprus in the ballad of 'Arodaphnoussa', sung until quite recently in the villages.

Peter inherited a kingdom seriously weakened by the Black Death – it is estimated that up to half the population may have perished during 1348–9 – and Turkish pirates took advantage of his absence in France to make two raids on the north coast of Cyprus, at Pendayia on the Bay of Morphou and on the remote Karpas peninsula. Following his return, Peter took his revenge by sacking the town of Anemouri, on the coast of Anatolia north of Kyrenia, and for a while he even held Antalya. Peter's life and rule became dominated by his dream of recovering Jerusalem. As King of Jerusalem and Armenia he made a vow to wage ceaseless war on the infidels until the Holy City was freed. It is said that he constantly wore a naked sword on a cord around his neck until such time as his task might be completed. This handsome, fervent young man, perhaps the last of the 'knights errant', his eyes burning with the intensity of his vision, came to Europe to enrol Christian knights in his 'Order of the Sword' and to raise support for yet another Crusade. He was received kindly by the Pope in Rome, by the Emperor Charles IV in Prague, and in London, where Edward III gave a magnificent banquet in his honour, attended by the Black Prince and the Kings of France and Scotland. Yet, for all the compliments and courtesies, there was no enthusiasm in Europe for more ruinously expensive expeditions to the Holy Land. The crusading spirit had died during the previous century, with the loss of Acre.

In 1365 Peter returned to Cyprus with little to show for his mission, beyond moral support for a new attack on the forces of Islam. Undaunted, he assembled a fleet at Rhodes and mounted an attack upon Alexandria, which he took and plundered to the applause of all Christendom, before he was persuaded by his nobles to retire in the face of a Mameluke army marching from Cairo.

As with many an earlier monarch, notably Richard I of England, Peter's passion for the Crusades led to neglect of his family and his kingdom. The love and jealousy of two women brought about his downfall. In 1353 he had been married to Eleanor, a princess of Aragon, an attractive and strong-willed woman with whom he said to have been very happy. When he travelled abroad he habitually slept with her shift at his side. Later he fell in love with a lady of the court, Joanna L'Aleman, a famous beauty celebrated for her kindness and wit. When in 1368 he left once more for Europe to canvass for support against the infidels, Joanna was pregnant with their child. The identity of the father was plainly known to all the court.

The Queen, roused to an insane pitch of jealousy by this blatant evidence of her husband's infidelity, lured Joanna to the palace, where she had her tortured in an attempt to destroy the child. In the words of the chronicler, Leontios Makhairas:

> . . . they brought a handmill and stretched her out on the ground and put it on her womb, and they held her firmly and ground two measures of flour upon her womb; and still she did not miscarry.

(Trs. R. M. Dawkins, *Recital Concerning the Sweet Land of Cyprus*)

Joanna was imprisoned and tortured in the dungeons of Kyrenia Castle, and here her child was eventualy born and taken from her, never to be seen again.

This prompted Peter to write a stern and threatening letter to Eleanor, who released Joanna, but forced her to enter the Convent of Santa Clara in Nicosia. Eleanor revenged herself by conducting an open affair with John de Morphou, the Earl of Rouchias, which precipitated such a scandal that one John Visconti was despatched to Italy with a letter to Peter. With all the fury of a wronged husband, he immediately returned to Cyprus, firstly visiting Joanna at the convent and offering her 1,000 silver piastres to renounce her vows and return to live openly with him at court. She agreed, and the King called together the Council of Nobles in order to try Eleanor formally for the crime of adultery, producing as evidence the accusatory letter which Visconti had brought to him.

But the nobles of Cyprus had never intended this, having merely wished to procure the return of their sovereign to attend to the affairs of his kingdom and to bring the scandal to an end. Fearing the consequences of the public arraignment of the Queen, daughter of a powerful European ruler, they instead turned on poor Visconti, accusing him of instigating a plot against the Queen and forging the letter. Visconti soon found himself immured in the dark pits below Kyrenia and later was moved to Buffavento Castle where he starved to death.

Peter's character had become warped by his experiences. Idealism had turned to suspicion and paranoia. He treated his faithless nobles with the open contempt he felt they deserved, and they in turn came to fear his dangerous, vindictive rages. They too came of turbulent Crusader stock, and began to plot the death of their king. Perhaps even Peter's joy in Joanna d'Aleman had turned sour, for he lay in the arms of a new mistress, Eschive de Scandelion, when they came to kill him, bursting into the chamber and butchering him between blood-soaked sheets. Chaucer in the 'Monk's Tale' wrote:

> O worthy Petro King of Cipres, also,
> That Alisaunder won by high maistrye,
> Ful many an heathen wroughtest thou ful wo,
> Of which thin oune lieges had envye;
> And for nothing but for thy chivalrie,
> They in thy bed have slayne thee by the morwe.
> Thus can fortune the wheel governe and gye,
> And of joy bringe men into sorwe.

Cyprus was more than just a beleagured outpost of Christianity in the East, being a vital trading centre for the spices and silks of Asia which were in great demand throughout Europe. Venice and Genoa, the two rivals for the trade in these precious goods, which reached the eastern Mediterranean by the long camel routes across the deserts of Arabia, vied with each other for influence over Cyprus and the great port at Famagusta. Matters came to a head in 1372 over the apparently petty matter of whether a Venetian or a Genoese should be accorded the symbolic courtesy of holding the right-hand rein of King Peter II as he rode from his coronation in Famagusta Cathedral. (By tradition, the Lusignans were crowned as King of Cyprus at Nicosia, and later King of Jerusalem at Famagusta, this city being the nearest to the Holy Land.) There was a riot, during which a number of Genoese merchants were killed and their warehouses pillaged. Their distress was sufficient pretext for Genoa to invade Cyprus; the King was captured and Eleanor of Aragon, the Queen Mother, was besieged in Kyrenia Castle with a force of Bulgarian mercenaries. The Genoese had Famagusta and Nicosia, but Kyrenia held firm and finally a truce was negotiated by which the King was released to regain control over the island, although Famagusta with all its rich trade was formally ceded to Genoa.

The troubles of the Lusignans continued through the fifteenth century. In 1426 the Mamelukes, the race of Circassian slaves who had captured Egypt, invaded Cyprus and captured King Janus. His family took refuge in Kyrenia; the Mamelukes approached the castle, examined the fortifications closely and went away, contenting themselves with the plunder of Limassol, Larnaca and Nicosia, before carrying the King back to Alexandria with them. Janus was ransomed for an oath of allegiance to the Sultan of Cairo and the payment of a considerable annual tribute in perpetuity. The authority of the throne was consquently weakened.

The rise and fall of Lusignan power, and their castles and cathedrals, can have been of little interest or concern to the native Greeks of Cyprus, any more than it is to the Turks who live in Kyrenia today. They had no cause to love these Franks who had taken the best of the land for their feudal estates, enslaving the Greeks as serfs, and whose Catholic Church rode roughshod over their Orthodox beliefs. In the *Bulla Cypria* of 1260, the Latin Archbishop was made the supreme chief of both the Catholic and Orthodox Churches. Orthodox property was seized (the Greeks, it should be remembered, believed that the Latin rite profaned a church), and all tithes were collected by the Latins. Orthodox bishops were obliged to take an oath of allegiance and obedience to the Latin Church. Until the time of the Turkish conquest, the Orthodox Church of Cyprus was not recognised by the Patriarch of Constantinople, for it was under the rule of Latin bishops. But the Cypriots never openly rebelled against their Crusader overlords, sullenly keeping their own counsel.

Towards the end, the introduction of Greek blood further weakened the monarchy as rival claimants to the throne were separately championed by the Latin and Orthodox Churches. In 1460 James II, the bastard stepson of Helena Palaeologa, a Cypriot Queen of ancient Byzantine blood, wrested the crown from his stepsister Charlotte, who held Kyrenia against him for four years. James employed Mameluke mercenaries and bombarded the castle from the roof of one of the churches in the town before the garrison was eventually starved out. James was to be the last of the independent Lusignan kings, for he made the mistake of becoming too closely involved with the Venetians, who helped him regain Famagusta from the Genoese. Venice provided him with a bride, a fair-haired beauty named Catherine Cornaro, who inherited Cyprus following the somewhat mysterious deaths of her husband and young son, said by some to have been poisoned. Queen Catherine ruled alone, though she was persuaded in time to award all key appointments to Venetians. At last, under intolerable pressure (her own brother, George Cornaro, had been sent by the Doge to work on her feelings), she formally ceded the Kingdom of Cyprus to the Serene Republic in 1489, before retiring to Venice, where she was ceremoniously greeted with every honour and courtesy. 'Our most serene and beloved daughter,' said the Doge, who had sent his own ship to collect her. Considering that she had given him a kingdom, this was, one might think, the very least he could do. On her death in 1510, Venice buried her as a queen; a bridge of boats was built to allow the funeral procession across the Grand Canal, and on her coffin was laid the crown of Cyprus.

The rule of Venice proved even harsher to the Cypriots than that of the Franks. 'We have escaped from the grasp of a dog to fall into that of the lion,' one of their clerics remarked bitterly. For their part, the Venetians had gained Cyprus without firing a shot, but were well aware that they would probably soon be called upon to fight the Turks in its defence. The Byzantine and Lusignan castles had been designed for defence against armoured knights and archers; now the nature of war had changed, and the Turks, said to be the finest soldiers of their day, would certainly bring siege cannon. At Nicosia and Famagusta huge modern citadels were built, among the largest the world had ever seen, while the walls of Kyrenia were thickened and strengthened by great stone-faced earthworks. All the sharp corners of the towers, so vulnerable to cannon fire, were replaced by curved bastions to deflect the shot, and embrasures were constructed at different heights to house the artillery of the defenders. If the earlier castle had been built around an inner harbour, as some claim, this was now filled in. These were the walls on which we now walked, 30 to 40 feet thick at the top, and enclosing grassy earthworks behind.

Strange to tell, when the Turks did invade Cyprus in 1570, taking first Nicosia and then Famagusta with great difficulty, Kyrenia surrendered without resistance to the Turkish admiral, Sadiq Pasha, who later died here and whose stone turban-capped tomb we had passed by the gatehouse. It is said that with his demand for surrender Sadiq enclosed the heads of two Venetian officers from Nicosia.

The castle might have been left to a peaceful old age, were it not for the revolt of its commander, Khalil Agha, in 1765, when it was blockaded into submission. And in 1955, during the EOKA campaign, the British army took the fortress over from the Antiquities Department and garrisoned it once more. The mountings of their guns and searchlights, a little rusty now, were still secured to the stonework at the corners of the walls, facing out over the white houses of the town and the mountains beyond.

Down in an overgrown corner of the courtyard was a double row of barred windows and stout grey-painted doors, the upper row reached by a balcony.

'EOKA prison?' I asked the guardian, and he nodded confirmation. The cells looked rather more comfortable than those of a Victorian-built English prison, secure but hardly inhumane. We peeped through some of the windows; a few cells were piled with odd tools and building materials, others were empty, but all seemed surprisingly light and spacious. There was something of an outcry in the Greek press about conditions, for many of the men and boys kept here were

42

only held on suspicion under the Detention Laws. A dramatic escape had been made from one cell; Marcos Dracos and others had climbed 60 feet down a rope made of blankets and sheets.

In another part of the court we came to the Great Hall, which has been turned into a museum to house the famous 'Kyrenia Ship', a galley from the time of Alexander the Great which was discovered by divers in 60 feet of water about half a mile offshore. An expedition from the University of Pennsylvania recovered it in 1969, together with its cargo of plates and amphorae. Now it stands in half-light, its timbers (of the Aleppo pine which still covers these mountains), carefully preserved in resin. The crew seems to have lived entirely on almonds, which must have become exceedingly dull.

The minaret of the old Jafer Pasha Mosque, not far from the castle walls, was severely damaged during the bloodletting between the communities in 1964, to be restored later. Then, the Turks lived in the upper town, known as Regiatiko, and in a few streets leading down to the harbour. Now the names of Greek streets – Hellas Street, 28th October Street, Korais Street, Pericles, Athena and Makarios II – had all been changed. It was the time of prayer, and a steady stream of men passed through the door, kicking off their shoes and moving forward to kneel on the worn carpets: business suits next to paint- and grease-stained workmen's overalls, and a smell of leather and sweat from the discarded shoes by the door. We went to eat at a little restaurant across the street which served *dolmades* and *keftedes*. Later the *hodja*, a youngish man dressed in baggy, black *shalvar* trousers, came in to collect his lunch. 'And God be with you,' he said, in the Arabic form, taking away a packet of *kebabs* and *pitta* bread.

At a nearby supermarket, an establishment western in that you served yourself, eastern in that the proprietor presided over the till with a tiny cup of coffee and a fly whisk, we loaded up with provisions for our kitchen. Everything was very cheap, except for imported goods such as the breakfast cereals which our children insisted on eating in the morning. To my surprise, our purchases were weighed in *okas*, the old Ottoman measure of approximately three pounds which the British adopted when they leased the island from the Sultan in 1878. I have seen this measure used in remote parts of Crete, but nowhere else, for Turkey itself changed to the standard European system of metric measurement long ago, during Kemal Pasha's modernisations. South of the Green Line, Greek Cyprus has also instituted metric measurement, but here in the North the *oka* lives on, together with the *donum* for measuring areas of land. The old iron weights were piled on to the scales while the Labrador lying by the door, a friend to everyone in the street, yawned sleepily and stretched its legs in the sunshine.

* * * *

We had long promised ourselves that when we approached St Hilarion, the fairy castle of the Kyrenia mountains, it should be on foot. We were determined to savour to the full the pleasure of that little winding road leading up to those romantic towers and pinnacles which we had seen on so many postcards. In practice, as so often in life, it was less simple. The forest road, which led away uphill to the west from the main Kyrenia–Nicosia highway, went past an army camp, an area of parked lorries, barbed wire and sentry boxes which overlooked the distant roofs of Kyrenia far below. 'Controlled Road' announced the signs, and 'No Photography'. The whole area had been militarised since the 1960s, when Turkish fighters had established themselves here to dominate the pass. The afternoon had become dark and it began to rain, while the sound of thunder occasionally echoed around the crags and through the woods. When we deemed ourselves out of sight of the military installations and radio masts, we pulled off the road under a fir tree and waited for the shower to pass, uneasily aware that we were probably contravening the regulations.

When the rain ceased and the sun flashed briefly from behind clouds which were still black and threatening, we pulled on waterproofs and began to walk up the deserted, grassy valley. Sir Samuel Baker had ridden the same way and found this little plain cropped with barley, while the cultivators lived in a nearby cave. The Lusignan knights had reputedly held their tournaments here, but now it had been turned into a field firing range. We passed through a narrow defile and on to high ground to the right of the lonely road. As we crested the ridge, St Hilarion was suddenly before us, a twin-peaked mountain of sheer cliffs and jumbled crags, into which the sand castle crenellations, battlements and towers merged as if they were growing from the rock, just as the cypress trees grew between them. It was a dramatic vision of pure magic, only enhanced by the fork of lightning which cracked down from the thunder clouds as we watched. Walt Disney's cartoonists used St Hilarion as their model for *Snow White and the Seven Dwarfs*, and our spirits were so lifted by this flight into architectural fancy that it was hard to believe it was ever intended for war. The Crusaders were moved to give the castle the charming name of 'Dieudamour', though this may have simply arisen from an inability to pronounce the Greek 'Didymos', for the twin peaks of the mountain.

It was plain that we could not scale the walls from this side, any more than the medieval knights had been able to, and so we returned to the forest road to take the long way round to the main gate. These were the strangest mountains I had ever seen. Their layers of Jurassic limestone had once lain horizontally under the Caramanian Straits. Then pressure from the Taurus mountains of Anatolia pushed them up against the igneous rock of the Troodos range to the south until they buckled and folded, and the now vertical layers of jagged rock broke and pointed into the sky like knives, or the broken glass atop a factory wall. To look to the east or the west was to glance along the cutting edge of a great saw. Writers have variously described these mountains as 'Gothic' or 'operatic' and perhaps the last adjective is the best chosen. The mountains of Kyrenia look very like an imaginatively painted backdrop for a performance of Wagner.

Although the long ridge is narrow and steep, the slopes are softened by a clothing of trees, for Cyprus has not been entirely denuded of her forests as have so many other Mediterranean lands. Remarkably, the British Forestry Commission contrived to build a dirt road along the top of almost the entire length of the range – at a cost of £300 per mile according to Patrick Balfour, who watched the construction after the Second World War. This road, although sadly neglected in places, was still passable for a four-wheel-drive vehicle.

In time, we arrived at the mountain's foot, where we eventually found the guardian behind the curtain wall, wandering among the ruinous outbuildings of the lower ward, where once Byzantine cavalry had stabled their horses. He was accompanied in this overgrown garden by his lame Alsatian, an amiable creature which liked to accompany visitors over the castle, hopping on three legs up the flights of rock-cut steps to the very highest tower. We bought our tickets and began the long climb, past the gatehouse and barbican, through the Byzantine arch and by ancient cisterns. This was only the first of a series of defences, for at the top of the path we came to a huge gatehouse guarding the approach to the middle ward: old Byzantine masonry again, modified by the Lusignans to take a drawbridge. Beyond is a large tenth-century church, which may have been part of the monastery which stood here before the building of the castle.

No one really knows who Hilarion was, although all seem agreed that he was not St Hilarion the Great, who founded the first monasteries in Palestine before coming to die at Paphos in AD 371. This Hilarion came from the Holy Land too, but much later, when it had been overrun by the Arabs. Here, on this mountain, he lived the secluded life of a hermit, although there is an old legend that a ruined temple to the Cypriot goddess Aphrodite then stood on the summit, and that the mountain was haunted by pagan demons who made the place hideous with their groans and shrieks until the holy man's presence exorcised them.

One of the hazards of a hermit's life in Cyprus seems to have been that others might be inspired by one's good example to forsake the world also, and set up house in the cave next door, thus ending one's dreams of peace and blessed solitude. This was the fate of St Neophytos at Paphos, and it seems that before St Hilarion died he too may have found his lonely contemplation overwhelmed by the brawling of a large monastery full of monks. The saint's memory and relics were reverently preserved for some centuries before being lost by some accident of history. Eneo Silvio de Piccolomini, the scholarly Pope Pius II who was so interested in Cyprus and its history, wrote as late as the fifteenth century that 'four furlongs from Kyrenia Castle is a mountain where the head of St Hilarion is kept'.

Still less is it clear exactly when the monastery became a castle; only that it was one of three, the Byzantine defensive chain of St Hilarion, Buffavento and Kantara, all of them perched in the splintered crags of the Kyrenia range. By lighting signal beacons at night, the garrison of St Hilarion could communicate with Kyrenia below on the north coast, and across the mountains with Buffavento, which in turn was in sight of Nicosia on the plain, and of Kantara, far away in the east.

We wandered through the maze of rooms which form the middle ward: the Castellan's quarters, kitchens and privies, all precariously built over an abyss, their vertiginous balconies giving views to the north, east and south. Here a modern restaurant had been contrived in a medieval hall, locked up today but open at weekends. On fine nights, one can dine by candlelight out on the gallery, the lights of Kyrenia spread out below; a pleasure tempered only by concern for the worm-eaten timbers on which one's life depends.

The castles in the mountains held out against Richard Coeur de Lion even after he had made Isaac Comnenus prisoner. Guy de Lusignan turned his attention to St Hilarion after Kyrenia, but this time met with fierce resistance until Comnenus himself was persuaded to order the garrison to surrender. Subsequently, Comnenus' daughter was kept safely here under a strong guard, lest the remnants of his supporters be tempted to set her up as a new Byzantine queen. The Lusignans continued to strengthen the castle, until it played a part in an extraordinary series of wars during the minority of King Henry I, who acceded to the throne in 1218. John d'Ibelin had been appointed Regent by the High Court of Cyprus, but he was challenged in this role by the crusading Emperor of Germany, Frederick II, whose own claim to Cyprus was preposterously obscure. St Hilarion was the stronghold of d'Ibelin and the boy-king during a protracted series of negotiations which eventually resulted in a truce, after which the pair of rivals happily set off on a Crusade together to the Holy Land. D'Ibelin's displeasure can be imagined when he returned the following year to find that Frederick's henchmen had taken the reins of government into their own hands, and he was obliged first to defeat them in open battle at Nicosia, and then to besiege them in St Hilarion for nine months before they surrendered.

D'Ibelin was accompanied during this siege by the soldier-poet Philip de Novare who, even when wounded, lay among the rocks beneath the castle walls taunting the defenders within. When word came that the garrison were so starved that they had killed a donkey, rather than a lamb, to celebrate Easter, he mocked the Emperor's bailiff with these lines:

Strange things at Eastertide by his behest,
Were brought about, when daringly he blest
And then devoured the lamb with the great ears.

(Trs. Patrick Balfour, *The Orphaned Realm*)

There seemed no end to Frederick's pretensions. (His Crusade had involved little fighting, rather an accommodation with the Sultan whereby he acquired the Kingdom of Judea for himself in return for his toleration of Islam.) In 1232, while the King and his Regent were in Syria, he sent a force of Lombards to capture Cyprus, investing St Hilarion where the King's family had sheltered. Young Henry himself saved the day on this occasion, returning from Syria to defeat the invaders on the Kyrenia mountain pass and so ending the Emperor's hopes of adding Cyprus to his possessions.

A zigzag path, overgrown with moss and wild cyclamen, led up through cypress trees to steep flights of rough steps and a Frankish arch set into the Byzantine fortifications, which let us into the upper ward. This area, within the walls, was thick with cypress and juniper, and made slightly hazardous by the presence of deep, open cisterns cut into the rock, the haunt of olive-coloured frogs. Here the Lusignans had maintained their royal apartments during 140 years of peace through the thirteenth and fourteenth centuries. St Hilarion then was not so much a fortress as a summer palace, a place to escape the sweltering heat of the plains in the cool pine-scented mountain breezes, a hunting lodge, a banqueting hall, a place to wear soft silks rather than coarse chain mail; a time, perhaps, when Dieudamour became as Lancelot's Joyous Garde.

The name of Lusignan was always associated with legend and mystery, and it was believed that fairy blood ran in their veins. The earliest historical record of the name is that of Hugh the Hunter, Sire de Lusignan in the late ninth century. But by tradition the name came from the Fountain of Lusignan, a spring deep in the forests of Poitou,

47

which was haunted by a beautiful nereid named Melusine. Here a young knight, Raymond, came riding through the woods, so the story runs, and found a lovely girl by the water. He was so enchanted that he begged her to marry him, but she would only accept on the condition that he swear never to try to set eyes on her on a Saturday. He agreed, and so they were married and lived for years most happily in the great castle of Lusignan which they built in the forest. Melusine bore her husband handsome children, though each had some minor blemish. And every Saturday, Melusine remained within her chamber and would not emerge until the Sunday morning.

Eventually, her husband could no longer restrain his curiosity, and one Saturday he peered cautiously through the door of the chamber. To his horror, he saw his wife, a beautiful woman above the waist but below formed in writhing coils like a water snake. 'Serpent!' he gasped in his astonishment, thus betraying his presence. With a piercing shriek, Melusine flew through the window and her family never saw her again.

The line of Lusignan continued, it was said, to be born with slight defects: a twisted finger or a mark on the skin. Guy de Lusignan was so affected himself, although he was much liked; a modest and honourable man according to his contemporaries. And the spirit of Melusine continued to watch over her descendants, so that her cries would be heard when the death of a Lusignan drew nigh. '*Poussez des cris de Melusine*' used to be a superstitious saying in Poitou, when impending evil or disaster was foretold.

Mythologists, of course, have suggested that early in the Christian era the Lusignans married into a family with a pagan tradition: priestesses of a sacred spring, or worshippers of serpents. But to the late medieval world, the old story only added lustre to the legends which grew around this little Christian kingdom and its rulers, who were famed for their wealth derived from the eastern trade. Above all, they were renowned for their chivalry, which belonged to an earlier, less complicated age, one whose passing many in the West may have regretted. Surrounded by an Islamic sea, they hawked and hunted, jousted and banqueted, all in such splendour and style that every traveller they entertained returned to Europe bursting with stories of the marvels he had seen. Their ladies, fabulously jewelled and dressed in all the rich fabrics of the East, wore always a black velvet cape in mourning for lost Jerusalem.

Lusignan Castle itself was razed in 1562 during the Huguenot wars, while the last direct descendant of the line, Eliza de Lusignan, who had lived obscurely as a Victorian governess, died in London at the turn of the century. Yet the Lusignan kings had married into the noble and royal houses of Europe and their blood still flows, even in the British royal family.

The Black Death came to Cyprus in 1349. Almost one-third of the population died, and King Hugh IV and his court retreated to St Hilarion in terror, saving themselves by their isolation. Here they must have fretted for long months, each concealing the dread in his heart that the terrible disease might have entered the walls with one of their company.

We climbed higher on the wall, to a gallery where windows looked out to the west and the blue mists around Cape Kormakiti; one of these, elegantly carved with Gothic traceries, is still known as the Queen's Window. Which of the Lusignan queens this refers to I am not sure, though it was pleasant to sit in the embrasure and speculate. Perhaps the name refers to that strange, mythical Queen who appears in so much Cypriot folklore, the 'Regina' who fought battles with giants and concealed treasures. It is said that there are 101 rooms in the castle; 100 can be found, but the last contains the bewitched treasure of the Queen. There are stories of men blundering into the secret doorway, falling asleep in a magic garden and reawakening many years later on the open mountainside. Similar legends are told of the other mountain castles, Buffavento and Kantara.

I have never liked heights, and I was tense and sweating by the time we had mounted a spiral of ancient steps, reinforced with twentieth-century steel here and there, left to crumble in other places, to emerge on the summit of Prince John's Tower. This seemed to me to be a place fit only for eagles or the insane, with sheer cliffs on three sides and a high walk along a narrow shelf protected on one side by a knee-high wall. Joan and the children, by contrast, strolled along with the utmost nonchalance, until my fear for them was added to my fear for myself. But once I had found a solid piece of rock to cling on to, I had to admit that the view along the 100 miles of the Kyrenia range was superb. This place is 2,559 feet above sea level.

During the Genoese invasion of 1373, Prince John of Antioch, uncle of King Peter II, occupied St Hilarion together with his bodyguard of Bulgarian mercenaries. These soldiers distinguished themselves in courageous attacks on the Genoese army encamped around Kyrenia Castle, besieging the Queen Mother, the indefatigable Eleanor of Aragon. Prince John had earned the hatred of this lady by his earlier involvement in the assassination of King Peter I, her husband and his brother. When a truce had been arranged with the Genoese, she contrived to poison his mind against the bodyguard which had served him so faithfully, sending word that they were plotting his death. The Prince fell into a fit of melancholic suspicion, climbed with his attendants to this highest tower, and had the unsuspecting Bulgars summoned up one by one, to be hurled out into the abyss. Unguarded, the Prince himself soon fell an easy victim to Eleanor's revenge.

The Venetians had no use for these antique castles of the mountains, for there was no prospect of making them proof against heavy artillery. Accordingly, they dismantled the defences and there the history of St Hilarion would have rested, were it not for the violence of recent times. During the fighting between the Greek and Turkish communities in 1964, a party of young Turks seized the castle and the Greeks were unable to fight their way inside the walls. St Hilarion has remained in Turkish hands ever since, and through the 1960s and early 1970s their militia occupied the upper parts, watching the countryside through high-powered binoculars and using the castle as a base to control the main Nicosia–Kyrenia road, denying it to Greek traffic. Even after the invasion the soliders remained in their eyrie, and for a long time visitors were restricted from visiting the upper ward, being conducted around the lower parts of the castle by a soldier doubling as guide.

A distant cry reached up to us through the clear air from the gatehouse. The tiny figure of the guardian could be seen waving his arms. He obviusly wanted to lock up for the night, so we began to make our way down, accompanied part of the way by his old dog who had come limping up to meet us. It took nearly twenty minutes to descend to where he waited, together with his son, who had arrived to drive his father home.

'But how did you get here? Where is your car?' asked the younger man.

I explained where we had left it and how we had walked up the valley. He gave me that look of incomprehension which Cypriots always reserve for anyone who walks when he might ride.

'I'm very sorry, but you mustn't do that. This is a military area and the road is controlled. It might be dangerous.'

We faithfully promised not to repeat the offence and were relieved, after hurriedly walking down the valley past the firing range, to find our car undisturbed beneath the trees.

The showers and thunder of the day had given way to a fine evening as we drove through the villages lying close under St Hilarion. Temblos, or Zeytinlik, once held by the Knights Templar, now consisted mainly of ruins surrounded by clustered palms, and Trimithi, or Edremit, which once had a reputation for slave trading, was now remarkable only for its dirt and poverty. Karmi, or Karaman, in full sight of the Queen's Window thousands of feet above, and so close under the mountain's north flank that its people are said to live in shadow for most of their lives, was in premature darkness when we reached it, leaving an impression in the headlamps' glare of tumbled almond blossom hanging over steep narrow streets.

The little seaside restaurant at Guzelyali formed a welcome oasis of warmth and light. It had not been easy to find; we had bumped over uncertain dirt tracks and open fields in the dark, and stopped to ask for directions at isolated houses where watchdogs barked and pulled their chains. By local standards there was a smart line-up of vehicles outside: a BMW and two Volkswagens, with a number of the ubiquitous AJS and Matchless motorcycles, for the British motorcyle still lives on in North Cyprus, even if the industry is only a memory at home. The restaurant belonged to Mr Hamit Ucok, a neatly dressed middle-aged man, who always shook your hand at the door as you entered and left. He and his children did everything, working in a large inner room, part kitchen and part family living room, so that the daughters would clean fish and make up salads at the large table while watching television. Sometimes they would knit, or the younger ones spread their homework books. One son waited in the restaurant, the other, Mr Ucok told me, had lived for seven years in England, at Watford. Above the kitchen door hung the huge, horned head of an African buffalo, which gazed with a baleful eye at the dishes passing beneath its nose. There was a long story attached to the acquiring of this trophy, which I now forget.

The *mezethes* were the restaurant's forte; up to twenty dishes would be brought in rapid-fire delivery to the table, containing toasted cheese, pickled artichokes, beetroot, onion, sliced tomatoes in oil, cucumber, cauliflower in vinegar, stuffed vine leaves, olives, *houmous* and *taramosalata*. There might be grilled red mullet to follow, sometimes octopus or squid, though there is less seafood in Turkish Cyprus than one might expect. More often there would be *sheftalia kebab*, the rich, spicy Cypriot sausage, or *souvlakia* – the Greek word for *kebabs* spit-roasted over charcoal. Of these last two dishes, the mainstay of every restaurant and café in Cyprus, it must be said that one could have enough as the days went by, especially as the meat is cut and served with great yellow wedges of fat. 'No more . . . ing *kebabs*' became the watchword of our family, and as time went by we began to dream of a spicy curry, a chop-suey, some Italian pasta, couscous – anything, in fact, except more grilled meat. But meat, especially mutton, was very cheap and most people who could afford to eat in restaurants at all ate prodigious amounts, accompanied by large glasses of *raki* and puffing at cigarettes between every course. By middle age many of these had achieved quite a considerable bulk, necessitating much grunting as they heaved themselves out of their chairs at the end of the evening, and waddled happily off to their cars, apparently lacking any inner sense of guilt. One evening I was moved to begin leafing through my dictionary, quite convinced that I would find no equivalent words in Turkish to 'diet' and 'heart disease'. Somewhat to my surprise, I found that I was wrong.

Accounts of earlier travellers indicate that this obsession with meat-eating might be a recent phenomenon, perhaps made possible by the higher living standards of the late twentieth century. A hundred years before, Sir Samuel Baker wrote:

> The principal food of the Cypriotes consists of olives, beans, bread and onions . . . whether this is owing to the scarcity of food, or whether it is natural in this climate to avoid flesh, I cannot determine: some say the people are too poor, and cannot afford mutton at twopence a pound, while at the same time they will not kill the oxen that are required for purposes of draught; they refuse the milk of cows and only use that of sheep or goats. The fact remains that the country people seldom eat butcher's meat, but subsist on olives, oil, bread, cheese and vegetables.

(Samuel Baker, *Cyprus as I Saw It in 1879*)

Mr Ucok and his son were always interested in our excursions and often used to pull a big framed map of Cyprus down from the wall and lay it on the table amongst the plates and glasses, in their enthusiasm to point out places they thought might interest us. Once they looked at our Greek map and Mr Ucok's forehead creased in bewilderment.

'What is this?' he said, his finger tracing the legend running across the north and his own village, 'Inaccessible . . . because . . . of the Turkish . . . occupation.'

'It's a Greek map,' I said, embarrassed, although I am not sure why. 'It's accessible to you and I at least.'

By unspoken mutual agreement we changed the subject.

'I am sure you liked St Hilarion,' said Mr Ucok. 'Everybody does. But I don't often go to the castle now. You see when I was a soldier, I spent thirteen years up there.'

CHAPTER FOUR

MORPHOU AND THE WEST

My early walk to the village shop had become a routine, and the figures among the lemon trees on the way up the hill were now familiar. There was the lorry driver who collected the sacks of fruit from the roadside, the women, wrapped in woollens and shawls, who picked the yellow globes with the aid of tall ladders, and the farmer who led his little Friesian cows one by one to tether them in the orchards among the lush grass and turban buttercups. A very old man used to sit on a wicker chair in the morning sunshine, surrounded by geraniums and cyclamen outside his daughter's house, and a young man in mechanic's overalls used to ride a smoky little motorcycle down the road towards the coast. All of these had a friendly '*Gunaydin*, good morning', though somehow the cheekiness and gaiety of their Greek counterparts were lacking.

The shopkeeper's daughters would fetch me milk and yoghurt, a packet of coffee, fresh eggs in a paper bag and bottles of beer, practising the excellent English which they learned at school. The new bread did not arrive until eleven, and so had to be bought elsewhere.

On emerging with my purchases, I would walk further into the village to take the long route home. An old gentleman with a grey beard and a long overcoat, invariably carrying an umbrella, was often waiting for a bus at the crossroads. As soon as he learned that I was English, he seized my hand and pumped it with an air of great pleasure, murmuring 'Welcome! Welcome!' – the only English words he knew. This little scene would be repeated every time we met, as though I was a friend he had not seen for years – and if I had come, in his eyes, to represent all the English, this was perhaps the case. Near the old mosque I would sometimes see an ancient crone, bent and twisted by arthritis, scuttling to the public water tap to fill her blackened kettle, mumbling to herself in a continuous monologue. She was quite crazy with age and poverty, seemingly unaware of the presence of any passers-by. She would duck back into a crumbling mud brick hovel in a jungle of overgrown garden, a building which must have

53

been in a serious state of disrepair in Ottoman days, and her bare feet would show through the worn and flapping soles of her shoes.

Every morning Mr Kemal would arrive, take a sort of huge shrimping net and spend a long time removing every speck of debris from the swimming pool, very slowly so as not to spill water on his beautiful suit. This pool was always in such magnificent condition that I began to feel guilty, for only three bungalows were occupied in the whole complex and I had never seen anyone swim. I went in once or twice, for the sake of Kemal's feelings, and found it desperately cold – far colder than the nearby Mediterranean. Nevertheless, as the spring advanced the days were getting steadily warmer and there was no more sign of rain. We took the glass sunroof from our old Renault and locked it away in the boot.

★ ★ ★ ★

To the south of Myrtou and its army camps, beyond the lonely rolling hills of the Dhirios and Karpasha Forests, we came out on to a vast steppe, slowly merging into the north-western part of the Mesaoria plain. Only the occasional tree dotted the sweeping fields of fertile land, freshly ploughed or planted with vegetables, which stretched out uninterrupted to the plantations around Morphou, the centre of this agricultural wealth. Beyond the town, the blue shapes of the Troodos mountains rose abruptly from the lowlands, less spectacularly splintered than the Kyrenia range behind us, but twice as high, and crowned with snow. The smoke of Nicosia was visible far to the east. The broad, pockmarked cheeks and expressionless, Asiatic faces of the soldiers at the checkpoints seemed in tune with the size of the landscape. If their steel helmets had been exchanged for the fur caps of the Khazaks or the Turkmen, the khaki battle dress for the tribesmen's padded coats, one might easily have believed oneself anywhere in that Turkish homeland where the horseman once reigned supreme – somewhere betweeen the Caspian Sea and the Altay mountains of Chinese Turkestan, between the river Oxus and Galodnaya Steppe. What extraordinary wanderers the Turks were, and how remarkable the history of their race. Once or twice we came across a Turk whose belief in the destiny of his people extended to a dream of one day recovering all this territory of Central Asia from China and the USSR, even to ideas of repeating the western conquests. Of course their fellow countrymen laugh at this pan-Turanism. 'Do you expect to be knocking at the gates of Vienna again?' they mock. But even here, and in modern, Kemalist Turkey, the dreamers exist.

Once sugar-cane, cotton and flax were grown on these plains around Morphou, whose population was almost entirely Greek. Now

Guzelyurt (to use the Turkish name, the Beautiful Homeland) grows immense quantities of oranges, and also strawberries, which crop twice a year. The production of oranges is now more important than ever, for this one crop is North Cyprus' main export. We passed a juice-processing factory, and then a large number of Friesian cows feeding on heaps of the rejected fruits. The sharp smell of fermenting juice pervaded the air. The open land gave way to the groves of trees and the road became crowded with pickers riding on the backs of lorries, clutching giant woven baskets. One of the brightly painted wooden buses had run a rear wheel into a ditch and now lay at a drunken angle, while the driver and the orange pickers he had been carrying stood in a group, staring at it disconsolately.

On a little green at the edge of the town, incongruously parked under some pine trees, stood an old narrow-gauge steam locomotive, resting on a short section of track; the remainder of the line had obviously been taken up years ago. As far as I know, this is all that remains of Cyprus' only railway, built in 1907 to carry produce across the island via Nicosia to the port at Famagusta. There had been a plan to extend the railway to Larnaca, but the mayor of that town turned the project down on the grounds that the camel drivers of his district would be discomfited. Later he was pilloried for the foolishness of this decision, but the railway closed before the Second World War and so, by a few years at least, the camel trains outlasted the steam ones. Though the red and white paint was streaked with rust, I could make out 'Philadelphia, USA' on the boiler plate and 'CMC No. 3' on the side. I surmised that it must have been a private locomotive, working on one of the branch lines for the Cyprus Mines Corporation. Mineral extraction was once the island's main foreign currency earner and the struggle between Cypriot miners and the American-owned CMC is part of the history of the Communist movement here. This little engine, quietly rusting and surrounded by foraging chickens, made a strange memorial to the futility of all that investment and all that strife, so many years ago.

The number of abandoned filling stations was a striking feature of the run-down economy and depopulated landscape of the Turkish sector. Much of the fuel seemed to be delivered by Turkish army tankers and some of the stations in use had a military guard. In Morphou we found two closed, although the dusty streets of the old part of town, still lined with the mud-brick and straw buildings which Sir Samuel Baker saw in 1879, were choked with market traders' vans, motorcycles and trucks. Eventually we found a pair of rusty pumps at the intersection of two streets. As our tank was filled, we asked the attendant to direct us to the Monastery of Ayios Mamas, once the pride of Morphou and famous throughout Cyprus. He had never heard of it, but thought that it might be on the north side of town where there were some old churches, and pointed the way along a muddy, potholed lane. Here we found a large nineteenth-century church, now converted into a mosque, for loudspeakers pointed in different directions from the campanile. Plainly this was not St Mamas.

Across the street was an old-fashioned laundry, busy with the noise of machinery and filled with steam from the presses. The owner, a bearded young man still wearing his army trousers, shook me by the hand.

'Hello English. Welcome. Sit down and drink a coffee with me and I will send out to find this place for you.'

The hospitable Cypriot cannot bear to welcome a stranger, even into a shop, without the symbolic gesture of offering him something. Everybody in the laundry was very nice, but none of them had lived in the Morphou they now called Guzelyurt before 1974, and no one nearby had heard of Ayios Mamas.

At last we found an open space where a number of roads intersected. Here a magnificent new mosque had been erected, with twin minarets flying the Turkish flag, and a glistening white dome surmounted by a crescent moon. This is one of a number of prestigious projects financed by Turkish money since 1974: for the most part schools and mosques, showcases for the new order. Nearby, a modest, traditional building was signed 'Guzelyurt Muzesi', and tucked away behind this we saw the warm ochre-coloured stones and tiles of the monastery we sought, locked up now, but with the undefaced Christian cross still standing on the belfry.

While we waited for the monastery key, we looked round the collections of the museum. The natural history section was one of those old-fashioned disorganised displays of badly stuffed and preserved curiosities which I rather enjoy: strange fish trawled up from the depths of the Mediterranean, the island's large snakes and lizards coiled up in bottles of alcohol, a deformed lamb, snarling foxes, motheaten vultures and eagles. The collection of birds was interesting, for Cyprus is strangely rich in songbirds and such delightful creatures as bee-eaters and hoopoes; I say strangely in view of the Cypriot passion for hunting and blazing away at anything that moves. We examined the finds from Toumba tou Skouru, the Bronze Age town to the north: ancient ostrich eggs from Africa, cylinder seals from Syria, pottery sherds and artefacts. Many years ago, a treasure trove of Lusignan coins was found nearby.

The assistant curator came with a large iron key and we walked across to the monastery church. This was originally built in the twelfth century, on the site of an ancient temple of Aphrodite, as is common in Cyprus where many holy places have been sacred since pagan times. The church has been much altered over the years, and the original Byzantine work acquired Gothic additions in the fifteenth century and a great dome in the eighteenth. The key grated in the lock and we were allowed into the gloom of the interior, where everything, including the chandeliers, was covered with a thick layer of dust. The dust and the dim light, however, could not hide the magnificence of the *iconostasis*: the gilt on the carved wood and the Venetian coats of arms, twisting dragons and angels. Some of the better icons from neighbouring churches which had survived the war were leaning against the walls, safe for the moment at least. A cupboard stood open, revealing magnificently coloured sacerdotal vestments, prey now to dirt and moths. On an arched doorway we say the graffiti of eighteenth-century visitors: the French Consul and a Russian in search of a cure.

The remains of St Mamas are contained in a marble sarcophagus, certainly Byzantine, perhaps even Roman, which has been built into the wall. This sarcophagus, according to one legend, was thrown into the sea after the holy man was martyred by the infidels in Asia Minor (where he had lived, feeding the poor with the milk of lionesses which he had miraculously tamed). The coffin floated away to Morphou Bay off Cyprus, and in the middle of the night the spirit of the saint appeared to a farmer of the town, commanding him to harness his team of oxen and drive them down to the sea. In spite of his fears, the man obeyed, only to find when he reached the shore that the waters rolled back before his beasts until the sarcophagus was revealed. The oxen dragged the white marble box as far as the town, where it stuck fast and would not be budged, a clear signal – as anyone familiar with the ways of saints should know – that a church should be built around it on this spot.

When the Turks invaded Cyprus for the first time, they were said to have bored holes in the coffin, hoping to find hidden treasure – there are so many stories of the Turkish obsession with treasure trove. Sweat then ran from the holes, a miracle which terrified the desecrators and restrained them from inflicting further damage. The strange liquid continued to flow on occasions over the years, a fluid with the property of calming the sea, if poured on the waters during a storm, or, alternatively, of curing earache. Alexander Drummond, HM Consul for Aleppo and Cyprus, who was here in 1745, claimed that the sweat was running at that time, not from the coffin but from St Mamas' face on the icon above, while the corresponding pictures of St George and St Demetrios remained dry.

A better story concerns the saint in his own lifetime, a quiet hermit here in Byzantine Cyprus, who lived in a cave, carried on no business and had no income. On receiving a tax demand, he was understandably incensed and refused to pay. As he was being escorted under arrest to the Governor's Palace, a lion leaped from the thick undergrowth to attack a lamb on the open pathway ahead. The soldiers were terrified (as well they might be, for lions have never been known to inhabit Cyprus in historical times), but St Mamas merely held up his hand and the lion became as friendly and harmless as the lamb, his erstwhile prey. The saint picked up the lamb, mounted the fawning, purring lion and rode on to the palace, right into the presence of the Governor, while the bemused escort tagged along at a safe distance behind. The Governor decided that he could stretch a point in view of the saint's obvious powers, and promptly excused him from paying taxes for life. Ever since, St Mamas, the patron saint of tax evaders, has been beloved above all the 110 saints accredited to the Church of Cyprus. We found the icon standing in a dark corner, St Mamas sitting demurely on his lion, the lamb tucked under one arm.

★　★　★　★

We continued westward through busy, agricultural land, where thick groves of eucalyptus shaded the road. '*Hos Geldiniz*, welcome' said the sign at the approach to each villge, and '*Gule-gule*, farewell' (literally 'smiling-smiling') as the houses came to an end. A crowded landscape, populated by soliders, peasants, schoolchildren, factory workers. The village of Ghaziveran is an old Turkish enclave whose name means the Place of the Veterans, and which may well have been founded by soldiers discharged from Lala Mustafa Pasha's conquering army. The village gained a reputation for heroism in 1964 when attacked by superior Greek forces. Twelve rifles defended Ghaziveran against some hundreds of Greek National Guardsmen during a long morning until an ultimatum from mainland Turkey directly to Makarios stopped the bloodshed. We saw the graves of the Turkish fighters later at Lefka.

This road was controlled, so we were not permitted to stop and stare as we emerged on to the coast and our senses were assailed by the magnificent sight of Morphou Bay, all glittering beaches and deep-blue water in the sunlight. In this anchorage, it used to be said, there is room for all the fleets in the world to congregate. The littoral is quite flat, swinging in a great arc between the distant mountains of Kyrenia and the Troodos to the south. Here, on the shore, were huge piles of red copper ore by a silent crushing works, rusting railway lines and goods trucks, a freighter holed and lying on its side on the beach, and a long pier with a conveyor belt, crazily twisted and distorted by high explosive in 1974. The waters of the bay were once stained green with the metal, and the ore carriers queued all night to load up under these warped and corroded arc lamps. Nearby Xeros was something of a rough town, with noisy bars full of sailors. Now the mines of Skouriotissa and Marathasa, only a short distance away in the foothills of the Troodos mountains, lay on the Greek side of the Attila Line which separated them from their sea terminal here in the Turkish sector. The copper was mined in Roman times and before, giving the island of Cyprus its very name, yet the traffic which once brought so much wealth to this coast was at an end.

We stopped at a little café surrounded by banana plantations, to find a room full of chairs upended on tables. All was apparently deserted, and we were about to turn and go when a small girl put her head round the door and then came back with an unshaven man carrying a hoe.

'Are you open?' I asked him.

'You are English? Welcome!' And he began to take down chairs and arrange them around a table.

'Where are you going?'

'To the ruins of Soli,'

'I knew it!' He laughed and slapped his thigh. 'Only the English go there. Nobody else. Not many English now. Please, you must stay and have a drink with me. I don't often speak English these days.' He collected bottles of beer and lemonade, and opened and poured them into dusty glasses.

'What's this?' I asked, looking at a map of the north, zoned in bright colours for no apparent reason.

'Oh, that's for hunting. Closed seasons in different places for different game you know. To tell the truth, there's not much to do here except shooting. No work here. We came from Paphos in 1974 – this was a Greek village before, you understand – and there has never been enough work. The copper is finished. What have we got? Bananas! Thank God my two sons are in London, both doing well.

'What about the café?'

'On this road? No one travels on this road, because it doesn't go anywhere. Once it went to Kokkina and Polis. Now, another six miles and there is the Line. Please stay, because I never speak English now . . .'

*   *   *   *

Karavostasi, or Gemikonagi to the Turks, was once something of a port and had a customs house in Ottoman times. We found a large and busy village, with an ASIZ checkpoint at each end of the street and a bridge over one of those Cypriot rivers which look so impressive on the map, but so often turn out to be dry stones or sluggish ditches except during rare floods. There were a couple of blue and white UN Land Rovers pulled up beside the road, and a sign to 'Viking Camp One' betrayed the presence of the Danish contingent. We stopped at the filling station to ask the way, just as a middle-aged man in farmer's clothes thumped on to the forecourt on a single cylinder Matchless motorcycle.

'Soli? Not far, up that road and you see a sign. English? English motorbike, see. Very good.'

Wondering how long it would take Honda, Suzuki and the rest to clean up this market when they finally broke into it, we arrived on a small hill a short distance inland, overlooking the broken copper conveyor and a grove of palms and eucalyptus. The site was still fenced, but there was no sign of a guardian as we walked by dry, white stones, fallen Roman columns and the tesselated floors of the basilica.

Authorities differ as to the founding of Soli. Legend has it that Demophoon, son of Theseus of Athens, built a city in the hills nearby, one of the first Greek city-states of the island and perhaps known as Sillu. Archaeologists, however, state that the colonists were Hittites from Asia Minor; moreover that the original mountain-city was named Aepia, which was once thought to have been the hilltop site of Vouni, to the south, but is now believed to have been somewhere quite different. Archaeologists always manage to create confusion and have a talent for spoiling a good story. It might be simpler to pass over all this and go on to the time when Solon, the famous Athenian legislator, was visiting the island and persuaded Philocyprus, the King of Aepia, to move his capital out of the mountains, down to this ledge above the coastal plain. It would be nice to think that the new city of Soli was named in honour of the eminent man from Athens. Incidentally, I have always had the greatest admiration for Solon since I read Herodotus' claim that he introduced from Egypt to Greece the inspired notion that every man should present himself annually before his *nomarch* (magistrate) in order to give firm proof of the honest and worthy trade or profession by which he supported himself and his family. Should he fail to do so, he would be instantly put to death. One might dream of this admirable practice introduced to the modern world. What price then advertising executives, double-glazing salesmen, property developers, politicians, architects, the people who ring you up to sell you tea-making machines, owners of pretentious restaurants, writers of bad travel books . . . ? The list grows endlessly before one even considers the more obvious criminals.

Soli's position proved to be well chosen because, during the Greeks' revolt against their Persian rulers, this little town under Philocyprus' son held out for four months until the enemy undermined the defences. The men of Soli also distinguished themselves in the campaigns of Alexander the Great and the King's son reached the Indus with the conqueror. The city managed to come to an arrangement with the Egyptian Ptolemies who later ruled Cyprus and retained its independence for some time after the other city-states had been subjugated.

Another story is that Soli was notorious for the barbarous speech of its inhabitants, and that from this we have the word 'solecism'. This is credible, for most of its people would have been miners and they are often strongly accented men the world over. Copper was mined and smelted on Cyprus in the thirteenth century BC and has been associated with the island ever since. Medieval alchemists used to apply the sign of Aphrodite, the island's own goddess, to the red metal. In the hills behind Soli are heaps of spoil left by the Mycenaean smelters, the slag being brown in colour because they used manganese as flux. But the Romans left over a million tons of their glistening black slag, and the hills are honeycombed with their galleries. The Cyprus Mines Corporation's opencast works exposed and destroyed some of these, turning out ancient pit props into the sunlight, even ropes and reed baskets. The modern miners found that the Romans had already taken the best of the ore, some two million tons, and that their workings, without the benefit of ventilation, went 600 feet below the surface.

Herod the Great paid a premium of 300 talents to the Emperor Augustus in return for the management and half the income of the Soli mines. The copper boom brought wealth to the town, which boasted a public library and in the second century AD built the theatre which stands higher up the hill. This was reconstructed in concrete 50 years ago by Swedish archaeologists (too neatly by half), and we sat in the breeze on the upper tier of seats, looking at the jangling colours of the coastline – blue sea, red ore and dull green trees – wondering whether a photograph would seem provocative to the army. Even before the Swedish expedition, the outline of the theatre had been visible beneath a thin covering of grass and soil. Richard Pococke had ridden past in 1738 and clearly made out the half-buried, semi-circular walls. A century earlier George Sandys had found himself near 'the city of the Sunne, with the Temples of Venus and Isis, built by Phalerus and Achaurus, the Athenians'. The early travellers had little to guide them beyond local tradition and their own knowledge of classical literature, which in many cases was remarkably extensive. So these lonely men, far from home in lands which were often hostile, patiently copied inscriptions from cracked tablets of stone, asked after antiquities in a hundred villages where ancient capitals had been incorporated into the walls of modern houses, scratched about in the undergrowth, pored over their books and wondered. In the circumstances, it is remarkable that they were so often right. With hindsight, their mistakes were sometimes ludicrous. Pococke left Morphou, for instance, firmly convinced that St Mamas was female.

The Christian basilica at the bottom of the slope was built in the fifth century AD, 200 years before the city began to empty as the corsairs raiding the coast made life by the sea too perilous. During the Lusignan period, the poor Orthodox Bishop of Nicosia retreated here, the Catholic clergy having taken over all the more lucrative livings in the central plains. He can have presided over little more than ruins. There would have been a good deal more of those to see now if the site had not been used as a supply of ready-cut masonry for builders all over the Levant for some hundreds of years. Large amounts of stone were removed by Egyptian sailing ships for use in the building of Port Said and the Suez Canal during the last century. As we walked in the basilica, by mosaics of flowers and a long-necked white swan, the guardian, who had seen our car, came bounding up the hill, just in time to sell us tickets before we left.

Where the road ran by the sea to the west, we came to a building occupied by the United Nations Police, outside which two white BMW cars were parked. Next door was a little taverna, a friendly place with tables outside in the sun, along the south-facing wall by the road. The proprietor took our order for grilled *kebabs* and fanned up the white charcoal in the chimney against the wall, setting over it a tin cylinder to draw up the fire. In a few minutes he was back with spits of lamb to prop in position, and glasses of cold Danish beer.

'I keep it for these boys,' he said, grinning at the three fair-haired young men in track suits at the next table. These were joined shortly by a fourth in swimming shorts who towelled himself dry and sat down to peel one of a pile of oranges.

'Which are you with?' one of them asked. 'Refugee Commission?'

We told him we were nothing to do with the UN, just travelling.

'You mean you are tourists?' He seemed to be taking some time to digest this.

'Is that unusual?'

'I've been here two years and I don't think I've ever seen anybody. Wait a minute, there were some Germans last year, I think.'

'How do you find life here?' we wanted to know.

'You can see,' he said, pointing around at the sunlit beach and the banana plants. 'To tell the truth I signed on for a second year to escape the Danish winter. How are things in England? I've got a girl friend in Epsom.'

We assured him that England had probably had as cold a winter as Denmark this year.

'We come down here to swim. We're restricted; we can only move a few miles along the coast road. For some reason the Turks decided a while ago that the UN forces were passing information about the North back to the Greeks. Now we are restricted to the Line and a few observation posts. Free movement on the Greek side of course.'

We had already become familiar with signs declaring various roads out of bounds to UN vehicles and personnel.

'How do you get on with the Turks?' I wondered.

'Fine. They're naturally friendly people. Take the man who runs this place; he's a really nice guy. Not just because we're customers, but because it's in his nature to be helpful.'

As if to illustrate his point, a lorry crammed with oranges rattled down the hill and pulled up by our table with a screech of brakes. The driver and his mate beckoned to me frantically, smiling brown faces craning out of the dusty cab. Slightly bemused I stood up, wondering what they wanted, and walked over to have my arms filled with sweet oranges, which they thrust on me without explanation.

'*Cok tesekkur ederim*, thank you very much,' I managed to stammer in my surprise, as they drove on with a cheery wave.

'They can see you're strangers,' said the Dane as I arranged my pile of fruit on the table and began to tuck into the plate of fresh *houmous* which the tavern keeper had brought. 'To be honest, I prefer them to the Greeks. I like this side of the Line.'

'The Greeks are a friendly people. Famous for their hospitality.'

'They're as friendly as hell, so long as you have money,' he replied shortly.

'How far is the Attila Line from here?'

'About two miles up there.' He pointed up an innocuous-looking path.

'Is there ever any trouble?'

'No, not really. Sometimes you hear firing up in the hills, but it always turns out to be a false alarm. Stray dogs set off the trip-wires.'

'What about the Turkish army? How efficient are they in fact?'

He smiled. 'You shouldn't really be asking us, we're telephone operators. But the word is they're good. If this lot here ever decided to advance, the Greeks couldn't hold them for a day, even in these mountains. Of course it's not an army like our army. Not a European army at all.'

'What do you mean?'

'Well, have you heard what they pay private soldiers? And we've seen how they treat the poor bastards. Some of the officers are the most arrogant . . . well, you don't want to have anything to do with the officers.'

With a howl from its cluster of exhaust pipes, a six-cylinder Honda motorcycle accelerated briefly along the waterfront before braking to a halt in front of the tavern, the huge engine throbbing with suppressed power. An admiring group of Danes clustered around the rider.

'Our boys buy those tax-free. You know, personal export. That one came from London. It's a little crazy with only a short piece of road, but he can use it on the Greek side.'

Before we left, a party of Turkish soldiers came down the road with a sergeant, engaged in laying a field telephone cable. They all seemed relaxed and good-natured enough, but the look of envy on one or two of the lads' faces when they saw the gleaming Honda was memorable.

⋆   ⋆   ⋆   ⋆

The road westward was controlled again. Joan had discovered that, if she waved to the ASIZ checkpoints, the soldiers usually snapped smartly to attention and saluted her. 'If in doubt, salute . . .' is the soldier's motto everywhere. Thus we progressed imperiously up a twisting road, drawing ever closer to the point where the Attila Line met the sea and the Turkish sector came to an end. We passed a little modern cross-in-square church with a tiled dome and, as no one was in sight, risked stopping to walk up the steps. Though disused for years, it was relatively undamaged. After another mile or two, we turned off on a track which wound around three sides of a precipitous peak, to emerge at the Palace of Vouni which occupies several acres at the summit.

Vouni is a place of wind and sunlight, an eyrie overlooking the sea on one side, with the majestic sweep of Morphou Bay stretching away towards the Kyrenia mountains, dimly perceived through the haze. To the west a series of rugged little hills covered by dense maquis projects into the sea. Somewhere beyond them, Greek territory begins, and further again is Kokkina, that strange, besieged, Turkish enclave which stands alone with the enemy on three sides and the sea at its back. By climbing to the crude, modern observation post built of breeze-blocks on the inland side, we could look at the secretive hills of Tillyria and a tumbling confusion of lonely valleys leading up the main Troodos massif and the Paphos Forest. This too was now Greek territory, but there was no sign of the Line across the thickly wooded hills. For the first of many times in Cyprus, I experienced that strange sense of the unattainable, of the distortion of ordinary geography which the Line has produced. From where we stood, we might have walked deep into those hills in the space of a few hours. A dog barking or the report of a shotgun would be clearly audible. One might see the smoke of a fire or the flash of sunlight on a car's windscreen. But in order to make that short journey, to stand in those woods, it would be necessary to fly first to London.

In fact there was no sign of any human activity at all, for many of the villages near the Line and the Kokkina enclave have been deserted since the invasion. This was once the land of the race known in Greek as the *Linobambakoi*, literally 'linen-cotioners'. All kinds of strange stories were told of these mysterious people, Crypto-Christians who masqueraded as Muslims to avoid taxation under Ottoman rule. Their ancestors were variously said to have been Latins who survived the Turkish conquest of 1571, the progeny of illicit love affairs between Greeks and Turks, or Christians who apostatised during the massacres of 1821, although their apparent Catholicism would indicate that the first theory might be the closest to the truth. All that is really known is that, while each dressed as a Turk, bore a Muslim name in public and prayed at the mosque, they used Christian names within the closed family circle, baptised their children secretly and held Christian rites behind closed doors. In this way they avoided the *kharatch*, the poll tax to which all *rayah*, the subject peoples of the Ottoman Empire, were liable. In later years they showed a greater tendency to switch between religions as it suited them. Thus in 1873 the Archduke Louis Salvator observed that:

The Christians pay, from the day they are born, twenty seven and a half piastres [about one guinea] a year, and are free from military service. There are also Greeks who pretend to be Mussulmans, and they are called Linopambagi, which means half linen, half cotton, When they attain the age to enter the army they would often like to pass to Christians again, but the Government enrols them nevertheless, saying that it is illegal to give up Mahomedanism: for that reason they do not follow that proceeding as they would otherwise like to do.

(Archduke Louis Salvator of Austria, *Levkosia*)

Only six years later, Sir Samuel Baker, who estimated that there were perhaps 1,500 *Linobambakoi* still in Cyprus ('two-faced time servers' he scornfully designated them), was given to understand that they had taken to having themselves baptised in the Greek Church. Thus they had successfully avoided their military service during the last days of the Ottoman administration. With the accession of British rule and full religious freedom, the whole *raison d'être* of the *Linobambakoi*'s strange way of life would seem to have disappeared, but a few of them lingered on in their old traditions, and in 1935 one of the last was pointed out to H.V. Morton in a remote village of the Paphos Forest, as a curious and anachronistic survival.

The name 'Vouni' means no more than a mountain peak in Greek, and the ancient name is lost. The Swedish archaeologists who excavated this site in 1928 dated it from the fifth century BC, and detected an oriental influence in the architecture. They conjectured that the settlement may have favoured Persia during the Ionian Rebellion. Perhaps it was set up by the pro-Persian city of Marion (near modern Polis to the west), in order to intimidate the Hellenes of Soli. When the great Athenian admiral Kimon captured Marion in 449 BC, Vouni may have fallen too, and there is a Temple of Athena from about this date. During the fourth century the Greeks of Soli successfully attacked their rival and sacked it, since when the palace has been uninhabited, lying open to the wind and sky. The country people used to call this the Eating Place of the Lords, for these nobles had left silver utensils among the ruins after their meal which were sometimes found by shepherds. We saw numerous fragments of delicate pottery drifted into the corners of the low walls, and Malcolm picked up a triangular sherd which clearly showed the decorative grooves a craftsman had traced into the soft clay two and a half millennia before. Beside the mouth of a deep cistern stood a stele, a solitary stone pillar which once supported the winding gear of the well, carved with the face of Athena. In spite of these traces, the open courts seemed so sterile and bleached under that bright light that it was hard to picture them, crowded with people as they had once been.

Twenty years before, a Greek visitor had carved his name into the bark of a sapling at the edge of the palace site and the name had swollen and grown with the tree. 'Stratiotis Socrates Kristodoulos of Limassol 14.7.65'. Kristodoulos, 'Slave of Christ', is a common surname in Cyprus. I wondered what his thoughts had been, up here in the sky at Vouni all those years ago. What was he doing now, and did he ever remember with nostalgia that day and this place, now beyond his reach?

* * * *

Beyond Vouni, the village of Yesilirmak, formerly Limnitis, had the impermanent appearance of a frontier town. The streets were littered with rusting agricultural implements and the chassis of cannibalised tractors. Most of the men were sitting outside the coffee shop and looked up curiously as we passed, while the gold earrings and brightly coloured *shalvar* trousers of the women indicated that these people were from the mainland. In a mood of curiosity and perhaps foolhardiness, we wondered how close the Attila Line might be approached. We climbed through silent, deserted countryside to a large red notice announcing '1st Restricted Military Zone'. Did this necessarily mean that no civilian could enter at all? Was there a 2nd Military Zone? We continued slowly over a series of little hills, the engine idling in second gear, ready to stop clearly and unequivocally if challenged. We passed a house, half-built but now overgrown with weeds, the work having been interrupted twelve years before. There were others, standing in tall grass which reached to their windows, the paint peeling off the woodwork of doors and shutters. Black Cyprus crows perched on the roofs, and the fruit trees in the gardens straggled untended.

As we crested a ridge, we caught a momentary glimpse of the snows of Troodos far above, and then we ran down into a hollow where the flags of Turkey and North Cyprus flew from the roof of a village school. A hundred yards beyond, an observation tower showing the blue flag of the UN was raised high on wooden stilt legs above the bushes. A group of teenaged soldiers came trooping out of the schoolroom door, almost young enough to be children let out for playtime, and then looked up in surprise to see us. They called inside and a corporal, very little older, emerged and smiled, but seemed non plussed by our presence and uncertain as to what course to take.

'Could we travel further along the road?' we indicated by signs. He shook his head and pointed back the way we had come. We turned around, and the corporal saluted and was still waving politely as the little group was hidden by a bend of the road. Just as we left the Military Zone, a taxi came up from the village and the officer in the back turned round and stared hard at us as we passed. We hoped nobody got into trouble.

★   ★   ★   ★

On Saturday night, the army restaurant was packed with the youth of Lapta and Karavas. Ibrahim waved a welcome as he rushed by with a laden tray of steaming pizzas, before squeezing us into a table by the wall. There were a few soldiers in uniform, including NCOs, but most of the young men were civilians. These were drinking at a prodigious rate, every table being littered with bottles of red wine and opaque glasses of *raki*, the 'lion's milk' spirit of Turkey. Perhaps a last fling before the abstinence of military service. There were a few girls, each carefully chaperoned. The young men drank and laughed among themselves, every now and then casting surreptitious glances at the girls, who sat demurely at separate tables with their parents, gazing straight ahead as if unaware of the boys' interest. The room was filled with an almost tangible atmosphere of frustration and I was rather reminded of end-of-term dances at school.

The band, which was modern, electric and as young as the audience, played a few American ballads to modest applause, and then settled down to play the oriental Turkish music which was really popular. The boys began to dance first and after a while a few of them plucked up the courage to ask the girls' parents for permission to dance with their daughters. But there were too few to go round and most of the boys danced with each other. Soon they were crowding the floor, undulating and snapping their fingers happily, while we finished our meal and left, feeling rather middle-aged.

CHAPTER FIVE

BELLAPAIS AND KYTHREA

Early the next morning, I wandered through Lapithos. It was Sunday and people were sleeping late, so the streets were almost empty. I came to a large church, stripped of all interior fittings and with faded blue and white Greek flags painted on the outer wall. 'ENOSIS' and 'EOKA' were quite plainly visible, for the Turks had either failed to scrub them away or not troubled to do so. In some parts of the village as many houses lay partially ruined and deserted as were occupied. I explored some of the empty rooms, all constructed in the same way, with one huge interior arch supporting timber beams, on top of which was laid a matting of woven reeds and seaweed. Earth laid above formed the flat roof, quite adequate for the dry climate and a method of construction still sometimes used today. Rats scrabbled in the far corners behind rusting olive presses and the circular stones of crushing mills. In one room domestic rabbits were penned behind wire netting, fattening for the table, another was full of sheep, dirty brown fleeces packed into the half darkness. There were ancient doorways of ornately worked stone, and carved wooden doors which had not seen paint for decades and were too massive to rot away for many years to come.

Old houses in the villages of Cyprus used to have their floor made of hard-packed earth, water being sprinkled daily to combat dust. As this damp floor was unsuitable for the storage of grain, flour and beans, and was uncomfortable to sleep on, a half loft would be constructed over part of the main room, reached by a ladder. Among the sacks of produce a great communal mattress filled with dry seaweed or straw would be spread. If the family was wealthy enough to afford a cotton mattress, it would have to be pulled apart every couple of years, in order that the cotton be reteased and made soft again.

In the low space against the wall below the loft would stand the great jars, sometimes of clay, sometimes of wicker-covered glass, for wine and olive oil. These can still be found in odd corners. Travellers always enjoyed the wines of Cyprus, but there were occasional cautionary warnings. In 1588 the Seigneur de Villamont wrote enthusiastically:

> The wines will keep, the common people tell you, for thirty years, and if you drink only two pegs of this in the morning you can easily pass the rest of the day without meat or drink, so remarkable is the strength and goodness of the wine. But taken in excess, it burns you up at last.

(Trs. C.D. Cobham, Excerpta Cypria)

Cheeses, too, were kept in jars, pickled in oil or brine. Otherwise, according to Pococke, 'when new they could breed a worm, and when old soon go dry'.

Cooking, if not carried out in the yard on a pan of charcoal, or in the clay oven, took place over the fire. Until quite recently all the utensils were of copper or clay, even forks being made of wood. When metal forks became available, they were hung up on a bamboo rack to keep them from rusting, together with a row of pottery mugs, one for each inhabitant and two for guests. There would be a water-cooling jar of clay and hollowed gourds for carrying water. As the water dripped from the porous jar, it would fall into a trough where the salad vegetables would keep fresh.

The bread would be kept in a basket of reeds and mulberry bark, the *tabayia*, suspended from the ceiling away from rats and mice. To prevent the more enterprising rodents from running down the cord, a bunch of sharp thistles was tied halfway up. The bread was made in a wooden trough and then placed on a curiously shaped board, with a row of hollows, for the dough to rise. These boards are still to be seen in Cyprus; in Greek houses they usually have eleven hollows for eleven loaves, thus commemorating the apostles with the exception of the traitor Judas. In monasteries, curiously, a board is used with a double row of six to make twelve, and Judas is reinstated. Some boards make ten loaves, for the Ten Commandments, or five, for the five loaves baked on a name day. For these saints' days, which take the place of our birthdays (all the Georges celebrate together on St George's Day and so on), the five loaves were stamped with a cross and taken to church to be blessed.

Greeks everywhere traditionally regarded bread as something mystical. In Crete, the remaining crumbs after a meal were ritually swept up and kept in memory of the Last Supper. Special loaves are still baked for the Easter holiday. There was a magic about the division of a loaf: 'One portion for each of us, one for the house and one for the stranger who may knock on our door.' The Greeks of Cyprus still bake each year the 'Bread of St Basil', a loaf with a gold coin hidden inside. (On the Greek mainland the coin is sometimes an

English gold sovereign remaining from those used by British agents during the last war). Whoever is fortunate enough to receive the coin when the bread is broken will have good luck for the rest of the year. And in the Paphos district, a girl about to be married would bake loaves to send as invitations to her wedding guests.

The village of Vasilia, or Karsiyaka (the Other Side), is a quiet little place tucked under the north face of Mount Kournos at the western extremity of the Kyrenia range. I stopped the car on a steep corner, beneath a cascade of almond blossom, to talk to a woman who sat outside her door on an old wooden chair, engaged in the interminable knitting that seems to occupy every spare moment of Cypriot women's time. The results of these labours – thick woollen stockings, jumpers and shawls – are worn in the warmest weather.

'The Sinai Monastery? Where can you mean, my child? *É!* The old monastery, of course! You follow the road up the hill and then when you see . . . but wait, my son will go ahead and show you the place. You will follow his car.'

A cheerful young man gunned the engine of an old Austin Cambridge, executed a rapid turn at the edge of a steep bank and charged at the slope in second gear. Eventually he pulled to the side of the road; we all got out and he pointed to a large stone building, half hidden by olive trees, some half a mile away on the mountain flank.

'That's the old monastery,' he said, 'but no one ever goes there. Are you English?'

This seemed to be all the explanation required, for after 82 years in Cyprus, the British established a reputation for eccentricity, if nothing else. He waved away our thanks and returned to his car while we climbed up through a *phrygana* of sharp thorn bushes. Goats moved away ahead of us as we approached, their bells tinkling melodiously as they bounded from stone to stone. The goatherd was standing like a statue higher up the slope, a lean streak of a man in leather boots to the knee, with a face burned almost black by the sun. A long shotgun was tucked under his arm and he carried a bandolier of cartridges over his shoulder. He raised his hand gravely and silently in greeting as we passed, before turning and making his way with long strides up a steep path which led between the crags towards a saddle higher up the mountain.

The windows of the monastery gaped black and empty as we climbed the grassy bank below the fortress-like walls, through neglected groves of trees: olives, almonds and figs growing wild. The yellow ranunculus of the mountainside gave way to the waxy white of asphodel, showing that man had disturbed the ground here. The sheer cliffs of Kournos loomed above, offering purchase for only the occasional stunted cypress tree. We broke into a courtyard filled with

71

nettles, smashed roof tiles and pieces of broken plaster. An old mill-stone lay on its side, beside the fallen columns of some earlier build-ing. A concrete conduit ran from the arches of the cloisters and diagonally across the quadrangle, evidence of the introduction of the water supply by the British administration. A marble-topped foun-tain, dry and cracked now, was engraved 'ER 1953'.

The monastery church, approached by overgrown and broken steps, boasted mock Corinthian columns and the double-headed eagle of Byzantium carved into the stone of the entrance arch. But the roof tiles were almost all fallen and the interior was a desolation of rubble, most of the slabs having been torn up and the stone altar sledge-hammered into fragments. Many of the floors of the monks' cells had collapsed and the earthen roofs above the cloisters were slowly trickling through the reed matting. The young man had been right; there was really nothing to see except a fine view of the sea between pinkish white sprays of almond blossom waving by the crumbling plaster of the walls.

★　★　★　★

According to the map, it should have been possible to drive along the forest road, south of Mount Kornos, following the ridge of the moun-tains to St Hilarion, across the main Kyrenia–Nicosia road, and so on to the village of Bellapais. At first we passed through charming alpine scenery in the Korphi Forest where the hut of a goatherd and his family was isolated high above the dust and heat of the lowlands, surrounded by flocks grazing in meadows spotted with wild cyclamen of the most delicate mauve and purple hues. But after a time the condition of the track began to deteriorate alarmingly. Twice, Joan and the boys got out while I inched the car past landslips which had removed most of the width of the carriageway. Eventually the gullies and potholes became so deep that it was clear that, once trapped, it would be the devil of a job to get out. It was another 12 miles to St Hilarion and this was plainly four-wheel-drive territory.

Reluctantly we turned back to the longer route on the main road via Kyrenia, to pick up the forest road again from the pass at St Hilarion. This track was in much better condition but, inexplicably and in-furiatingly, closed to civilian traffic by the army. Once more we were forced back on to the main road, and so finally, late in the morning, we approached Bellapais on the paved road through the green fields and orange trees around the old Turkish village of Kazaphani. Al-ready we could see the honey-coloured walls of the famous abbey above, punctuated by the exclamation marks of the tall cypresses which Konstantinos Kollis planted in 1940.

Perhaps it is a pity that so much has been written about Bellapais, and that most travellers will arrive with a preconceived picture to match up to the reality. Indeed the little square in front of the abbey's gate seemed like a stage set, deserted by the (Greek) actors who made it famous. Lawrence Durrell, author of *Bitter Lemons*, has something to answer for here, because this tiny village is the only really commercialised place in Turkish Cyprus. (Poor Mr Durrell must be used to these criticisms; he says that people write to him complaining that Alexandria is not the magic place he made it seem, as if he should refund the price of their tickets.)

The visitors to Bellapais now are largely diplomats, UN personnel and Cypriots at weekends. We found the square crowded with cars, including the only Lotus in the Turkish sector, and the coffee shops were doing a brisk trade. The Tree of Idleness Café had been rebuilt and renamed the Tree of Idleness Pub, while the tree itself, surrounded by concrete and reinforced with metal splints, looked about to die from extreme old age, or perhaps a broken heart. We gathered that many of the houses in the village were now second homes, for the wealthy of Kyrenia or Nicosia.

There was no Greek Mr Kollis now to usher us into the grounds of the abbey, but for all that the French Gothic building, strangely set among the lush vegetation of the Mediterranean, stood as magnificently as ever on the edge of its cliff, looking down on Kyrenia and the sea. We fell in with an English diplomat and his wife, newly arrived to take up an appointment and thoughtfully provided by the Foreign Office with a Land Rover. I was intrigued to hear that they had free access to both sides of the Line.

'Harry's been solidly bogged down with paperwork for the last month,' the wife confided, 'reading up the political situation and so on. I thought it was about time we took a couple of days off to do some sightseeing and Bellapais seemed a good place to start.'

Armed with a selection of guide books, we rambled together through the gardens and cloisters.

The Orthodox Bishops of Kyrenia may have taken refuge here from Arab pirates through the seventh to tenth centuries, and the first name of the abbey was 'Episcopia'. The present building dates from about 1200 and is totally Latin and Frankish in style. Over the years the 'Abbaye de la Paix' came to be known as 'Bellapais', the most remarkable example of Gothic architecture in the East. Aimery de Lusignan established the Augustinians here after they had lost the Church of the Holy Sepulchre at Jerusalem. Later the white-robed Canons of St Norbert held it, when it became known as the 'White Abbey'. Under the patronage of Hugh III, who may be buried here, the abbey became immensely wealthy, the treasures including a

73

fragment of the True Cross. This wealth attracted the attention of the plundering Genoese in 1373.

In those days the Abbot was a powerful figure, entitled by royal decree to wear a gilded sword and spurs, and spending most of his time at his Nicosia residence where he quarrelled frequently with the Archbishop. In truth, the monks themselves were less than exemplary in their observance of the faith, for the voluptuous and fertile climate of Kyrenia is not one to mortify the flesh. By the Venetian period, the situation had become quite scandalous, some of the brethren having taken as many as three wives. It was said that the monks would only accept their own progeny as novices and that the village of Bellapais which grew up from around the abbey gate was populated by their children, while the abbey itself was sadly neglected.

The Turks pursued their usual policy of encouraging the Orthodox Church while suppressing the Catholic. So the abbey itself, stripped of its monks, gradually became a picturesque ruin among its overgrown gardens, while the villagers continued to worship in its church, suitably converted to Orthodox use. The Greeks of Bellapais continued to use the church of the abbey until they left for the south after 1974. Now it was locked and we were unable to see the combination of thirteenth-century Gothic with a Greek *iconostasis*, or the little opening where lepers were once allowed to listen to the service. But we were able to walk through the cloisters, delicately arched and carved with strange medieval beasts, the fine traceries of the decoration matched by the fronds of the palm trees in the court. Travellers of the eighteenth and nineteenth centuries, some of whom had carved their names into the lintel of the refectory door, wrote of the beauties of Bellapais, and also deplored the ruinous state of the grounds, together with the villagers' use of the abbey as a source of stone for their own houses. The refectory, a magnificent hall with six fine windows overlooking the sea, was treated with remarkable callousness by the British during the nineteenth century, having been used as a small-bore weapons range by the army, while the floor had earlier been torn up and cemented over with the idea of making it into a fever hospital. There was even talk of using the abbey's stone for road making.

The care of antiquities was one of the many areas which suffered from a ludicrously inadequate budget during the early British period. In 1903 the Legislative Council of Cyprus sent a formal protest to Chamberlain, the Colonial Secretary, which, apart from the routine expression of the Greek desire for *enosis* and complaint against the iniquitous tribute, expressed concern for the preservation of antiquities from casual despoilers and tomb robbers. In 1885 a commercial consortium had quite openly excavated at the Polis tis Khrysokhous site, and had profitably sold their finds at a Paris auction.

74

We emerged from the rose gardens of the abbey to find that the guardian had called it a day, locked the gate and gone home for his lunch.

'You'll have to climb over,' called the customers at the café tables on the other side of the wall, and so we scrambled across and took our places in turn at a table beneath the scanty shade of the Tree of Idleness. I had always wanted to do this, since reading the warning given by the *muktar* (mayor) of Bellapais to Lawrence Durrell:

> I must warn you, if you intend to try and work, not to sit under the Tree of Idleness. You have heard of it? Its shadow incapacitates one for serious work. By tradition the inhabitants of Bellapaix are regarded as the laziest in the island. They are all landed men, coffee-drinkers and card players. That is why they all live to such ages. Nobody ever seems to die here. Ask Mr Honey the grave-digger. Lack of clients has almost driven him into a decline . . .

> (Lawrence Durrell, *Bitter Lemons*)

At the time of writing, our long sojourn under the Tree – for service in the café was very slow – appears to have made no noticeable change to the energy, or lack of it, exhibited by any member of our party. But this may mean nothing, for I suspect that some of us were already dwellers under its shade by nature.

English voices from the next table; more diplomats from Nicosia: 'Excuse me, do you have Turkish delight?'

The young waiter looked startled and embarrassed, trying to work out the implications of this question.

'The lady means *loukoumi*,' someone interjected.

'Ah, of course. I regret no.'

Surrounded as we were by the memories of Durrell's friends, we climbed the steep little street after lunch, in search of the author's old house. I knew what I was looking for: high up on the hill, mud-brick and straw, carved doors of Anatolian timber, a garden filled with tangerines, lemons, pomegranates and mulberries. There would be a view of the abbey, Kyrenia and its castle, and the sea stretching to Turkey beyond. The mountain behind would be encrusted with the ruins of Buffavento Castle. It might have been almost any of these houses, most of which had been modernised by absentee owners in recent years. I asked a youth, who was idly kicking a football over the cobbles with two or three younger boys. There was something vaguely familiar about his face and I realised that I had seen him at Heathrow Airport.

'You're looking at it,' he said, in an accent which came from Clapham or Battersea, and left us staring at shiny brown, varnished

75

woodwork and a newly whitewashed wall over which the tops of fruit trees showed. It struck no chords at all.

As we regained the square, the visitors' cars were leaving and the wildly unsuitable Lotus went roaring and bumping down the hill, striking sparks from its underside on the stones. As if to provide a contrast, a very old man with an enormous moustache was making his way across the open space with the aid of a stick. He was dressed in the handmade clothes of old Cyprus: an embroidered waistcoat and loose-sleeved shirt, long woollen stockings, a broad sash and breeches so enormously loose that they almost touched the ground between his feet.

★　★　★　★

Here the women are not chary of their favours.
Here Buffavento looks to every side.

(Isolario, Bartolomneo Zamberti, 1485)

People seemed uncertain about Buffavento, the castle which straddled the very summit of the Kyrenia range, looking down at the sea on one side and at Nicosia in the plain on the other.

'I don't know whether you can go there now,' they would say dubiously. 'It's difficult. The military use that area a good deal. Have you seen St Hilarion?'

One afternoon we took the road beyond Kyrenia which crosses the mountains beneath the clenched fist of Pentadactylos: the old road to Nicosia in fact, now being widened by giant earth-moving machines. A procession of lorries was cautiously grinding down the hill at walking pace, each containing a single white boulder weighing many tons. I was reminded of the way worker ants each carry an egg away to safety when the nest is breached. To the left of the road, an area of cleared trees and barbed wire guarded something very secret indeed. Sentries stared down from searchlight towers and skull and crossbones signs on the fence warned of minefields.

Mount Pentadactylos is associated with the legendary hero Dighenis Akritas, the frontiersman, defender of the Byzantine Empire from the incursions of the infidels. Tales of Dighenis are told not only in Cyprus, but in all Greek-speaking lands, and he occupies an equivalent position in folklore to that of King Arthur in England. Endowed as he was with superhuman powers, this mountain shows the imprint of his giant hand as he leaped over the range to attack the Saracens. Dighenis was the codename chosen by General Grivas during the EOKA guerrilla campaign against the British.

The forest road which leads along the ridge towards Buffavento had a chain padlocked across it and the usual notice: 'Restricted Military Area'. Grumbling under our breath we used the map to identify and find a second track which follows the southern flanks of the mountains towards the Monastery of Ayios Ioannis Chrysostomos which lies beneath the castle. This road was badly cut about by heavy bulldozers, for all these foothills were being eaten away by opencast quarrying. Moreover, there were still sloughs of red mud left from the rains and we lurched and slid our way precariously over ridges and gullies, until we skidded round a corner to find ourselves suddenly surrounded by soldiers. Their blue berets confused me for a moment into thinking that they must be a UN patrol. The young officer was looking up from his map. He had a tanned, brown face and very blue eyes, and spoke in English with an American accent.

'Buffavento?' he said. 'Straight on.'

'Where are you from?'

'Turkey,' he replied, looking more surprised than ever, and we realised that they were Turkish commandos on exercise.

Reassured that our presence appeared to be acceptable, we continued to slide through the sticky mud for several miles until we came abruptly to a crossroads and a gateway in a barbed-wire entanglement, guarded by a sentry. One track led uphill towards the mountain pcaks, but it was closed off with a steel cable. I parked the car and walked over to talk to the soldier, who looked uncertainly at me. We obviously did not fit in with any instructions he had been given.

'*Selam. Lutfen Buffavento Kalesi nerede?*'

He pointed up the track towards the mountains. High up on the crags, thousands of feet above, I thought I could just make out ruined walls and crenellations. When I looked over the sentry's shoulder I appreciated the reason for the nervousness about this area, for we were standing at the gate of a huge camp. Hundreds of lorries and jeeps were parked in rows, and further back, under the slope of the mountain, were the bulkier shapes of tanks under camouflage netting. On the far side of the enclosure I could see the tiled roof and cypress trees of the monastery. The soldier gestured behind him and made a barring movement with his carbine.

'Here no. There yes.' He pointed up the track leading to the mountains.

'But it's wired closed.'

He shrugged his shoulders.

'But are we permitted to walk up?' I made what I thought was an appropriate gesture to indicate a long climb. But he did not understand and shrugged again.

'Tashkent, yes. Kaynakkoy yes. Here no. Not permitted.'

Tashkent! The name sounded outlandish, unreal. I wished I could string just a few words of Turkish together in order to ascertain exactly which paths we were allowed to use. We held a rapid conference and concluded that, even if we could leave the car by the gate and climb up to the castle on foot, it was too late in the day to complete the round trip by nightfall.

Promising ourselves that we would return for another attempt, we turned downhill to Gungor, once known as Koutsovendis and inhabited by Maronites long ago. The only occupants were a group of UNFICYP soldiers playing football in the dust of the little square. The blue and white laurel wreath flag drooped from its pole by the schoolhouse which accommodated the observation post. They were Austrians.

'Wherever have you come from?' one of them asked. We explained that we had been trying to reach Buffavento Castle. Did they know if access was permitted?

'I wouldn't think so. I'm surprised that they allowed you even as close as they did. They won't have us any nearer than this. But if you want to try and walk up another day, you can leave your car here.' He grinned. 'Who are we supposed to inform if you don't come back for it?'

To the south of Koutsovendis we found ourselves in a desolate landscape, which I assumed had been hopelessly eroded during years of overgrazing by the ubiquitous goats. Herds of these animals still wandered over the barren ground, crystalline and streaked with gullies where flood water had washed to the bedrock. Small eucalyptus trees had been planted in a forlorn attempt to bind the topsoil, but their position looked precarious, particularly as the goats had not been fenced out. This is the rain-shadow side of the Kyrenia mountains, deprived of the sea moisture enjoyed by the northern slopes. Later, a Turkish forester told me that I was wrong to pin the entire blame for this desert on to the goats, for the original damage had been caused by mineral extraction. And indeed Sir Samuel Baker had reported severe erosion in 1879, for which he blamed the lime-burners who lived and worked in the district and who systematically cut every sapling to its very roots in their search for firewood.

The depressing scenery matched our mood of frustration. Nobody in Turkish Cyprus ever seemed to be quite clear as to what was permitted and what was not. Perhaps, as it was late on Sunday afternoon, the guardian from Buffavento had gone home, wiring the road off behind him? It did not seem very likely. If only we had had a Turkish speaker with us. Perhaps we should go into Nicosia and enquire at the Ministry of Tourism. How could the authorities possibly expect to encourage tourism while denying access to one of the most famous beauty spots of Cyprus?

We emerged from these low, denuded hills on to the grassland of
the Mesaoria plain, which stretched unbroken to the outskirts of
Nicosia. At intervals, even at the very edge of the city, we could see
brown clusters of goats, each attended by the solitary figure of a
herdsman standing a little apart. In the distance, the main Nicosia–
Famagusta highway was busy with traffic. We joined it ourselves for a
short distance near Haspolat, which the Greeks called Mia Milea as it
was one Greek mile (or three English miles) from the capital. In the
surrounding fields we could see jeeps and armoured vehicles under
camouflage netting, for the Line runs very close to the road here,
before turning south to divide the city.

A few yards beyond the next turning back north, a small road
leading to the old Maronite enclave of Kythrea, we almost missed a
small blue and white sign low down on the verge. This one simply
read: 'Entry forbidden to Foreigners'.

'Oh come on,' Joan snapped, 'that one was so small that I didn't
even see it. I'm quite prepared to desist from taking photographs, but
I'm damned if I'm going to spend the rest of my time here sitting on
the beach at Lapithos.'

So we continued across the plain towards Kythrea, which the Turks
call Degirmenlik, the Place of the Mills. It lies, together with a cluster
of attendant hamlets, at the foot of the mountains, surrounded by
luxuriant palms and fruit trees. Out on the prairie to the cast, a rig was
drilling for water, the ground newly churned by vehicle tracks and
stacked with drums of diesel fuel, the derrick spidery against the sky.
Water, in Cyprus, is almost more precious than oil. Cypriots, both
Greek and Turkish, are an amiable people and generally slow to
anger. Nevertheless, a number of judicial executions for premeditated
murder took place during the British administration; water theft, an
unforgivable crime to a Cypriot farmer, was the provocation for many
of these killings.

The *kephalovryson* spring which burst from the mountains here
under the Pentadactylos Forest brought people to this area from the
earliest times. Neolithic remains have been found, and the ancient
Greek city of Chytri stood nearby. There is an old story that the
marvellous spring water came not from Mount Pentadactylos above,
but through a channel beneath the sea, all the way from the Taurus
mountains of Turkey, to well up and spread prosperity over these dry
plains. (A similar legend attaches to the Lapithos spring, and another
involves a gold chalice, dropped into an Anatolian pool, to emerge
later from a Cypriot fountain.)

The Romans built an aqueduct to supply the water into the great
city of Salamis, or Constantia, which stood 30 miles away on the east
coast, and the ruins of this watercourse can still be traced over the

Mesaoria plain. The whole area is littered with relics of the past, and ancient stones, tiles, pottery and coins are often found in the soil of these fields. In 1928 a Turkish farmer ran his plough into something heavy under the ground; he dug down and unearthed a bronze arm, and then the rest of a large statue. The stomach was smashed open in the hope of finding coins – again that Turkish obsession with buried treasure – and the arm was sold for scrap, before the Antiquities Department came to hear and paid £25 for the rest. The statue was of the Emperor Septimius Severus, the able African soldier who was raised to the throne by the legions in 193 and died in York while rebuilding Hadrian's Wall. Once it adorned the Kythrea terminus of the Salamis aqueduct and it is now one of the finest exhibits of the Cyprus Museum – although one arm, of course, is a reconstruction.

A Christian bishop had his palace here until the Arabs sacked the city in about 800. (St Demetrianos, Bishop of Kythrea, is said to have fallen to the raids of the 'Babylonians' and his saint's day is celebrated on 6 November.) But in time the farmers returned, and the market gardens became famous for their succulent olives, mulberries, lemons, cotton and, above all, cauliflowers, which originated here and were first sent to Europe in 1604. The stream was powerful enough to drive a whole line of water mills, and when Sir Samuel Baker came in 1879, conscientiously cataloguing the assets of Britain's new possession, he found no less than 32 still in operation. These mills had ground the flour for all Nicosia and the countryside for miles around since Byzantine times. Indeed, so important were they that during several revolts against the Turkish governor the insurgents blockaded Nicosia by first capturing the mills of Kythrea. Baker observed that the water emerged from an arch in the mountainside and that there was a fall of 400 feet in all. Wheat was carted from as far away as Larnaca. Whereas the millstones used on the north coast were brought from Athens, those for the Kythrea mills came from Alexandretta. And while Baker lingered here, noting these details, he chanced to meet a young soldier, Lieutenant Kitchener, who was busily engaged in surveying the island in order to produce the first detailed and accurate map.

There is one more remarkable thing about Kythrea. Travellers as recently as the nineteenth century reported that the women were exceptionally beautiful and also rather lax in their morals. It may well be that some of them were influenced by the classical accounts of this island of Aphrodite and its reputation for orgiastic religious rites – 'Here the women are not chary of their favours' reflected popular, though not necessarily accurately informed opinion. There is more than a hint of wishful thinking in some of these writings, mixed with a little salacious gossip. Ali Bey, possibly the strangest traveller ever to set foot on these shores, reported in 1806 that he met no beautiful women here, but that they were indeed lacking in chastity and that this failing led to numerous lawsuits:

> Possibly the heat of the climate, the isolation of the houses which stand each apart, the mulberry thickets, and the absence of the men, who are away during the day in the markets of Nicosia, are the causes to which one may assign the dissolute character of the women of Cythera, for all these are circumstances favourable to debauch.

(Trs. C.D. Cobham, *Excerpta Cyria*)

A strange reputation this, in an island where sexual morals were generally strict, and one which must have caused a good deal of embarrassment to the men of the town. Perhaps Aphrodite's influence lingered on in this place from some ancient and undiscovered temple.

Mindful of all these stories, we had stopped in the main street while we checked our map and looked out for any sign of a water mill, a cauliflower or a loose woman, when our car suddenly became the object of anxious attention and people began to gather round it. A bus driver blew his horn frantically as he passed on the other side of the road. Then a lorry pulled up, and the driver leaned out of the window:

'Where do you want to go? Nicosia? Kyrenia?'

'We wanted to come here, to Degirmenlik.'

A middle-aged man pushed his way to the front of the crowd: 'Can I help you? Are you looking for the main road?'

'No. If we may, would like to visit your town.'

'That is absolutely impossible. Foreigners are not permitted here. I am afraid you must leave at once.'

'May we drive through and leave by the Kyrenia road?'

'Yes, but you must go quickly please.' Then a worried look crossed his face like a shadow. Had he seemed rude? Had he seemed inhospitable? After all, he was a Cypriot.

'Where are you from?' he asked us.

'England.'

'English! Oh how do you do? Welcome to Cyprus.'

Once on the move we seemed to attract less attention as we made our way through a maze of ancient wooden houses. There were dovecotes in the courtyards and bright flowers planted in rusty petrol tins. We passed a deserted monastery, a new school built in 1975 and a derelict church, one half of which had been converted into a shop and coffee house. There were crumbling mud-brick walls, beehive-domed ovens, coiled irrigation pipes and thick beds of bamboo. A black-uniformed police sergeant seemed unconcerned about our presence when we stopped to ask for further directions.

As we slowed past a grove of trees, we saw something strange; a white marble pillar, obviously some kind of memorial, inscribed in Greek characters, stood in a graveyard. I could only make out the date as we passed: 1958. But at some time red paint had been daubed over it, and crudely wired on top was the figure of a wolf baying at the crescent moon, the symbol of TMT, the Turkish terrorist organisation.

Just before we left the controlled area, we saw one, at least, of Kythrea's famous products. A sunken field lay below the road in a narrow valley, irrigated by little concrete channels and planted with enormous cauliflowers, larger than I had ever seen. Three men, one of whom spoke German having lived and worked in Germany, were piling the vegetables into wheelbarrows. Then a soldier guarding a red and white painted barrier across the road swung it up to let us out of Kythrea with a salute.

'Kythrea is a difficult place,' said Mr Ucok later, as we sat in his restaurant eating grilled red mullet which had been brought all the way from Bogaz, near Famagusta. 'They wouldn't allow you to stay there of course. But you can never be quite sure. One day there is an exercise and the roads are closed. Next day there are no soldiers and you can go where you please.'

He brought me a *soumada*, a drink of hot sweetened almond juice, to ease a sore throat which I had developed.

CHAPTER SIX

FAMAGUSTA

Salih and I sat in deck chairs with our coffees, watching the sun coming over the Kyrenia mountains. I declined one of his strong Karpas tobacco cigarettes, for my throat was still troubling me. Salih puffed and coughed happily. The workers on the building site nearby had begun their day and persuaded their concrete mixer into noisy life. A farmer wheeled a barrow-load of cabbages past the swimming pool, bound for the hotel's kitchen. The recent rainstorm had resulted in a veritable explosion of wild flowers, so that the fields before us were now carpeted with yellow and red anemones.

'Is a strange thing about Kythrea,' Salih remarked. 'Very old place. Very old peoples lived there: Greeks, Romans. Always they had water, too much water. And now, just now, the water is finished. All finished. And all the clever men, professors, scientists, cannot say why the spring is dry. They bring a machine to dig in the ground, but they still cannot find the water.'

Curious indeed for such a copious supply of water suddenly to cease. The presence of the drilling rig on the nearby plain was explained. We sat for a while, pondering this strange phenomenon, and then I remembered something which had amused me earlier.

'I saw something this morning,' I remarked. 'There were three men on the main road, just outside here, who flagged down a friend driving a lorry for a lift. But they made him stop after only a hundred yards, where the side road is, and they all climbed out again to carry on walking to Lapithos. It couldn't have been more than a hundred yards, rather less in fact, but they preferred to go to all the trouble of climbing in and out of the lorry, rather than walk it.'

Salih gave an appreciative and admiring chuckle.

'Lazy Turkish mens,' he murmured. 'Cyprus no is *Evropa*.'

★   ★   ★   ★

From Mia Milea the road ran eastward across the Mesaoria, a dreary place even during this spring of green grass and bright flowers. An occasional thorn tree struggled for existence by the dried-up irrigation channels. A steady stream of lorries moved along the narrow road between Nicosia and Famagusta and our progress was slow. Four out of five filling stations were closed, the concrete of their forecourts cracked and grown with weeds.

Each of the strange villages rode like a ship on the sea of the plain, a derelict church tower for a mast, around which clustered dusty mud-brick houses in varying states of decay: Trakhoni, where the Church of St Nicholas was turned first into a mosque and then into a stable during the first Turkish occupation; Palekythro, where the Turks built a harem with the stone from an ancient temple of Aphrodite; Angastina, once a commandery of the Templars, whose Church of St Therapon was sacked and the icons stolen by the Turkish army in 1974. A few years ago Gaidhouras, or the Place of Asses, tried, in a fit of Hellenism, to change its name to New Sparta. But the new name did not take, and the rest of Cyprus has been laughing ever since.

The village of Pyrga was always said to have been an unlucky place, ever since the inhabitants betrayed the revolutionary monk Ioannikios to the Turks in 1833. Ioannikios had fought in the Greek War of Independence, and began a rebellion in eastern Cyprus with the support of the people of the Karpas and disgruntled Albanian troops. The Turkish forces suppressed the revolt with very little difficulty, hanging the ringleaders, torturing many more and burning the crops of villages which had aided the insurgents. But before his death Ioannikios cursed the whole village of Pyrga, which had sought to save itself by informing on him. Apparently the village suffered constant ill fortune ever after. Now it seemed that the curse had really taken hold, for Pyrga, or Pirhan, had been completely taken over by the Turkish army, and there was no civilian population left, only barracks, firing ranges and assault courses.

The eastern part of the Mesaoria seemed particularly desolate, the villages ruinous and infested with flies, mainly populated by immigrants from the mainland. The men were dressed traditionally in huge baggy pantaloons and Turkish slippers, while women in brightly coloured head-dresses tended large flocks of sheep and goats, grazing right up to the denuded foothills to the north. Only a few tractors were working the land, which seemed to be slipping back into pastoralism. As we approached the hinterland of Famagusta, we came to empty factories, deserted warehouses and half-completed buildings, on which no work had been done since 1974. Some of the factories had a military guard on the roof, watching far across the plain from their elevated platform. On the outskirts of the city, it was a relief to find a carpenter's shop making furniture, a Sun Zest citrus-packing factory and a plant making lubricating oils, all apparently thriving.

Famagusta is really two cities: the old walled town which was the traditional Turkish quarter, and the modern high-rise suburb of Varosha to the south. Varosha was the Greek quarter, a temple to twentieth-century commerce, which now stands eerily empty, wired off and penetrated only by Turkish army patrols. Once again the Line is close, as is the British Sovereign Base Area of Dhekelia, so that Famagusta, now known by its Turkish name of Gazi Magusa, is enclosed on three sides by the sea, Greek and British territory.

The massive Venetian walls of old Famagusta have not been breached in the interests of modern traffic flow; indeed they are so huge and thick that no contractor would lightly undertake to slight them. They still stand as proudly as the Venetian military engineer intended, although now the city has fallen twice into Turkish hands. Today the traffic still queues to squeeze through the narrow gates, the diesel engines of lorries and buses roaring under the stone archways. After the extraordinary modern sculpture at the roundabout outside the city, we pased the Land Gate and the Ravelin, and the Bastions of Santa Napa, Andruzzi and Camposantio, before entering the city by the Djamboulat, or Arsenal Gate.

Famagusta is a relatively recent settlement by the standards of Cyprus. It may have been named the Fame of Augustus, in honour of the great Roman Emperor, but it achieved no great importance until Salamis, the ancient city a few miles to the north, fell to the Arabs in AD 648 and the inhabitants fled here. It has also been suggested that the name derived from the Greek *ammochostos*, meaning 'lost in the sand', although the city, far from being hidden, now sits squarely dominating the plain for miles around. But if Famagusta was once a little-known Byzantine fishing port among the sand dunes and ancient ruins of this rather dull coastline, its fortunes changed almost overnight when Acre and the seaports of Syria fell to the Saracens in 1291. King Henry II of Cyprus was far-sighted enough to offer the displaced Christian merchants of the Levant this obscure town in which to continue their interrupted trade. Over the next hundred years Famagusta became the most important Christian city of the East, excepting only Constantinople.

The wealth of these merchants, Venetians, Genoese and Franks, founded on ivory, silk and perfumes from Asia, together with the export of Cyprus wine and silk, became the wonder of Christendom. Every visitor had tales to tell of the extravagance of the inhabitants. The German priest Von Suchen wrote:

> Cyprus is the farthest of Christian lands, so that all ships and all wares, be they what they may and come they from what part of the sea they will, must needs come first to Famagusta, and in no wise can they pass it by;

and pilgrims from every land journeying to countries over sea must touch at Cyprus. And daily from the rising of the sun to its setting are heard rumours and news; and the tongues of every nation are heard and read and talked.

(Trs. C.D Cobham, *Excerpta Cypria*)

The talk would seem to have been mostly about money, and even the visitors became infected with the general obsession as, like modern tourists, they struggled to calculate the exchange rate. 'In Cyprus there is also a silver coin called Bizanti,' mused Rieter of Sebaldt, a pilgrim from Nuremburg. 'One is worth thirteen marks and of these Bizanti, ten are worth a ducat.'

Von Suchen described the betrothal of a merchant's daughter; the jewels which she wore in her head-dress alone were finer than all those of the Queen of France. Richest of all the merchants were the Syrian Lachas brothers, one of whom once ground up a jewel to sprinkle on his food as a spice. Sir Francis Lachas, who built the Nestorian or 'millionaire's' church, evidently basked in the affection of the king, and with good reason. 'Yesterday,' he wrote to Peter I, 'I did a stroke of business and gained thirty thousand ducats and these I am sending to your lordship, and I beg that you take it not amiss.' Happy monarch, to rule over such subjects!

Even some of the courtesans of the city possessed more than one hundred thousand florins, according to Von Suchen, who was appalled at the immorality of the people. Nevertheless, behind the strengthened Byzantine walls they built 365 churches, so it was said that a man could pray in a different one on every day of the year. In Famagusta he might hear Mass said in Greek, Latin, Syriac, Chaldean or Armenian, rubbing shoulders variously with congregations of Gregorians, Maronites, Nestorians, Jacobites and Copts. A remarkable number of churches still stand in old Famagusta, some of them almost side by side.

Famagusta's decline began with the quarrel between the Venetians and the Genoese which came to a head in the riots at the coronation of Peter II. When the Genoese invaded Cyprus in force, they sacked the city, and it never recovered the old wealth and brilliance of the fourteenth century. Many of the buildings remained in ruins, even as they do today, for we found large areas of wasteland within the walls, and Famagusta is still half-empty.

Once inside the gate, we parked by an old coach with the name of an operator in Bromley still stencilled on the side; Cyprus, where they still drive on the left, is a ready market for second-hand British buses and lorries. The Djamboulat Gate was named after Djamboulat Bey, a Turkish hero who died in an attempt to capture the arsenal during the great siege of 1571, and who lies buried in the bastion nearby. Here too we found a cemetery for the Turkish dead of 1974: people of all ages, most of whom had died on 20 July. Across a jumble of ruined walls, wrecked cars and dilapidated shacks we could see St Nicholas' Cathedral: French Gothic architecture incongruously framed by dusty green palm trees and surmounted by the minaret which the Turks added when they took the city and converted it into the Mosque of Lala Mustapha Pasha. This is the dominant building of Famagusta and one catches glimpses of it from all over the old city.

As we walked inside the wall towards the Land Gate, we came to a more populated district. Whether it was due to the sight of the mosques, the palm trees, the features of the mainland Turks who crowded the streets around the market, or the obvious poverty of the shops and houses I am not sure, but it seemed to us that this was an oriental city. One might imagine oneself in the old quarters of Damascus or Jerusalem, but surely this could not be Europe? Street vendors pushed barrows of fruit, sweet pastries and Turkish pizzas through the traffic, surrounded by flies and shouting in loud, harsh voices as they went. Peasants and their wives, in to market from the villages of the Mesaoria, stood out in their homespun traditional clothes as they carried reed baskets along the pavement. I caught a glimpse of a narghile being lit in a crowded coffee shop. And, just for a moment, the wonderful sight of a Turkish bride in the dramatic, winged head-dress of Central Asia.

The Land Gate was built by the Turks, and the narrow bridge which takes motor vehicles across the moat under the control of traffic lights is more recent than it appears, having been built during the nineteenth century. The original 'Limassol Gate' of the Venetians could still be seen beside it. We clambered down into the ditch which seemed to be in general use as a lavatory. From here we could look up at the great Ravelin, or Rivettina Bastion, the place where the Turks concentrated their attack. But it was not until we gained the top of the wall, and gazed down at the diminutive figures of off-duty soldiers walking by the parapet of the bridge, that we appreciated the monumental work of the Venetian engineers. This must be the most perfect example remaining of a walled city, from an age when the art of fortification had reached its height. Such is the width of the wall that British colonial officials once used to amuse themselves by playing golf along the grassy top. Natives of the city do not often trouble to climb up here, and we met no one as we walked around the better part of Famagusta.

The Venetians had Cyprus for only 80 years before the Turkish invasion, but they were not caught unprepared. Here at Famagusta the angular Byzantine fortifications were modified into heavy, rounded walls designed to withstand cannonfire: 50 feet high and nearly 30 feet thick. The stone was taken from the ditch and the ruins of ancient Salamis nearby. Jodicus de Meggen, who later became the first commander of the Vatican Guard, saw these works in 1542 and was suitably impressed:

> On August 1st we arrived at Famagusta before dinner. This lies about forty thousand paces from Nicosia, and is very strong and well fortified, especially on the side which faces the land. For the Venetians, after they had become masters of the island, fortified it remarkably with new and exceedingly strong ramparts so that it seemed quite impregnable, partly because the ground just outside the city walls is sloping (and thus easily averts the shots from siege trains) and partly because the walls are set with very hard stones and so cannot be undermined with passages or other subterranean devices. Besides, there is an astonishing thickness of some thirty-three feet of earth packed against the walls on the inside.
>
> (Trs. C.D. Cobham, *Excerpta Cypria*)

Venice was fully occupied with preparations for the coming storm. Cyprus was regarded purely as a military base to protect Venetian shipping, and the island itself, its people and its commerce were generally neglected at this time. Indeed the Cypriots led a miserable life under the Venetians. The pilgrim Von Baumgarten, who passed through Cyprus in 1508, had observed that

> All the inhabitants of Cyprus are slaves to the Venetians, being obliged to pay to the state a third part of all their increase or income, whether the product of their ground, or corn, wine, oil or of their cattle, or any other thing. Besides every man of them is bound to work for the state two days of the week wherever they shall please to appoint him . . . And which is more, there is yearly some tax or other imposed on them, with which the poor common people are so flayed and pillaged, that they hardly have wherewithal to keep soul and body together.
>
> (Trs. C.D. Cobham, *Excerpta Cypria*)

This wretched condition of the Cypriot Greeks goes far to explain their later attitude to the Turkish invaders.

By September of 1570, Famagusta stood alone in Cyprus, for, following the fall of Nicosia and the massacre of its population, the rest of the island was in Turkish hands. Now, according to the Venetian historian Paolo Paruta, 50,000 additional Turks came over to Cyprus from Karamania and Syria, in the hope of enriching themselves with plunder:

> . . . the Grand Signor had sent so vast a host that if every man of them had thrown a slipper into the ditches of the fortress they would have filled them up, and made a platform reaching to the top of the walls.

(Trs. C.D. Cobham, *Excerpta Cypria*)

Thus the Turkish army under Lala Mustapha Pasha, known as the Tutor, numbered over 100,000 when it came up against the walls of Famagusta, which was defended by 2,500 Venetians, 2,500 Greeks and some 200 Albanian cavalry, all under the command of the Venetian Marco Antonio Bragadino. This governor must have been loved and respected by his people, in spite of Venice's oppressive treatment of the Cypriots, for in a speech which an ancient Greek or Roman general would have envied, he was able to inspire them to stand bravely against appalling odds:

> 'No glory that warriors have earned in any age could be greater than that which is reserved for you who, in defending against the might of the Ottoman Empire a fortress so far from other Christian lands, will ensure the preservation of our flourishing kingdom from enslavement by barbarians . . . do not let the enemy's numbers frighten you for a moment. They are certainly less than what we hear by report, or than what is indicated by a pompous array of tents. Most of them, or at least the bravest of them, are exhausted by toil, or have returned home to enjoy the riches acquired in the siege of Nicosia.'

(Trs. C.D. Cobham, *Excerpta Cypria*)

The Turks dragged the huge siege cannon known as basilisks to bear on the walls, and began an intense bombardment. A hundred and fifty thousand cannonballs were fired into the city over the ten months of the siege to create the ruinous, bombsite appearance which remains in parts of Famagusta today. The Armenians of the pioneer corps constructed a maze of trenches over the plain in order that their troops could move safely up to the wall under the Venetian guns: trenches so deep that only the lance tips of the cavalry showed above ground. The walls were undermined and battered by artillery. Bragadino, for his part, organised a remarkable number of sorties, partly to forage for food, but also to give the impression that the garrison was stronger that it actually was. 'Fireworks' were thrown as grenades from the walls on to the Turkish sappers. In military terms their situation was hopeless, but the defenders constantly turned their eyes to the sea in expectation of help from Venice. This proved to be a vain hope, for the Turkish blockade remained unbroken and the supplies for Famagusta, as Alexander Drummond put it, 'loitered in Crete four months.'

The fighting became desperate and both sides claim their heroes. Djamboulat, Bey of Kilis, rode his horse into the gate of the Arsenal Bastion to force a way through for his followers. Here the Venetians had mounted a fearsome machine of war, a kind of rotating wheel covered in knives and spikes. The Bey and his horse were impaled, but the machine was broken. For the rest of the siege his ghost was seen with its head held under its arm, encouraging his fellow countrymen in the thick of the battle. His grave, marked by a fig tree, later became a place of pilgrimage. Childless couples would eat a fig in the hope that the hero would bring them fertility.

The fighting around the Ravelin, the great bastion projecting into the moat at the Land Gate, was the most severe. The wall was damaged by the explosion of a mine, and in July the Turks finally gained a foothold and fought their way inside. The design of the inner chambers was such that the defenders found themselves limited in their movements by the lack of space. The Venetians then fired a great charge that had earlier been buried beneath the Ravelin. A thousand Turks and a hundred Venetians are said to have died in the explosion, but still the attackers flooded through the breach among the smoking rubble. Here, the Turks claimed first to have seen the white flag flown by the defenders, and they still call this bastion the Akkule, the White Tower.

Although the fortress was breached, the Venetians fought on behind improvised barricades for a few days. 'Candiot carts' packed with earth were dragged into place so that men might fire from behind them. The two sides were now separated by only a few yards. According to Paruta:

> The ravelin lost, there remained between besiegers and besieged only the breadth of the second line of defence, constructed, as we said, of carts and sacks full of earth. The men on either side often talked together and, as soldiers use, flouted one another, the Turks deriding the vain hopes of our men, and telling them that the Christian fleets had by this time fled as far as Venice. Ours, in turn, mocked the enemy who, more like peasants than warriors, trusted so little in their arms that they used spades and shovels.

(Trs. C.D. Cobham, *Excerpta Cypria*)

Only a quarter of the original garrison was now left alive, while as many as 50,000 Turks may have died. On 1 August, Bragadino negotiated a surrender with Lala Mustapha, under which the Cypriot inhabitants of the city would remain unharmed, while the surviving Venetians would be granted safe conduct to Crete in Turkish ships. Thus the defenders emerged, and for the first time the two armies were able to examine each other properly. Paruta wrote:

> Our men were staggered at the prodigious number of the force they saw in the Turkish camp. For over three miles from the city it stretched over a vast circuit, and was everywhere so full of troops that the turbans, which on every side showed white above the trenches, covered the ground like snowflakes. The Turks, on the other hand, when they saw the defending force so small in numbers, the emaciated bodies and pale faces of our soldiers, who seemed as though they could hardly stand, much less offer so long and gallant a resistance to a foe, marvelled at their courage and felt some touch of shame. They let natural pity, and the generous workings of true courage, have their way; they began to offer them refreshments, to speak courteously, to praise their steadfastness, and to encourage them to hope for the best.

> (Trs. C.D. Cobham, *Excerpta Cypria*)

On 5 August, Bragadino went with his three principal commanders, Quirini, Baglioni and Martinengo, to deliver the keys of Famagusta to Lala Mustapha Pasha in his camp, Bragadino riding in style under a red umbrella. Lala Mustapha received the keys politely and formal compliments were exchanged while a meal was served. 'Up to this time,' according to the Venetian Calepio, 'Turks and Christians had maintained with each other friendly and trustful intercourse, in all courtesy of deed and word, eating and drinking together.'

But after a time Lala Mustapha insisted that he wanted the young Quirini to remain behind as a hostage, to ensure the safe return of his vessels from Venetian Crete. Bragadino protested that no mention had been made of this condition during the negotiations for the surrender. The conversation grew heated, and Mustapha accused Bragadino of executing a group of 50 Turkish pilgrims in his hands after the surrender, a charge which the Venetians hotly denied, then and later. But the Pasha's terrible rage, a trait for which he was notorious among his own people as well as enemies, had seized hold of him and he called for his executioner. Bragadino was forced to watch as his three officers were dismembered on the spot. According to Angelo Calepio:

> Then twice and thrice he made Signor Bragadino, who showed no sign of fear, stretch out his neck as though he would strike off his head, but spared his life and cut off his ears and nose, and as he lay on the ground Mustafa

reviled him, cursing our Lord and saying, 'Where now is thy Christ that He doth not help thee?' The general made never an answer, but with lofty patience waited the end.

(Trs. C.D. Cobham, *Excerpta Cypria*)

For ten days the unfortunate Venetian was left chained in a dungeon without attention. Lala Mustapha's vindictive fury was no passing mood, for on the tenth day Bragadino was again dragged out and forced to carry earth up to the wall which was being repaired, and to kiss the ground at his tormentor's feet each time he passed. Finally he was taken to the square in the front of the Cathedral of St Nicholas, shortly to become the Lala Mustapha Pasha Mosque, and chained between two pillars. There, as the Turkish commander watched from the terrace of the Governor's Palace, he was flayed alive, and witnesses stated that he bore all these tortures silently and with great courage until his death.

The Pasha's treatment of the defeated commander and citizens of Famagusta horrified many Turks. According to Paolo Paruta:

It was mere madness which stirred him to rage even against the dead. He entered the Episcopal Church of Saint Nicholas, caused the graves to be opened and the bones scattered. He destroyed the altars and the images of the saints, and committed other bestial and cruel acts for which he was much blamed even by his own people.

(Trs. C.D. Cobham, *Excerpta Cypria*)

The humiliation of poor Bragadino continued beyond death. The skin was stuffed with straw and, under the same red umbrella which had shaded the Venetian on his way to the Turkish camp, was mockingly paraded through the city. Then, tied to the mast of a galley, it was displayed at all the ports of the Syrian coast, before being sent to the Sultan at Constantinople, together with the heads of his three commanders. The skin was displayed for 25 years at the principal prison of the Sultan, in sight of the Christian captives. Finally, Bragadino's family managed to acquire the sad relic for a huge bribe and brought it back to Venice, where it lies preserved in an urn in the Church of SS Giovanni e Paolo to this day.

From the repaired Akkule Bastion we looked beyond the Land Gate to the old Turkish cemetery. Not far away are more recent graves belonging to Turkish prisoners from the First World War. Captured in the Dardanelles, in the Hedjaz and by the Suez Canal, some 2,000 of these soldiers were brought to Cyprus to be confined in the Karaolos camp (or concentration camp as the Turkish guide book terms it). This same, sad camp was used as a detention centre for many of the 51,000 illegal Jewish immigrants to Palestine after the Second World War, who were intercepted by the British authorities and kept on Cyprus for a while.

The moat of the citadel was filled with water until 1900, when it was drained in an attempt to combat the malaria which was rife in this district. Early in the British period, earth infested with locusts' eggs had been dumped here during an attempt to dispose of another of the perennial plagues of Cyprus. These flatlands long had an unhealthy reputation, though of course the connection with the anopheles mosquito was never directly made. For many years the Turks' trenches remaining from the great siege were held to be responsible for the prevalence of fever. And in the fourteenth century an anonymous English traveller had blamed the wine:

> . . . in this place the mortality is so high among the foreigners who have to learn to abstain from unwatered wine, nor to rule themselves according to the habits of their countries so that it might be called a burial ground of all Christendom.

Nicholas Martoni more accurately considered that the surrounding marshes 'and the great number of courtesans' were the main hazard to the health of the Famagustans. Famagusta always had a reputation for its brothels. 'Famagusta used to be a bit of a wild town,' a friend who was stationed there shortly after the war stated delicately. 'A soldiers' town, if you know what I mean.' He was referring, no doubt, to Aphrodite Street, off Desdemona Square.

Below the wall on the city side stands the Akkule Mesdjid, an oratory built by the Turks in 1619. Rather than take the street which runs along the base of the wall, the Kemal Zeytinoglou, we continued to follow the ramparts, past the Diocare and Moratto Bastions. We descended by the old Nestorian or 'millionaire's' church, built by the Lachas family in 1359 for this Syrian sect, sometimes known as the Chaldeans from their use of that ancient language in their liturgy. These followers of Nestorius, the fifth-century Patriarch of Constantinople who preached the heresy that the human and divine were not merged into one in the person of Jesus Christ, still survive in Persia and Kurdistan. But their church in Famagusta was deserted and used as a stable for camels for many years, until it was taken over by Orthodox Greeks who worshipped here until they abandoned the old city to the Turks after the violence in 1963. Since then, it has stood empty.

Finding the door locked, we walked around the walls to which local housewives had tied the ends of their washing lines. Just as we were leaving the dusty graveyard, a car pulled up in the street and a man in a dark suit climbed out, balancing a bunch of enormous keys in one hand. He smiled as he saw us.

'Would you like to see the church? You're lucky; I come only once a month to check that all is well. I'm from the Antiquities Department.'

The rusty key turned with difficulty in the lock before the door was pushed ajar and we walked into the echoing gloom of the interior. Leaning against every wall, stacked four and five deep, were painted wooden icons, the details obscured by the thick dust which lay everywhere.

'After 1974, we collected all the icons of any importance from the churches of the district and brought them here for safety,' explained our guide. 'You must appreciate that we are a new state – with all our problems there is very little money for antiquities. So we must save, we must preserve, but for the moment we cannot restore.'

The Greeks knew this church as Ayios Yeoryios Xorinos, St George the Exiler, for there is a legend that the dust from the floor has magic properties. A small quantity of it, dropped in an enemy's house, will kill him within the year, or at the very least bring him such ill luck that he will be forced to leave Cyprus. I picked up a pinch of the fine powder which lay so liberally over the stone flags and ran it speculatively into my palm. Then I thought better of it, and let the dust trickle back to the floor. Our companion was watching me with amusement.

'So you have heard that old story. We used this church as a hospital during the bombing in 1974 you know. I remember there were stretchers all along that wall. Are you staying in Famagusta long? Come and see us at our office before you leave. We are down at Othello's Tower, near the Sea Gate. I can show you some interesting things there.'

Beyond the Nestorian church the city is even more depopulated, with fields of dry grass between the ruins. We passed the Latin Church of St Anna, dedicated to the mother of the Virgin, and the Tanners' Mosque, originally a sixteenth-century church. At the north-west corner of the wall is the great Martinengo Bastion, or Tophane, so formidable that the Turks left it strictly alone during the great siege. This is the work of Giovanni Girolamo Sanmichelli of Verona, whose uncle Michele built the famous walls of Candia, in Crete. It was named after the popular Venetian soldier Hieronimo Martinengo, who died at Corfu on his way to a command in Cyprus. The gun ports and passages run deep into the stone and there are even ventilation shafts for the powder smoke to escape. During the Second World War it was used as a petrol store.

We could not approach too closely, for this empty part of the city had been occupied by the Turkish army and was cut off by an entanglement of barbed wire, guarded by sentries every few yards. Among the beaten earth of parade grounds, barrack huts and assault courses, the ruined shells of yet more churches stood starkly. The Latin Church of St Mary of Mt Carmel was once attached to a monastery which has now disappeared. Peter de Thomas, known as the Blessed, the Latin Patriarch of Constantinople who was fatally wounded during the siege of Alexandria in 1366, lies buried humbly under the floor so that all men, high or low, might walk over him. In the Armenian Church of St Mary beside it, a series of acoustic jars have been cemented to the ceiling and inscriptions in the Armenian language are visible below frescos of the saints. This church, out of bounds to civilians, now, was once the chapel of the Monastery of the Caller; so much is known from the survival of a manuscript written by one of the monks, one of the most haunting voices to come out of Cyprus' past:

This book was written by the hand of the senseless and sinning Houhannes, servant of God, in the year of the Armenian Calendar 1317, in the Island of Cyprus, at the Door of the Cathedral of the Mother of God, which is a monastery and is called the Caller, in the city of Maghusa.

(Trs. C.D. Cobham, *Excerpta Cypria*)

The effect of the first Turkish occupation on the people and economy of Cyprus is still wrangled over by the respective Greek and Turkish racial propagandists. The Turks claim with truth that they abolished serfdom and permitted the Orthodox Church freedoms and privileges which had been denied them by the Latin hierarchy of the Lusignans and Venetians. The Turkish system was to rule their subject peoples through their own leaders and institutions. Thus the Autocephalous Church of Cyprus, provided that it collected the taxes specified by the Sublime Porte, was virtually free to govern the Greeks of the island as it wished, and indeed to levy whatever extra taxes it pleased. Archbishop Makarios III, the elected Ethnarch of the Greek Cypriot people, was one of a long line of such independent leaders, in secular as well as religious matters, a concept which the British always had difficulty in grasping.

The Turks also claim to have restored the local trade which had suffered from Venetian neglect and to have built aqueducts here to channel water into Famagusta. But such public works appear to have been few and far between, according to the reports of independent travellers. After 70 years, although many of the veterans of Lala

Mustapha's army, the ancestors of today's Turkish Cypriots, had settled here, most of the Catholics had fled abroad and the total population of Cyprus had shrunk to a quarter of the previous figure. Christians were forbidden to live within the walls of Famagusta; indeed they dared not approach the city closely in those early days lest they be forced to embrace Islam. In 1683, more than 100 years after the siege, the Dutchman Van Bruyn was refused entry at the gate and warned away from the walls. Later Christian travellers from abroad were obliged to dismount from their horses before entering, and were barred from the Mosque of Lala Mustapha Pasha. Pococke, in the eighteenth century, reported that half the space enclosed by the walls was overgrown wasteland and that many of the remaining houses were empty. In 1751 the young Swedish Dr Hasselquist found the fortifications so neglected as to be useless and the ramparts grown with aloes, while the inhabitants of the city then numbered only 300 dwelling among the ruins. And Dr Sibthorp, who visited the city in 1787, described 'streets now deserted, a melancholy picture of Turkish desolation; the gateway by which we returned to the convent was paved with cannonballs'.

Life in Cyprus was regarded virtually as exile by the Turks themselves. Near the Sinan Pasha Mosque is the tomb of Chelebi Mehmet Effendi, the janissary who became a writer and diplomat and was appointed Ambassador to Paris in 1720. Implicated in the Patrona Halil rebellion of 1730 in Constantinople, he was dismissed from public office and sent to Cyprus, where he died two years later. Outside the city wall stands the tomb of Kutup Osman, philosopher and tutor to Sultan Mehmet IV. His influence over his old pupil became so great that it earned him the enmity of other members of the court, who engineered his downfall and banishment. More recently, the radical nineteenth-century writer Naimik Kemal, who outraged the Sultan and the establishment with his play *Vatan yahut Silistre*, was imprisoned for three years in the old Venetian Governor's Palace. There were a number of political prisoners still in residence when the British took possession in 1878, including Subh-i-Ezel, the religious leader of the Persian Babi sect, whom the Sultan regarded as a threat.

Famagusta, even at the end of the nineteenth century, was still described as 'a confused mass of ruins and filth', although many of the churches had been shipped away to Egypt to provide stone for the Suez Canal. Indeed, Sir Samuel Baker was all for knocking down the remaining ruins as a health hazard and using the masonry to build a new harbour.

St George of the Latins is the oldest of the Gothic churches in Famagusta, possibly even older than the Lusignan walls, for the building was originally heavily fortified. Little remains but part of the choir, for the roof was blown away during the siege by the Turkish bombardment. There is, however, one beautifully carved doorway, through which we could see the minaret of the Lala Mustapha Pasha Mosque formed against the sky. A cluster of bats is carved on one of the stone pillars – strangely apt, for these ruins are now haunted by the silent forms of real bats at dusk.

We were approaching the populated part of the city once more. In the grounds of a school, a class of children were hoeing the soil for vegetables under the watchful eye of a young teacher – a practical kind of education. At an arch in the wall near the Sea Gate, the dockers were knocking off for lunch, pouring past the heavily armed police at the entrance to the port and dispersing to bars and restaurants. Quite a number were Negroes, for the descendants of slaves are mixed with the Turkish population, and one sometimes comes across Turkish Cypriots who are quite black. In 1881, according to the Archduke Louis Salvator, there were a considerable number of Negroes and mulattos in Cyprus, some of them Christians, and female slaves were still being imported, though quietly by Kyrenia, for fear of offending the European consuls at Larnaca. Interestingly, there appears to be no colour bar in operation against these people, although it has to be said that Turkish Cypriots are generally highly prejudiced against their fellow Muslims from Africa and Asia.

We followed the crowd into the narrow streets and found a tiny restaurant where we drank cold beer and ate rice pilaff with spiced chick peas and lady's fingers. One hard-pressed youth did all the work, cooking the food as well as serving it, while the plump proprietor sat with a cup of coffee, guarding the till and working out the bills with a kind of abacus.

After lunch, more churches. St George of the Greeks is an odd mixture: Byzantine weight and presence combined with Gothic intricacy. It was built by the Orthodox community in an attempt to rival the nearby Latin Cathedral of St Nicholas and demonstrates a merging of the two styles. Indeed as the centuries passed, the religious distinctions themselves became blurred and many Latins drifted towards Orthodoxy. By contrast, the ruins of the original Orthodox Cathedral of St Symeon are pure Byzantium. So too are the little fifteenth-century Church of St Nicholas, which looks as if it belongs in a small Greek village, and the Church of Ayia Zoni, dedicated to the sash of the Virgin. The Church of the Knights Hospitallers stands cheek by jowl with that of the Templars, though the two orders quarrelled continuously through the Crusades. Somehow this extraordinary collection of religious sects managed to live together within these walls, united by their mutual interest in making money and their mutual fear of the infidels across the water.

Near the Church of St Peter and St Paul, once a mosque, used as a grain store by the British and damaged by earthquakes, a group of sweating men, bare to the waist, were excavating a foundation hole with pneumatic drills. The air was filled with dust and the smell of diesel exhaust as the compressor roared and hammered. Joan and the boys joined the little crowd which always forms at the scene of such operations. One of the young workmen looked up and saw Joan, and wiped the black hair from his eyes.

''Allo,' he said, 'you're not a local are you?'

'Neither it seems are you,' said Joan.

'Oh, we're Turks all right. But we live in England. I was born in London. We've got an ice-cream business in Bromley.'

'So why are you digging a hole in Famagusta?'

'It's not just a hole. Gonna be five new shops in here. No, it's this lot.' His wide gesture took in the rest of the onlookers and all the people of Famagusta. 'Too bloody lazy to do it themselves. So we have to come and do it for them. We're all here, father and brothers; spend the winter on the contract and be back for summer to open our business. Personally I can't wait to be off.'

'How did you get here?' Joan asked.

'Overland. Drove an old coach and sold it when we got here.'

'What about military service? Don't you risk being conscripted?'

'No problem, I sussed all that out. They can't touch me until I've been here six months and I'll make sure I'm away by then.'

★   ★   ★   ★

'A sea port in Cyprus,' Shakespeare wrote when setting the scene for *Othello, the Moor of Venice*, and there is little doubt that Famagusta was intended. To this day the citadel by the Sea Gate is known as Othello's Tower, although the evidence for the existence of a real Moor in the service of Venice is slim. Shakespeare had the bones of the story from the Italian Cintio, this at a time when fashionable England was enthusiastically reading Italian fiction. A possible source for the character of the Moor was Francesco de Sessa, a southern Italian mercenary who served Venice in Cyprus and was known as 'Il Capitano Moro' for his dark looks. In 1544 the Council of Ten tried and banished him for some crime which has become lost to history. Intriguingly, two of his subordinate officers shared the same fate – Iago and Cassio? But even earlier, between 1506 and 1508, the Lieutenant-Governor of Cyprus was a Venetian named Christophoro Moro. This surname was apparently not uncommon in Italy: as well as Moor or Negro, the word means mulberry tree, and this governor's family coat of arms is known to have included three mulberries. It is also known that his wife died on the voyage home to Venice.

It has been said that there are three lions of Cyprus: the English lion of King Richard, the Lusignan lion and the winged lion of St Mark. Above the door to Othello's Tower (the massive structure does not open now and one enters through a smaller hole cut through the baulks of timber), is a fine frieze of the Venetian lion, which can still be seen carved into the stone in odd places all over the city. The guardian recognised us from his little wooden office and came out to greet us.

'Hello my dears, have you seen enough churches? Come, and I will show you Othello's Tower. What you must first understand is that once this was a castle for defending against swordsmen and archers. High walls with battlements and narrow slit windows. The towers were square. Look, I have a model here. Then the Venetians came here and Nicolo Foscarini rebuilt it for warfare with artillery. This is what you see now. The walls are lower and much, much thicker with gun ports. The corners are gone, everything is round so the shot bounces away.'

He continued to talk as we climbed to the top of the crumbling but massive walls. Here and there, unguarded ventilation shafts led down to unseen chambers. The guardian kept a watchful eye on the children.

'Be careful where you walk; some of these shafts are dangerous. Look boys, see these cannonballs. Everywhere in Famagusta we find them from the time of the siege. In the gardens. Under the walls of old houses.'

Sir Samuel Baker had been impressed by the size of the shot, which made it plain that the Turkish and Venetian guns had been of much larger calibre than the English ones of the same date. At Famagusta he was shown marble balls of 11 inches diameter, and at Kyrenia stone shot measuring fully 19 inches.

We had reached the top of one of the towers on the seaward side. There was a tang of salt in the air, and the red flag of Turkey flapped in the wind. In Venetian days there used to be a floodgate near here, so that galleys could be hauled up safely within the fortifications. Now we found ourselves looking down at a single long dock outside the walls, where four or five freighters were unloading. There was plenty of activity, but virtually no mechanisation, not so much as a railway line. Ships were unloading with their own derricks and mobile cranes mounted on lorries. Nevertheless, this single port is vital to Turkish Cyprus: the only sealink with the outside world and a key target of the Turkish army's advance in 1974. From here a ferry now runs to the Anatolian port of Mersin.

Seated amongst the thistles growing on the stone capping to the wall, where some United Nations soldiers had once carved their names, the guardian told us that he had worked for the Antiquities Department since British times. He remembered Mr Theophilus Mogabgab, the Lebanese Christian who fought so hard to preserve the antiquities of the historic city from builders and developers, and who compiled the *Supplementary Excerpts on Cyprus* to complement C.D. Cobham's amazing *Excerpta Cypria*.

'It's not a bad job, you know. I think I am a lucky man. Of course there were not many opportunities for Turks in the time of the Republic, after 1960.'

'And now?'

'Oh, we have our problems as you can see. But we are safe. Look over there.'

Beyond the funnels of the ships we could see high-rise buildings to the south: blocks of flats and hotels.

'That's Varosha, the Greek quarter. The north part has been settled by people from the mainland. But the rest has stood empty for twelve years. If you go down to the beach you can see it from quite close. Rauf Denktash is talking about allowing some Greeks back, to run those businesses for the good of our economy. But it seems to me that it would be very difficult to arrange this. I just heard on the radio that Denktash has been in London today, talking to Mrs Thatcher. So maybe we will hear something soon. We have waited a long time for recognition. This is what we need more than any other thing.'

He pointed in the other direction, back up the coast to the north.

'While you are in Kibris you must go to the ancient city of Salamis. You know what you see now is only part of the city – the rest is under the sea. I had an English friend, an army captain from the Sovereign Base Area, who used to come up here with diving equipment – unofficially, you understand – and we would go out in a rubber boat, perhaps half a mile. More recently I have been with divers from the United Nations. The divers brought up pieces of marble, mosaic and tiles. There were amphorae which were too heavy to lift, and one diver came up to the boat and said that he had seen a great statue, half sunk into the mud.'

Beyond Salamis the bay curves away to the north-east and the long Karpas peninsula. We asked the guardian if it was true that some Greeks still remained there.

'I am not sure. There may still be, and certainly the Apostolos Andreas Monastery on the cape is still occupied. There are a lot of people from mainland Turkey up there. There are still some Maronites in the North, you know. An interesting people.'

'Are there any Armenians remaining?'

'No, they all went to the Greek sector. Look, this moving of people may seem very cruel to you, but believe me, it was for the best. There was nothing else to be done. Of course, if the British had stayed . . .'

We descended once more to the courtyard, and he showed us a rusty Turkish helmet which he kept on his desk and the Great Hall: a huge and lofty chamber. Then he led us into a curved gallery, deep within the stonework of one of the towers.

'These walls still have hollows and cavities which we have not discovered. In 1966, under the Martinengo Bastion, we found two great chambers dating from the time of the siege. During the bombing in 1974, 2,000 women and children hid there safely. Parts of Othello's Tower are Lusignan, incorporated into the Venetian work. Sometimes the Venetians filled the hollows with stone, and sometimes they simply cemented the Lusignan chambers up and built over them. This little room here, for instance, was part of the old Lusignan wall.

'Now, there is a great mystery here which many have tried to solve. We know the Venetian merchants were enormously rich. They were famous for their wealth. Yet when the Turkish army attacked Cyprus, they had no chance to escape with their treasure. When the siege was ended, Lala Mustapha entered the city and the Venetian commander was . . . well, killed . . .'

'He certainly was.'

The guardian looked put out, but continued: 'The Venetians were allowed to leave empty-handed, but of their great treasure there was no sign. Obviously they had buried it somewhere during the siege in the hope that one day they might return in strength to recover the city and their gold. What else could they have done?'

'Surely such a treasure trove could be hidden anywhere in the city. How would you know where to look?'

'No, no, we believe that it must be here within the citadel. It is the strongest place, the place which might have held out after the rest of the city had fallen. But to find the cavity . . . Look, this wall here is nearly 30 feet thick. The roof above us, the same. It would take an army of men years to tear Othello's Tower down stone by stone.

'Listen, there is a professor in Italy, a very learned man. He is researching this matter in Venice, studying old documents in the libraries of the city. He writes to me regularly, and three times now he has come and we have dug together. Last year we pulled up these flagstones we are standing on. Another time, further down the passage, where the wall turns. This is not official, you understand. I think about this problem very much, even in my sleep. Perhaps I walk right over the treasure every day . . .'

The search for the Venetian treasure is an old one. In 1870 the Turks dredged out the harbour hoping to find it, but instead recovered a cannon which Henry VIII had presented to a Grand Master of the Knights of St John after the fall of Rhodes. Certainly many valuable objects, sacred as well as profane, disappeared after the siege. The Water Pitcher from the Marriage of Cana in Galilee, which in 1560 was said to be preserved in the city, was never seen again. And though I said nothing about it to the guardian, when the Turkish army took Famagusta for the second time, in 1974, they found their treasure surely enough. Twenty million pounds worth of goods in the bonded warehouse of the port were captured together with the loot of all the Greek quarter. Nor is the present Turkish administration's record on antiquities good, because during the months and years following the invasion a large number of valuable and restricted items found their way on to the black market.

★　★　★　★

In the courtyard of St Nicholas' Cathedral, we craned our heads to see the pinnacles high above us. In spite of the damage caused by the cannonfire in 1571 and a severe earthquake in 1735, and in spite of the addition of the minaret, this is one of the most remarkable examples of Cypriot Gothic, for the Turks did not restore or embellish the building in later centuries. Thus the purity of the original concept, probably that of a fourteenth-century French master-builder named Jean Langlais, still remains. This is where the Lusignan kings came to receive the Crown of Jerusalem, long after the Holy City was lost to them, and this is where Catherine Cornaro, the last queen, formally renounced her title in favour of the Doge of Venice.

Joan sat on a block of stone near the two pillars where poor Bragadino had endured his terrible fate. These pillars were brought from the ancient city of Salamis: one was once surmounted by a statue of St Theodore, and the other by a lion of St Mark. Venetian coats of arms were still engraved in the marble wall of the loggia nearby, and a frieze from the Roman temple had been incorporated into the wall. St Bridget of Sweden once preached a sermon here in front of the cathedral, castigating the Famagustans for their immorality. And there is an old story that, in the steeple above, a flask of holy water from Persia was once preserved which had the magical property of dispelling the locusts that periodically plagued the island. But after the siege, a Turk climbed into the steeple and in his ignorance spilled the precious liquid; thus the remedy was lost for ever.

A couple of young boys sat down, removed their shoes and washed their feet in the fountain before entering the mosque. I went quietly after them, Malcolm and Steven at my heels. It was the hour of prayer, and there were rows of prostrate figures along the floor as the

Imam chanted into a microphone at the far side of the building. A well-dressed man carrying a rosary brushed past me, removed his shoes and walked forward to kneel with the congregation. The interior had been gutted, the walls covered in whitewash, and every statue and painting removed. There was nothing coloured or rich to catch the eye, except for the carpets before the priest and the green symbols on the wall which indicated the direction of Mecca.

★　★　★　★

A short distance along the road to Varosha we came to a barrier of barbed wire and a sentry. Beyond, nothing moved between the tall concrete buildings except two soldiers on patrol in a jeep. We parked the car and looked over the wire. It was quite uncanny; a scene from a science fiction film, or like looking at London after the atomic bomb had dropped. The shop signs were all in Greek, together with familiar trade names in Roman script – Lotus Cars Agency, Grundig, Coca-Cola. The concrete of the roadway was cracking, grass forcing its way upwards into the gutters and around the kerbstones. The soldier, who had been looking uncertainly at us, accepted a cigarette which he tucked into his tunic, then smiled and saluted as we made a tight U-turn and drove back towards the old city. Some while later there was a certain amount of excitement in Varosha, when a teenaged sentry on the Attila Line nearby, apparently under intolerable pressure from an NCO, hysterically opened fire on his fellows before running across to claim asylum in the Greek sector. This incident was still unresolved when we left the island.

Townhouse in the old city of Famagusta

CHAPTER SEVEN

SALAMIS

We came to Salamis on a cloudy, windy day, driving north from the Land Gate of Famagusta and through the marshes among which the Pedhieos and Yialias rivers find their uncertain route to the sea. Sir Samuel Baker had been much concerned in 1879 at the flooding caused by the silting of the estuaries and the need for proper drainage works. So low is the land that the distant sea was almost invisible, and the tall shape of a freighter on its way into Famagusta port seemed to be ploughing its way through the fertile silt of the plain. This was a difficult area for the UN peace-keeping force during the 1960s; fighting broke out in November 1965 over the Turks' construction of defensive positions in concrete and their desire to search Greek vehicles travelling through the district.

Near the modern village of Enkomi lies the Mycenaean city now known as Enkomi-Alassia. The site had been dug over and robbed for many centuries, but in 1896 an expedition organised by the British Museum opened a number of untouched tombs, to find beautiful bronzes and ceramics. Swedish, French and Greek expeditions continued to excavate until 1974, uncovering an extensive grid of narrow, intersecting streets and the foundations of numerous buildings. Now the treasures are variously dispersed between the British Museum, the Cyprus Museum (which is in the Greek sector of Nicosia) and, since 1974, the European black market in antiquities.

The Mycenaeans reached Cyprus towards the end of the Bronze Age, at a time when the Achaeans, iron-equipped charioteers from the north, were already pressing towards the old Mycenaean homelands in the Peloponnese. The identification of this city with ancient Alassia, mentioned in the writings of the Hittites, is still not absolutely proven. The tablets found at El Amarna in Egypt refer to Alassia, whose king exchanged Cyprian copper with the Pharaoh Akhenaten in return for perfumes, a golden bed, horses and a fine bull. It would seem that the Alassians also traded with the Canaanites of Ras-Shamra in Syria. Two tablets found in Alassia were engraved with a strange script, not unlike Minoan Linear 'A'. One of these has been claimed to refer to Ajax and Teucer in the Trojan War.

The Achaeans followed the Mycenaeans to Cyprus, as did later waves of Greeks and Anatolians. The religion they followed is not clear. At Enkomi-Alassia a strange horned god, perhaps a primitive Apollo, made from bronze during the twelfth century, has been unearthed. During the next century, an earthquake or a fire devastated the city, whose inhabitants eventually moved on to nearby Salamis, while the ruins of their houses and streets were gradually submerged by silt from the river.

The coast road to Salamis was dominated by huge empty hotels, visible for many miles across the Mesaoria, their forecourts and car parks overgrown by weeds, the blinds drawn, and furniture covered in dustsheets. We nearly drove past the rusty little sign which directed us through groves of stunted eucalyptus and pine towards the sea. Salamis was once a huge city whose ruins lie scattered for miles over the plain and, if the man from the Antiquities Department is to be believed, under the sea as well. In ancient times there were reported to be islands off the coast; these have long disappeared, for all this area has been shaken and inundated by earthquakes and tidal waves. We passed the guardian's hut, padlocked and untenanted, before parking by the shore. There was no one to be seen and nothing to be heard, except for the steady crash of the waves on to a narrow beach.

Salamis is said to have been founded by the banished Teucer, brother to Ajax and the son of King Telamon, who ruled the original island of Salamis in the Saronic Gulf, where the Athenians were later to gain their famous victory over the Persians. There is no direct proof of this, but the Athenians evidently believed it to be true. Thus, Euripides (who traditionally was born on Saronic Salamis on the very day of the battle) has Teucer declare:

> How I may steer my vessel with success
> To Cyprus' isle where Phoebus hath foretold
> That I shall dwell, and on the walls I rear
> Bestow the name of Salamis, yet mindful
> Of that dear country I have left behind

(Trs. Theophilus Mogabgab, *Supplementary Excerpts on Cyprus*)

So perhaps this city, founded as Alassia declined, was first settled by men of the Heroic Age, hardened veterans of Troy. The culture and traditions of the citizens of Salamis were indubitably Mycenaean–Achaean–Greek, and the city became the most powerful and civilised of the island's kingdoms. Although Cyprus was successively dominated in later centuries by the Phoenicians, Assyrians, Persians and Egyptians, Salamis and the other city-states managed to retain their identities and a measure of independence.

During the sixth century BC, King Evelthon ruled Salamis, minting his own coinage and enjoying considerable autonomy within the Persian Empire. Herodotus describes him attempting to avoid providing aid to the deposed King of Cyrene, without wishing to offend the King's mother, who was his enforced guest:

> . . . his mother took refuge at Salamis in the island of Cyprus. Salamis was at that time ruled by Evelthon, the same who offered at Delphi the censer which is in the treasury of the Corinthians, a work deserving of admiration. Of him Pheretima made request, that he would give her an army, whereby she and her son might regain Cyrene. But Evelthon, preferring to give her anything rather than an army, made her various presents. Pheretima accepted them all, saying, as she took them: 'Good is this too, O King! but better were it to give me the army which I crave at thy hands.' Finding that she repeated these words each time he presented her with a gift, Evelthon at last sent her a golden spindle and distaff, with the wool ready for spinning. Again she uttered the same speech as before, whereupon Evelthon rejoined – 'These are the gifts I present to women, not armies.'

> (Trs. George Rawlinson, *Histories*)

Evelthon's grandson, Onesilos, whose elder brother Gorgos ruled Salamis and favoured the Persians, became a Greek hero during the Ionian Revolt of 499 BC. Having failed to influence his brother to join the rebellion, Onesilos shut him out of the city by a trick and persuaded the other kingdoms – Kition, Paphos, Tamassos, Marium, Kyrenia, Soli, Kourion and Lapithos – to attack their Asian rulers. Only the Phoenician city of Amathus, near modern Limassol, would not be swayed. A great battle was fought near Salamis, which resulted in disaster for the Greeks when the men of Kourion, together with the charioteers of Salamis, turned traitor and went over to the Persian side. Onesilos was killed outside Amathus and, according to Herodotus, the men of that city severed his head and hung it over the gate. Some twenty years later, King Gorgos of the Cypriot Salamis fought for Xerxes and the Persians at the great naval battle of Salamis in 480 BC.

Nevertheless, relations between Athens and many of the Cypriot cities remained good. General Kimon, whose father Miltiades had commanded at Marathon, attempted to liberate Cyprus from Persian rule after his victory at Eurymedon in Pamphylia. The Persians were defeated off Salamis by Kimon's triremes, but later, after Kimon's death, a treaty was concluded with Artaxerxes which left Cyprus in Persian hands.

Perhaps the greatest king of Salamis was a Greek mercenary named Evagoras who claimed to be descended from Teucer, the original founder of the city. In 411 BC he seized the crown from the Phoenician King Abdemon and forced the other cities into a confederation in order that they might act in unison to resist Persia. This was a Golden Age of Hellenism in Cyprus, when many Athenians came to settle at Salamis which became renowned for its culture and civilisation. His friend Isocrates described Evagoras as an ideal ruler and general: noble, patriotic and brave. Apart from Athens, Evagoras managed to enlist the support of Egypt and the cities of Cilicia, while his armies succeeded in capturing the great port of Tyre. For ten years he successfully defied the might of the Persian army, even when they landed on the Karpas peninsula to attack him on his own ground. Even at the last, when all seemed lost, he so harassed his enemies that they were forced to sue for peace, and Evagoras kept his throne, though for the rest of his life he paid a tribute to Persia for the privilege.

When Alexander the Great defeated Darius and a mixed Persian and Greek mercenary army at Issus in 333 BC, the cities of Cyprus supported him faithfuly and well, sending 120 ships to the siege of Tyre in the following year. (Indeed it was in their interests to do so, for the fall of Phoenician Tyre relieved their fears of domination from that quarter.) Pnytagoras, the King of Salamis, particularly distinguished himself, and the little kingdoms of Cyprus subsequently found themselves basking in the warm regard of the ruler of the world. Pnytagoras was rewarded with the famous copper mines of Tamassos.

The freedom of the Cypriots was as short-lived as Alexander and the unity of his empire. In 306 BC Demetrios Poliorcetes, the Besieger of Cities, was battering at the walls of Salamis in an attempt to add it to his Asian satrapies. The island eventually fell into the control of Ptolemy and remained an important and wealthy part of the Egyptian Empire for more than 200 years, supplying copper and building ships under the direction of a viceroy.

The old cities of Cyprus as usual retained some power, forming *To Koinon ton Kyprion*, The League of Cypriots, to administer internal affairs. This society later grew to have a religious significance under the Romans who ruled Cyprus from 58 BC. There was one further brief period of Egyptian domination, when Mark Anthony made a present of Cyprus, 'supreme in beauty', to Cleopatra.

The Romans moved their capital from Salamis to Paphos in the south-west. But Salamis remained a large and thriving city, benefiting from the new roads which encircled the island. It was the Levite Barnabas, a Jew from Salamis, who first introduced Saul to the apostles at Jerusalem, confirming his miraculous conversion. At this time, Salamis certainly possessed a large and powerful Jewish community. According to the Acts of the Apostles, St Paul's first foreign journey was with his friend Barnabas to visit his native Cyprus in AD 45. At Salamis they 'preached the word of God in the synagogues of the Jews' before travelling to Paphos, where they converted Sergius Paulus, the Roman Governor. This conversion took place despite the evil influence of Bar-Jesus, the sinister Jewish astrologer of the Governor's household, whom Paul blinded for a time as a demonstration of the power of Christ.

Cypriot legend has it that Paul and Barnabas were in Cyprus for only ten days before leaving for Pamphylia. Barnabas' return is also a matter of tradition rather than established fact. Certainly the Acts state that the two friends quarrelled over Barnabas' wish to take his cousin Mark on their second journey, for 'the contention was so sharp between them that they departed asunder one from the other: and so Barnabas took Mark and sailed unto Cyprus'. Paul, in a huff, went separately to Syria with Silas. It is believed in Cyprus that, when the vengeful sorcerer Bar-Jesus learned that Barnabas had returned to the island, he aroused the various Jewish communities into a fury against the 'blasphemer'. Ugly disturbances broke out, preventing him from speaking at Amathus and Kourion. There was a riot when he tried to speak on the racecourse of Kition, and a mob at Salamis became so frenzied that he was stoned to death as he attempted to preach in the hippodrome. His cousin Mark obtained the body afterwards, and buried Barnabas secretly in an old tomb somewhere outside the city, St Matthew's Gospel on his breast. Here the body lay, unknown and undisturbed for 400 years.

During the reign of Trajan, a major Jewish revolt spread through Egypt, Cyrene and Cyprus. It is estimated that a million people lost their lives as a consequence of this desperate fight against Rome: 250,000 or 15 per cent of the population, in Cyprus alone. When the Cypriot revolt was finally suppressed, virtually the entire Gentile population of Salamis had perished. The city, which had been seriously damaged by an earthquake during the previous century, was once more in ruins. From this time, the settlement of Jews in Cyprus was absolutely forbidden by Imperial decree, and it is said that even shipwrecked Jewish sailors were executed if found on the shore. Not until the year 1160 was any Jew permitted to land on the island, and no substantial colony was ever formed again.

It would seem that the people of Salamis spent most of the late Roman period in rebuilding their city after a series of earthquakes. The most damaging were those of 332 and 342, when a tidal wave destroyed the port and the thriving shipyard. After this final reconstruction, the city once more became the capital of Cyprus and was renamed Constantia, in gratitude to the Emperor Constantine II who, sympathising with their troubles, kindly relieved the inhabitants of taxation. Life in Byzantine Salamis came to an end in 647, when the Arabs under Mu'Awiyah sacked the city. The few survivors abandoned it for the more defensible town of Famagusta, returning only occasionally for a cartload of masonry.

The gymnasium of Salamis, at first sight a most imposing classical ruin, is a good example of the constant battering and reconstruction which took place in the city. This was built by the Romans over the site of an earlier Hellenistic building. But the 40 or so marble columns which archaeologists re-erected in the early 1950s to stand around the courtyard are themselves part of the Byzantine rebuilding, having been taken from the nearby theatre, often with the wrong capitals. The pagan statues which once embellished this temple to the human physique had their heads struck off by the narrow-minded Christian rebuilders, while those showing the naked body were ruthlessly toppled from their pedestals.

Nearby are the baths, where all the complexities of hypocausts, frigidaria and sudatoria which made up the social centre of a great Roman city are still visible. Not far way, the theatre stands with its back to the sea, originally built during the reign of Augustus and repaired later. The columns of the frons scenae have been removed to the gymnasium, but the eight lower rows of seats are still perfect and elegantly faced in marble. There are now twenty tiers in place, following archaeological reconstructions, but when we walked around the back we could see from the exposed buttresses that vast quantities of masonry have been removed over the centuries. There were once 50 tiers, and 15,000 people could be accommodated in the auditorium with ease.

We made the old experiment and found that, surely enough, a voice little above a whisper from the centre of the stage could be heard perfectly clearly from the uppermost seats. Strangely, while standing by the white marble pillar which marks this central position, where sacrifices were made to Dionysus before the performance of a play, one could hear a constant hissing susurration, like the voice of a seashell, focused from the semi-circle of stone. From the upper row of seats, we could look out over the remains of the city wall, built by the Byzantines to hold back the Arabs, and across the plain to the distant blue of the mountains around Kantara Castle.

To the south of the theatre, the ruins straggle through the woods, and fragments of mosaic and pavement litter the ground. There is part of a private villa, the Granite Forum (named for the huge columns which were brought from Aswan in Egypt), a Byzantine cistern with frescos painted on its upper walls, a water clock and, close to the

Roman harbour, the Campanapetra Basilica, only recently discovered. Besides the Agora, sometimes called the Stone Forum, stands the Temple of Zeus, dedicated in memory of Augustus' wife Livia.

The great metropolitan church of the city was built by St Epiphanius, the original Bishop of Constantia and Archbishop of all Cyprus, first in a line which continues to this day. (The full title of the head of the Cypriot Church is Bishop of Salamis and Archbishop of Cyprus.) He died in 406, and was said to have been buried here before his remains were taken away to Constantinople in the tenth century. Only the foundations of this enormous church remain, although a small part was rebuilt after the Arab raids and made into a triple-domed chapel, which the Greeks of the surrounding countryside used until the fourteenth century. Nearby is the tank which the water from Kythrea once filled, and a few sections of the aqueduct can still be seen far away over the plain.

We wandered across the fields to the west, until we found ourselves outside the towers of the Byzantine walls in a strange area known as the Necropolis of Salamis, or the Tombs of the Kings. Here stands the Prison of St Catherine, a blockhouse-like structure incorporated in a mound, isolated on the plain. Until recently Cypriots would come to this place to invoke the intercession of the saint, light a candle and leave an ex-voto of wax. The Cypriot version of the legend of St Catherine is that she was the daughter of Constantine, sometimes described as the King, or more accurately the Roman Governor, of Salamis. When Constantine arranged a marriage for his daughter, she refused, and her father imprisoned Catherine here in this desolate place outside the city walls, until she should learn obedience. But Catherine had become a bride of Christ; in a vision an angel had descended to her with the ring. Finally it was her father who relented and had her released.

Catherine accompanied her father when he was transferred to Alexandria, and there enraged the Emperor by successfully debating the Christian religion with 50 professional orators, specially hired to make a fool of her – and, what was worse, converting the Empress, one of her attendants and a large number of Roman soldiers. The Emperor condemned her to death by torture as a blasphemer. She was strapped to the famous toothed wheel, but when it began to rotate it miraculously broke into pieces which flew about, the razors and knives cutting the throats of the pagans who stood watching. Catherine was then beheaded and her body taken to Mount Sinai, where for centuries pilgrims came to visit her tomb, which was guarded by the Knights of St Catherine.

Another legend attaches to St Catherine's Grove nearby: a group of thorny Egyptian acacia, or *Zizyphus spina christi*, said to have grown

111

from the Crown of Thorns. This is said to be an ill-fated place, where it is dangerous to sleep or collect firewood, and death to cut down a tree.

All of this was of great interest to me as we looked in at the little chapel under the overhanging roof of St Catherine's Prison, but the truth, as revealed by archaeologists, is more dramatic than the legend. In fact, the great blocks of stone are Roman, but the tomb below dates back seven centuries before Christ, and under the floor the sacrificed chariot horses of a dead Achaean king were found, still yoked together. The Achaean culture is believed to have survived longer in Cyprus than in its homeland and, looking around at the ancient tumuli of the plain, one could almost sense the presence of that heroic age. Many of the round tombs have been robbed over the intervening millennia, but in others the archaeologists who dug into the entrance ramps found spears and shields, swords of the type which Homer described at Troy, an ivory bed, the bones of servants who willingly followed their masters to the Dark Realm (although the hands of some were tied), a silver wine-mixing bowl and always the war horses. Some of these, still armoured in bronze and yoked in pairs to light-weight chariots, had twisted and plunged in terror at the moment of sacrifice, and so broken their necks.

Not far away, close to Enkomi, which the Turks call Tuzla, the Salt Pan, lies a tumulus known as the Cenotaph of Nicocreon, the last free King of Salamis. Under Ptolemy, Nicocreon wielded great power and ruled for a time over all Cyprus, but in the end he was accused of treachery. Rather than surrender to his Egyptian overlord, he and all his family committed suicide after setting fire to the palace, which collapsed over their bodies. No human remains were found in the tumulus, only precious ornaments and clay statues of the dead, baked hard by the symbolic funeral pyre.

This eastern part of the Mesaoria has a sinister, watchful feel to it, peopled as it is by the ancient dead and almost deserted by the living. In every direction we could see little hillocks, parts of the ruined aqueduct, overgrown masonry, sections of ancient road leading nowhere, strange unexplained ditches and embankments. Even the few poverty-stricken villages had the appearance of being abandoned; distant mosques and decaying mud walls stood with the sea of the plain lapping around their feet. We came to a burned-out church: the graveyard torn up, the bell removed and the door torn from its hinges. 'ENOSIS' could still be made out, inscribed in blue over the entrance arch. 'Nationhood now!' the Turks had painted over the walls, repeated endlessly. The slight wind blew with a mournful sound between the pillars of the empty nave, and the smoke of a shepherd's fire, many miles away, made a lazy staircase towards the clouds.

The shadows were long when we came to the Monastery of Apostolos Varnavas, which stands on the prairie with a small grove of trees. A short, shaded avenue extends to a tiny chapel nearby. The late sun illuminated rich ochre tiles and the gold crosses still standing on the main dome and campanile. We were not sure whom, if anyone, we would find in the monastery. From 1917 to 1976 three remarkable brother monks ruled here: Barnabas, Chariton and Stephanos, who earned a living by selling honey and turning out large numbers of icons with a kind of assembly-line technique – not great works of art by all accounts. But they worked away diligently for the glory of God, and appreciative pilgrims went happily back to their villages with the brightly coloured pictures. Oddly enough, I have a copy of a photograph of Father Barnabas painting an icon in 1935 (taken by H.V. Morton), and another, now with a beard grown white and patriarchal, but still painting, taken in about 1970. How the old monks lived from 1974 to 1976, or the final manner of their leaving, I do not know – or indeed whether all three survived so long, for they must have been a great age by then. They would have needed all their faith to survive such a disaster at the end of their simple, harmless lives.

This place has a very great significance in the history of the Church of Cyprus. In the fifth century a conflict arose between the Bishops of Cyprus and the Church of Antioch. The latter, as an Apostolic Church, the first See of St Peter, claimed jurisdiction over Cyprus. The Cypriots claimed that their own Church was fully independent and of equal importance, for had it not been founded by the Apostle Barnabas? Unfortunately, after 400 years there was no more than tradition to prove that Barnabas had returned a second time to the island and founded a Church. It seemed that the Syrians' arguments would prevail at Constantinople, and Cyprus become subordinate.

However, at this point St Barnabas himself took a hand on behalf of his native island. He appeared in a timely vision to Anthemios, Bishop of Salamis and Archbishop of Cyprus, and showed him a certain place outside the city on the Mesaoria, where a carob tree grew. The next day, the Achbishop and a great crowd went out from Salamis to the place and, digging down, found the old Roman tomb and the bones of St Barnabas with the mouldering Gospel of St Matthew (the Hebrew original, it is said), which Mark had placed in his arms. The Archbishop at once packed up these relics and set off for Constantinople, where he gave them to the Emperor, Zeno the Isaurian, who was suitably impressed. A special Synod was convened to adjudicate on the matter of the Cypriot Church, and it was agreed that Cyprus and Antioch should remain independent.

Moreover, the Emperor conferred some remarkable privileges on the now Apostolic Church of Cyprus. It was to be autocephalous, with the right to elect its own leader, as the Archbishops of Cyprus are still elected today by the Orthodox Christians of the island. Cyprus is the senior of the autocephalous churches, only the four original Patriarchates of Constantinople, Alexandria, Antioch and Jerusalem having precedence. The Archbishop would also have the right to sign his name in red ink, as the Emperor did on state papers, to wear the Imperial Purple and, instead of the pastoral staff of a bishop, to carry a sceptre. All these privileges remain to this day, and Chrysostomos, as Makarios before him, signs his name in red, carries a sceptre and wears a cape of Roman purple.

The Saracens destroyed the original monastery erected near St Barnabas' grave, but it was restored, and rebuilt once again during the fifteenth century. The present church is relatively recent, dating from 1756, and was repaired after earthquake damage in 1941, when the belfry was added. Nevertheless, there are columns from ancient Salamis incorporated in the structure, and the floor of the older building can still be found in the garden. It was while we were wandering among the overgrown roses and fig trees of the courtyard, looking at the gravestone of a Greek woman, that a voice made us jump. There was a solitary guardian still, who had been asleep in his little office by the entrance to the church. When we had inspected the interior, containing a large number of icons, he handed me an iron key. 'Now you should look at the tomb of St Barnabas,' he said, pointing from the gatehouse to the little shrine at the end of the avenue of trees.

We walked down, hefting the weight of the key, and pushed open the wrought-iron gate which had cut grooves in the pavement because the hinges were worn. The mother of the three old monks is buried here, under a white marble cross. The sun was sinking below the rim of the plain, and the cypress trees by the door were turning black. There was a smell of dampness and earth inside, and I fumbled for the light switch before we made our way down a winding stair into the rock. We found a crudely cut chamber, with an empty shelf in the wall: very like one of the catacombs at Rome. Someone had laid offerings of fresh laurel on the shelf; we came to realise that in Cyprus the boundaries between the religions are in many ways blurred. The Turks often venerate those Christian saints to whom miraculous powers are accredited, while the Greeks are pantheists by nature. Many of the old pagan deities live on, disguised but thinly. St Barnabas has the power of curing skin diseases, and the miraculous property is embodied in a well close by the tomb whose water is famous throughout Cyprus.

We emerged as the light finally faded behind the monastery, silhouetting the twin crosses, the bell tower and the eucalyptus trees. As I handed the guardian the key, he was locking up the main gate, his car ticking over in wait, for no one spends the night in St Barnabas now.

★   ★   ★   ★

In the dusk we began to make our way across the plain, from one village to the next. Dortyol (Four Ways), once Prastio, was a place of grinding poverty: hovels and muddy lanes. But in the midst of all the dirt, the door of the church, now a mosque, stood open. The *muezzin* was calling the faithful to prayer, and we had a glimpse of the brightly lit interior, rich carpets and a chandelier. There were huge cacti, the size of trees, growing on the road to Torunculo, the Greek Strongylos, a village where nearly all the houses had been destroyed by bombing. A handful of mainland Turks were eking out a miserable living in the few undamaged buildings, surrounded by rubble and blackened beams. The marks of fire were everywhere.

On the main road to Nicosia I pulled into the forecourt of a café. It was quite dark and we still had a long way to drive, but I was tired and my head was aching. I just wanted a quiet coffee and to rest my eyes for a few minutes before going on. It was only a little café, dominated by a huge television and video-recorder showing a rock concert from Ankara. An old man in down-at-heel slippers brought us coffee, and then one of a noisy group of men in their thirties came over to our table, carrying a bottle.

'Hey English. You drink *rakı*?'

I had not the energy to try to refuse. In a minute they surrounded our table and were pressing drinks, cigarettes and cakes on us. They were all off-duty policemen, and they wanted to talk about everything under the sun, but especially politics. There were times when I began to believe that half the male population of the Turkish sector were employed as policemen. A man named Mehmet, with a cousin in Leeds, was dissatisfied with the pay and with the prospects in Cyprus generally. What did we think his chances of entering the British police would be if he received permission to emigrate? He complained about the political stalemate and the run-down economy. His eyes glanced around in vague disgust at the dirty tables, the tired-looking tinsel draped around the shelves and the dusty windows.

I was becoming concerned about one of his friends, who was show-ing a remarkable interest in Malcolm and Steven, particularly the former, whose fair hair he was patting and stroking, murmuring to him in Turkish. My companion followed my glance and explained: 'My friend is very unfortunate. Always he wanted sons, but he has four daughters. This is a great sorrow for him. When he sees sons like yours, he is very envious.'

115

The conversation went on, and my headache grew worse. I wondered how we could get away. They were talking about the days of the Republic, Greek atrocities, TMT, the invasion . . . The world was black and white to these men; what had happened was no fault of the Turks to any degree; Greek perfidy was entirely responsible. If only this was explained to foreigners, surely the justice of their case must be obvious? Even allowing for the fact that they were slightly drunk, there was something edgy and nervous about their talk, something extreme in their pronouncements which caused concern. They seemed to have lost all sense of balance and reasonableness, and their mind's eye had hardened into a kind of tunnel vision. These were the type that TMT and EOKA thrived on: apparently decent, hospitable men, but with a blind spot of rigid, unquestioning racism which could be manipulated, so that under the right circumstances they might be capable of . . . I kept thinking of the sectarian murders of the 1960s, and how often both Greek and Turkish police were involved. The more I listened to them, the more dangerous they seemed.

The man with four daughters was now hand-feeding Malcolm from a plate of sweet *baklava*, one arm around his shoulders. Malcolm was frozen with embarrassment, unable to cope with the situation. I took out my wallet and extracted a couple of notes.

'I'm sorry,' I said to Mehmet, 'we've enjoyed talking with you, but we have a long way to drive tonight and we must go on.'

I looked round for the proprietor, to pay for our coffee. At the same moment one of the men behind me reached over my shoulder and took the wallet and notes from my hand before I realised what was happening. There was a moment of tension. He handed them to Mehmet, who gently tucked the notes back into the flap.

'You don't pay when you are our guests,' he said, pushing the wallet into my pocket again. We shook hands, and they all came out to the car, the father of daughters with an arm each around Malcolm and Steven before reluctantly bestowing them on the back seat, to their intense relief. Even Mehmet and the others looked embarrassed.

'You must forgive him,' he said to me. 'Such sons!'

CHAPTER EIGHT

THE KARPAS PENINSULA

I was in a bad humour and slightly hungover.

'I've just been all the way up to the village,' I told Salih, 'and the shop's still closed.'

'When do the shops open in England?' asked Salih.

'Nine o'clock. Half past eight sometimes.'

'Always at the same time?'

'Pretty well. Give or take a few minutes.'

'England is *Evropa*,' Salih recited triumphantly. 'Cyprus no is *Evropa*. Besides, Turkish mens shop in the afternoon after work finish.'

There never was an answer to this kind of thing and I was slowly beginning to learn patience.

'Why does your head ache?' Salih asked. 'Have you been drinking *raki*?'

'Some.'

'I never drink now. Not even beer. But when I was a young man like you, I loved to drink. Too much wine, too much *raki*. In your army, in the NAAFI, they used to sell a drink made from apples.'

'Cider.'

'Yes, that's it. I used to drink that too much. Sometimes I was in trouble.'

'But isn't drink forbidden to Muslims?' I asked him.

'Turkish Muslims drink if they want. But drink and work, no good. Now finished. No more drinking.'

We were about to set off for the Karpas and I wanted to hear what Salih could tell us about it. A lonely place, he said, which was once inhabited by a strange mixture of peoples, different from those of the rest of the island. There were Greeks and Maronites, even a few with fair hair and blue eyes. Some of them, he thought, might still be there. But talk of the exchange of populations put him in mind of his own uprooting from his beloved Paphos, and this was always painful for him. He was one of the very few Cypriots I met who disliked discussing politics. 'Cyprus finished, Cyprus finished,' he would say, shaking

117

his head sadly. Having lost all hope of mankind regaining its reason, he had turned his attention now to growing things, and only talk of plants and trees kindled his enthusiasm. He was constantly asking me about English agriculture, and never tired of hearing me describe the dairy cattle standing deep in lush summer grass near our home. The idea of more rainfall than the land could possibly need seemed to Salih to be an infinity of wealth.

★   ★   ★   ★

Beyond Kyrenia, where the main road runs past the military camp to climb across the mountains under Pentadactylos, we turned on to the narrow road which follows the north coast. Two barriers of red and white painted oil drums had been erected to slow down the traffic and force it to zigzag right and left in front of a checkpoint. The soldiers waved us through, and a mile or two later we passed Kyrenia's power station, built at the water's edge, with a guard in a tall steel watch-tower. Then we were clear of the barbed wire and were out in sunlit, open fields, looking ahead to rolling foothills running down to deserted beaches. We were not to see another soldier for 50 miles on this road – one of the reasons we grew to like it so much during the following weeks.

Ever since the Saracen raids, the north coast has been a wild place, the few settlements, as usual in Cyprus, being a short distance inland under the mountains, safely away from the dangers of the sea and its pirates. Since 1974 and the depopulation of the Turkish sector, the countryside has become even lonelier. Every few miles there would be a shepherd and his flock, and in time we came to recognise them, each in his own territory. There was the bald-headed man with a large ginger moustache who used to wave at us from beside the bonfire which he built on the beach below the road, while his animals foraged among the dunes nearby. The woman who had made a sheepfold between the walls of a ruined hut, and who spent her time gathering wild herbs. The rather simple lad who used to lie down on the tarmac of the road, his water bottle beside him, in order to bask in the reflected warmth of the sun (vehicles were few and far between). The ragged little girl with dark, tangled hair, who should have been in school, and who waved shyly at our boys. The young man with earphones and a personal stereo, who passed his lonely days in a private world of cassetted Turkish music. And the old woman from the mainland who dressed in the spectacular white head-dress and purple robe of the eastern nomads. We found her seated among her sheep, in a field of anemones – purple, white and yellow – her crook before her, spinning a hank of wool on a heavy wooden distaff. All these figures,

St Hilarion Castle, in the
Kyrenia mountains

St Hilarion Castle: the
ruined Byzantine chapel

The castle and harbour of Kyrenia

The reconstructed theatre of Soli

The gothic abbey of
Bellapais

The cloisters of Bellapais
Abbey

The gymnasium of
Salamis

Famagusta: the ruined
church of St George of the
Latins

*Abandoned houses in the
village of Karavas*

*The church of the Apostle
Barnabas Monastery on
the Mesaoria plain*

*Turkish shepherdess in the
Karpas peninsula*

The palm groves of Lefka

*The Beuyuk Hamam, or
'Great Bath', of Nicosia*

*Abandoned houses along
Nicosia's Green Line*

In the backstreets of Turkish Nicosia

isolated in the landscape, were pleased to talk to strangers who stopped their car. But in most places, there was only an empty sea, blue mountains above and untenanted beaches below.

The first part of the route was dominated by the knuckles of Pentadactylos, rising above the haze on the southern horizon. Sheep and goats were grazing amidst bright yellow-flowering gorse, smelling sickly-sweet through the open sunroof. Groves of olive and carob were turning wild with no one to tend them. Stunted Aleppo pines overhung the dry, stony streambeds, which the road crossed on ancient bridges, switching back and forth along the contours. Someone had once made a shelter from a cave in the rock, walling in the entrance with a door and windows, but it was abandoned now, and the nearby patch of vines had grown entangled like briars. Towards Ayios Amvrosios we came to a desert-like area of cliffs and ravines.

In ancient times this district was more populated, and sites have been excavated at Vrysin and Alakati. But a less obvious reminder of the past was the road itself. We had been travelling for some time before we noticed that we were continually running between borders, almost hedges, of tall, white asphodel. This is a plant which likes to grow on ground that has been disturbed, even if the disturbance took place many centuries before. On pushing the vegetation aside to investigate, we could see that the narrow, oiled ribbon of the modern road had been laid thinly over the regular, square stones of an older, much wider pavement. We wondered if it had been laid by British military engineers during the nineteenth century, using masonry taken from some ancient source. I suspect that it is much older, but nobody locally could tell us the answer. As far as they knew, the coast road had always been paved.

We stopped to sit for a while on a promontory of tawny-coloured rocks above an aquamarine sea. A huge lizard ran with a regular undulating movement over the cliff face, before disappearing into a crevice. A dragonfly came shimmering over the bushes, to hover around us, indicating that there must be fresh water somewhere inland. An occasional dull clank came from the bells of the goats cropping steadily nearby. I undressed and slipped into the water, rising and falling with the swell, a few feet away from the elephantine boulders which reached down to the depths. The gutted shell of a chapel, with a small dome and barrel roof, stood at the water's edge across the little bay. In red paint, over the fading white of the walls, someone had daubed the slogan: '*Kibris Turktur*, Cyprus is Turkish.'

Hadjigeorghakis Kornesios, the Dragoman or Interpreter who represented the Sultan in Cyprus, landed on this part of the coast in 1804 with 2,000 soldiers to put down a rebellion of the garrison and the Turkish population of Nicosia. This was only one of a long series of mutinies by the Turkish army and settlers against the taxes imposed by the Governor and Christian Archbishop, not only on behalf of the Porte, but also for the benefit of their own pockets. Hadjigeorghakis himself was said to have grown immensely wealthy during his appointment. Two years later, another rebellion was led by the Turkish Colonel Altiparnak (the Six Fingers), and again innocent civilians were murdered and villages burned. Altiparnak was eventually caught and flayed alive in the familiar Ottoman manner. ('None the worse for a good flaying,' one may imagine Selim III remarking). Hadjigeorghakis fared little better himself, being summoned to Constantinople in 1809 and executed for his misuse of public funds, while Chrysanthos, the Archbishop, was exiled to Euboea.

We came unexpectedly on a tiny Garden of Eden, where a stream ran down into the sea through a steep valley between stalks of giant reed. A farmer had terraced and irrigated this suntrap with meticulous care, and every foot of available space was packed with tomato plants and fruit trees. Already the figs were bursting into leaf and the branches were noisy with finches. The little space was only a few yards across, and in a moment the road had crossed a stone arch over the stream and we were climbing once more over the dry hillside. A white Land Rover passed us, with a sign proclaiming that it had been donated by the UN, the only car we had seen since Kyrenia.

As we approached the ancient village of Akanthou, which the Turks call Tatlisu, or Freshwater, after a village on the south coast, the land became more fertile. Palm trees began to appear, followed by carob plantations, market gardens and dried mud-brick shelters for poultry. We had to wait for a group of men who had been using the flat surface of the road to fold sheets of polythene, which had protected the tomatoes over the winter months. They were amiable, smiling people; the women dressed in brilliantly coloured scarves and trousers, while the men wound chequered cloths around their heads like turbans. A group of very pretty girls, dressed in sequinned *shalvar* trousers and Turkish slippers, were walking down the road in the shade of the fruit trees. They turned to laugh and wave as we passed. High above us, the village nestled under Kyrenian Olympus and we could see pleasant houses and vineyards. The hot sun and bright colours gave the whole district an air of cheerful industry and prosperity. Surely these immigrants could not be accused of failing to use the land profitably, or of ruining it with sheep and goats?

There were unusual stratifications in the rock above the roadway, and a view ahead to the mountains of the Kantara Forest. The beaches here were strewn not only with driftwood, but with sun-bleached, shredded plastic and debris from the more populated shores of the Levant: a sad reminder that this far eastern end of the

Mediterranean, from Syria round to Egypt, is almost as polluted as are the waters around Italy and southern France. Jackdaws hopped among the rubbish, turning over each find with a speculative beak. A flock of white doves wheeled over the roofs of Dhavlos, their wings catching the sunlight, and butterflies wavered unsteadily over the gorse bushes. And in an olive grove, carpeted beneath the gnarled trunks with a mass of yellow flowers, we saw for a moment the flashing colours of a bee-eater.

The mountains were lower now, and near the ruins of an old aqueduct at Galounia the road turns away from the sea and climbs up through pine woods. Twice, a partridge dodged across the road before us: not the rare Cypriot francolin, but the red-legged partridge introduced by the British. At the top of the saddle, we were looking down over the plains dotted with trees to the Bay of Famagusta on the far side. The long, low Karpas stretched 50 miles into the haze towards Syria, like the blade of a swordfish.

The main village of this district is Komi Kebir, which used to be famous for its Church of Ayios Auxentios. Auxentios was a German hermit who once lived in a cave on the north flank of these mountains. When he died, his body remained miraculously sweet-smelling and a team of oxen, unguided by human hands, drew it to this spot. The street of Komi Kebir, which is now called Buyukkonuk, or the Great Mansion, was filled with tractors and men sitting outside the coffee shop enjoying the sunshine. Patriki, however, which is now called Tuzluca, was half empty. The walls of many houses were noticeably scored and marked by bullets, while one church, with the inevitable 'ENOSIS' in blue paint over the door, lay derelict. The other had been converted into a mosque. The new inhabitants would seem to have come from the mainland, judging by the name and the spectacular red, sequinned dress of a shepherdess who watched her flock in the rich pastureland near the village. Many of the houses were built of mud-brick and straw.

The Greeks who once lived in Patriki were famous for a strange custom. On Easter Monday, all the married men would meet in the churchyard, take off their jackets, and one by one attempt to crawl through a hole in an ancient stone which lay there. If a man found himself unable to complete the passage, it would be concluded that he had been cuckolded, and that his invisible horns were preventing him. Meanwhile, the wives waited nervously at home for the results of the experiment. Apparently a divorce case arising out of this ceremony, actually reached the courts in 1935.

After crossing some marshy land and seeing more partridges beside the road, we came to Ayios Theodoros, or Cayirova, an attractive place with fine gardens full of lemon trees. This village once had the distinction of being the first place in Cyprus to possess a telegraph office, the cable having been laid under the sea from Latakia in Syria during the last years of the Ottoman administration. Now it boasted a magnificent new mosque, whose minaret towered over the dusty, white road.

A dark-skinned man carrying a parcel hitched a lift from us at the crossroads towards his village of Ziyamet, further up the peninsula. He waved to friends in all the villages we passed through. We had not enough language in common to say much to each other, but I gathered that he had been born in the Karpas. The Moorish cast of his features reminded me of the reputation which the native Karpassiots (the district was predominantly Greek before 1974) held for being a different kind of people to other Cypriots.

This was always a remote and vulnerable district. Persians, Greeks, the truculent Antigonid Poliorcetes on his way to attack Salamis: all chose this lonely peninsula to begin their raids on Cyprus, and in more recent times the dwindling population was constantly depleted by Arab and Maltese pirates. These invaders, together with the Crusaders, Venetians and Negro slaves of the Turks, all left their mark on the people, who must have lived their lives in fear of the sea. Constantius, the Archbishop of Sinai who visited Cyprus during the eighteenth century, wrote in his affected pompous Greek that 'the inhabitants of Carpas in the East are little better than savages.' Sir Samuel Baker noted perceptively that even in the late nineteenth century the villagers continued to store their grain in large clay jars buried in the ground. This, he felt, was a sure sign of insecurity.

The people of the Karpas were famous for their craftwork, particularly elaborate embroidery, and their flourishing folklore and traditions. But Baker found them reduced to a sad condition by disease. He noted the enlarged spleens caused by chronic malaria – all the women, he remarked, appeared to be permanently pregnant for this reason. Ophthalmia was also extremely common, as it was in many parts of the East.

On the coast near here, the wreck of an old steamship is still visible, to which a curious story attaches. During the war between Turkey and Russia in 1877–8, large numbers of Muslim Circassians arrived in Turkish territory, refugees from the advancing Russian armies. Most were settled in Turkish Kurdistan, where it was hoped that their presence would intimidate the Kurds and Bedouin nomads who had always been a thorn in the side of their Ottoman rulers. It was planned to send a small contingent of 600 to Cyprus, but this provoked a vehement protest from the Greeks of the island who feared the Circassians' reputation for brigandage and the blood feud. Meanwhile, 3,000 more Circassians were embarked in Constantinople on an Austrian ship, to be sent to Latakia in Syria. These immigrants mutinied at sea and threatened the lives of the officers, so that the captain was forced to run the ship aground on this remote part of the Cyprus coast. Most of the Circassians drowned, and reports are unclear as to the fate of the survivors, although the officers and crew were sent on safely to Famagusta. After this incident, the 600 colonists intended for Cyprus were despatched to Antalya instead.

On a hillside near Tavros, or Pamukla, which has another fine new mosque, a large Turkish moon and star had been laid out in stones. Koma tou Yialou, near the Koronia Forest, is an ancient village dating from the Classical period, whose population was once sufficiently great to justify four churches. The one by the road was gutted and adorned with the usual Greek graffiti, which seems so hopeless in the light of subsequent developments: 'ENOSIS', 'EOKA'. This village has now been renamed Kumyali. I remember a house with beautiful wrought-iron decorations on the door and windows.

The soil now became chalky and the low slopes were covered with vines, until, after the Skalifourda Forest, we came to Leonarisso, now Ziyamet. The Greeks used to hold a big fair outside the church here every autumn. Now, the church was a mosque, and many of the people had come from Turkey. Most of the men were sitting outside the coffee shop, and here our passenger alighted to be greeted by his friends. An elderly woman was sitting out on her verandah, working an old sewing machine by hand, and doves were nesting in large earthenware jars, wired high on the walls of houses. But the petrol station was closed and there was a general impression of neglect.

Although the wild flowers were magnificent, and once more we began to catch enticing glimpses of the sea through the olive groves, the villages now became poorer and more run down. Ayios Andronikos, or Yesilkoy, and the large, sprawling settlement of Yialousa, now named Yeni Erenkoy (for the Turks of Kokkina who settled there), were depressed, dilapidated places, although the women were all sitting communally, knitting in the sunshine. On the south side of the peninsula close by is the Greek Lythrangomi, with the ruined Church of Panayia Kanakaria, famous for its fifth-century mosaic of the Virgin and Child. Much of this is missing; Saracen pirates have been blamed, but it is also true that Cypriot country people believed that a piece of mosaic carried in the pocket was sovereign against diseases of the skin. In the same church used to be kept an icon of the Virgin of Kanakaria from the fifteenth century, a copy of an earlier work. A Saracen was said to have shot at this picture with an arrow and, miraculously, it bled. Another icon from this church had the power of rain-making. In a dry season, the picture would be taken down by the priest from its place on the screen, and at sunset a procession would make its way down to the shore. The congregation would pray and the icon would be immersed three times in the water. By the time the painting had been replaced on the *iconostasis*, the night sky would be filled with thunder clouds and the first heavy drops would already be falling into the dust.

This area of fertile land, where most of Cyprus' tobacco is grown, is rich in antiquities and superstitions. An enchanted grove surrounds the ruined fourteenth-century Church of Ayios Theodoros; it is said to be death to cut wood from there. At Neta are the remains of a pagan temple, while at Ayios Simeon an ancient cave tomb is cut into the cliff, a haunt of the mysterious Queen. There is a deep well at the back of the cave and, not so long ago, an old countryman told the writer Colin Thubron a story of ghostly chanting from a subterranean church and incense rising from the ground.

Beyond Yialousa, we did not see a soul for miles. The land here is barren, covered with a low *phrygana* of lentisk and thorns, with occasional clumps of fennel. The coastline consists alternately of low cliffs and extensive sand dunes covered by stunted pine trees, spaced far apart. The little hamlet which clusters by the fifteenth-century Church of Ayios Thyrsos above the sea was deserted and falling into ruins. The church was full of ornate wood carvings, still largely intact, but sadly covered in dust and pigeon droppings. The boys clambered over the rocks and dangled their feet in the sea where it sucked at the margin. Later, we drove on through the Karpasia Forest, where miles of open, sandy beach showed through the trees on our left.

We could see from our large-scale map that Rizokarpaso, the last town of Cyprus, spread itself untidily over these low hills, before a single road led for the last 15 miles through a landscape empty of people but abundant in ruins, to the remoteness of Cape Apostolos Andreas and its famous monastery. Rizokarpaso had once been the centre of a Lusignan province, and churches were liberally scattered around the outskirts of the town: Ayia Marina, the Monastery of Panayia Eleousa, and Ayios Synesios, which was a cathedral when the Bishop of Famagusta was exiled here by the Latins.

The women of Rizokarpaso long had a reputation for great beauty and green eyes. More recent travellers found no evidence of this: Drummond in 1750 'did not see one handsome woman in the place', while Sir Samuel Baker thought they were 'the ugliest, dirtiest, shortest and most repulsive lot', which is indeed plain speaking. But I was more concerned as to whether we would find any of the original Greek inhabitants at all. Several years earlier, I had read a description of a beleaguered group of elderly men, considered by the authorities to be too old to move to the south, nervously spinning out their days in a coffee shop under the watchful eye of the police station, and surrounded by their enemies. Would they still be there, and would they want to talk to us?

Dipkarpaz, as the Turks have renamed it, turned out to be no thriving county town, but an uninspiring and dreary place amidst its isolation. The main activity was taking place on the outskirts, where workmen were laying out a new cemetery. Already a neat row of headstones was forming in one corner, each surmounted by a stone turban. The Turks who had come to live here were now beginning to die here. The Greek cemetery nearby was a wilderness of smashed monuments and broken fragments of tombs.

The village sprawled untidily over the valley with no easily discernible centre. The narrow, potholed lanes were clogged with rubbish and the wrecks of old cars. Chickens and a few cows wandered aimlessly about. The filling station was abandoned and many of the crumbling, single-storey houses were empty. The few people sitting drowsily in the streets looked at us with dull curiosity, before relapsing into torpor.

We left the car by a little fountain and shrine, and successfully located the police station. Nearby, a new mosque was nearing completion, while a Christian church had loudspeakers wired to the wall, although two crosses remained on the roof to proclaim its original use. Across the tract of dried mud which served as the main street were two small coffee shops, side by side. A few men sat at tables on a terrace, and as we climbed the steps we found ourselves the centre of their attention. Both the proprietors' names over the doors were Turkish, I noticed. One of them emerged from the interior, wiping his hands on a grubby apron. I asked him for two beers and two orange juices. No, there wasn't any. 'How about Coca-Colas?' I asked, looking at an ancient corroded sign. No Coca-Cola either. We were too thirsty to want coffee. I was engaged in trying to remember the Turkish word for water, when a man in a dark green uniform detached himself from a group of card players and came over to us. He was the only English speaker there.

'I am sorry,' he said, 'but they only have coffee and tea here. No alcoholic drinks. There is a drink made with yoghurt and some herbs. Would you like to try that? It is very refreshing.'

We asked him to join us, as I think he had intended. He was very interested to know who we were, and why we had come so far into the Karpas, one politely phrased question following another. I had the strong impression that he made it his business to keep an eye on strangers. Eventually he must have decided that we were harmless and began to relax slightly. The drinks arrived: a kind of sour, liquefied yoghurt flavoured with mint, which was indeed very refreshing. We learned that we were doomed to disappointment in our plan to continue our journey to the Cape.

'That is impossible. All the Cape beyond there is a military area. No one is allowed beyond Dipkarpaz without a pass. Even I can't go there.'

'Are there still monks at the Monastery of Apostolos Andreas?'

'I think so. But no one can go through without a pass.'

'And how would we get a pass?' I asked.

'From Lefkosa. You would have to ask the authorities there. Then, if they say yes, a soldier would go with you. But, to tell you the truth, I don't know if they would give you a pass.'

I thought I might as well ask straight out.

'Are there any Greeks still living in this town?'

'No Greeks in Dipkarpaz now,' he replied shortly. 'They've all gone to the South.'

The green uniform, we learned, was that of the Forestry Service.

'It's interesting work, although I am new to it. The forests have been badly neglected, and the land is eroded.'

'Because of the troubles?'

'No, no, they have been badly managed for many years. The British administration had no thought of the future.'

'Really?' I asked, surprised. 'I understood that the Forestry Service achieved a great deal. Didn't they build the forest roads and conserve woodland?'

'That is quite wrong. I have been researching this matter, with the idea of writing a book. The British were too greedy. Particularly during the First World War trees were being felled all the time. They failed to prevent the Greeks from taking more timber than they even needed. There are 100 houses in this town built at that time, using maybe 70 or 80 big beams in the roof. I have seen this myself in many houses. That is 70 or 80 trees – far more than necessary. The British were much too free.'

In ancient times, Cyprus was famous for its forests which covered the whole island, and ship-building timber was one of the main exports. Indeed, because robbers hid in the trees, forest clearance was actively encouraged, and men were offered all the land they could clear. But ever since, the forests have been ruthlessly exploited, with no real attention being paid to the consequences until the nineteenth century. Thus in 1873 we find the Kaimakan of Larnaca, worried by the increasing felling of timber to drive wood-burning engines, issuing an edict banning this, together with the exporting of locally cut timber. A few years later, Sir Samuel Baker wrote almost in despair at the profligate waste of timber by peasants who would cut down a whole tree for one piece of wood and leave the rest to rot. In particular, he reported massive felling of the cypresses of the Cape, where ships arrived from Asia Minor and Egypt to help themselves to the trees,

126

while the Abbot of the Apostolos Andreas Monastery, the owner of the land, was powerless to prevent them. There was some truth behind the forester's allegation, for many trees were cut during the First World War. And during the Second, when the fuel shortage became extreme, a tanker had to be directed at great risk to Cyprus, in order that the felling might be reduced. Since that time, and this he did not mention, the greatest damage had occurred during the invasion of 1974, when the Turkish Air Force deliberately began a major blaze in the Paphos Forest.

The forester passed round a packet of cigarettes. Men at the next table were playing a game like dominoes with little wooden tablets. An ancient man with a crooked stick sat alone in a corner, staring at us without blinking. I felt that British forestry deserved a little defending.

'What about goats? Aren't they responsible for much of the deforestation? And I still see goats grazing free in parts of the forest.'

'Of course. Always we are fighting against goats. They eat everything down to the roots, and then they eat the roots. But look, the government must tread carefully in this matter. Many of these people are very poor; they live from their goats. How can the government take away a poor man's living?'

'We saw some very eroded land in the mountains near Degirmenlik,' I remarked.

'Ah, that is different. That's not from goats, but from mining by the British and during the Republic.'

I though of all the pastoralists and flocks which we had passed earlier in the day.

'I think that we saw many immigrants from the mainland, on our way along the coast,' I said.

'Why do you say that?'

'Their dress.'

'Yes, they are very happy here. Many of them were nomads before they came. And their loose trousers; they must be very comfortable. I'm going to ask a friend of mine to get a pair for me.'

Why did we have to be fencing with each other constantly? Behind the smooth public relations phrases, I could sense an astute, if uneducated mind working overtime. Did he think I was a journalist fishing for politically sensitive information? I asked him what he had done before he joined the Forestry Service. Had he come from the South? And the answer to that question was very illuminating.

'I come from a place where the Line goes like this.' He drew a semicircle, a kind of bight, in the damp on the table-top.

'You mean the Red Village? The Kokkina Enclave?'

'That's the place. It is my village, although there are only soldiers there now.'

127

Kokkina, or Erenkoy, was famous. It lies, as already described, beyond the western end of the Attila Line. From the very beginning of the struggle, it was a stronghold of Turkish nationalism and a supporter of Volkan, the Volcano or, as it later became, the Turk Mudafaa Teskilati, or Turkish Resistance Organisation.

When the Turks effectively seceded from the Cypriot Republic, and retired to their own strongly guarded positions, most of their arms and supplies from the mainland were secretly landed at Kokkina. In August 1964, after nine months of intermittent fighting and growing tension between Greece and Turkey over the situation on the island, matters came to a head. The Greeks feared that the Turks of Kokkina and Lefka planned to link up and cut the roads which supplied a number of Greek villages. At this time, 10,000 troops from Greece were on the island with the idea of forestalling an invasion by Turkey, a possibility which seemed daily more likely.

Following an incident on 3 August, when Greek Cypriot patrol boats were fired at from the shore near Kokkina, an attack on the enclave was carried out by 3,000 Greek National Guardsmen, led by Grivas. It was estimated that about 500 Turkish fighters were barricaded inside. UNFICYP forward posts were withdrawn in what appeared to be a hopeless situation. The initial reaction from the mainland was for Turkish jets to buzz the nearby Greek town of Polis and fire warning shots. The fighting around Kokkina was intense, but the Turks retreated from their outlying positions around Mansoura and Ayios Theodoros on the morning of 8 August. In the afternoon, and on the following day, Turkish jets appeared in large numbers and Greek villages in the area were strafed with rockets and napalm-bombed. Most of the casualties were civilian, including women, children and the staff of a hospital. Greece and Turkey, both members of NATO, were on the brink of war. Athens threatened 'intervention' and effectively delivered an ultimatum via the United Nations Security Council. Cyprus herself appealed for military aid from Egypt and the USSR. The Russians declared that if Cyprus was invaded by Turkey 'the Soviet Union will help Cyprus to defend her freedom and independence'. The American Sixth Fleet cruised offshore, but made no move to intervene.

Somehow, under the watchful eye of UNFICYP troops, a fragile ceasefire was negotiated, and it held. But if it can be said that there was a point when the Greeks and Turks of Cyprus finally parted ways, this was truly that point. From then on, the Turks of Cyprus effectively formed a separate state, with their crescent and star flag replacing that of the Republic, and their own police and military and civil administration. Cyprus was now a land of roadblocks, no-go areas and guarded villages. The inhabitants of many mixed communities were separated forcibly.

The nationalists of Kokkina continued their embattled existence, joined now by refugees from outlying villages. The outskirts were patrolled day and night by sentries. The roadblocks remained in place. No Greek set foot in the enclave and no Turk set foot outside it. Supplies came in by sea, or by convoys of lorries under the protection of UNFICYP. When the Turkish army invaded in 1974, they made a point of holding Kokkina, in spite of its position beyond the perimeter of the northern sector which Operation Attila was designed to capture. It must be expensive to maintain and hold, but presumably this is more a matter of honour than of military expediency.

'Kokkina? If you could have seen it once,' proclaimed the forester, 'you would have said that it was a paradise. Gardens, farms. But that was long ago. After 1964, I stayed for thirteen years until it became like a prison to me. Sometimes you could get out by boat at night, and then you might see people. But it had to be very dark, no moon, and if you even spoke loudly the Greeks might hear you and open fire. It is my home village, but in the end I left and came here. There are only soldiers in Kokkina now. It has been hard here, but I think now things will begin to get better. It seems to me that our new state is very young; it is like a baby. It must learn to walk slowly, but it will grow and we must be patient.'

'And recognition?'

'Recognition will come. If we had been a Christian country we would have had it by now, together with all the aid we wanted,' he added bitterly.

'Do you receive no help from your fellow Muslims?'

'We are Muslims, but we are Europeans, not Arabs or Africans. Only Turkey helps us.'

Had he been a member of TMT, we eventually asked.

'Of course I was. We all were. We wanted to defend our village, our houses and our families. Wouldn't you have done the same? And we wanted freedom. Freedom from the British, freedom from the Greeks. Isn't that worth fighting for? A lot of our people wanted the British to stay, but I could never agree with that. The only man I'll trust with my freedom is another Turk. Listen, my sister is married to an Irishman [I remembered the Irish UN contingent posted around Kokkina]. They're still fighting for their freedom, and you British have the same problems in Ireland that you had in Cyprus.'

I did not wish to get into this, tempting as it was to raise the matter of the Armenians and Kurds in Turkey. Instead, we steered the conversation to easier subjects, such as the wines of Limassol and Paphos, which he admitted to missing. And he told us an extraordinary story about a bottle of Commandaria, which he had seen found beneath the floor of an ancient house. The wine was literally hundreds of years old and the liquid had turned completely solid, like wax. But when a piece was broken off and dissolved in water a most delightful spicy scent arose from it, and when it was drunk there was an amazing strength and sweetness of flavour. Was he mocking us? I looked closely at him, but he had retreated behind a mask of good humour, and his eyes gave nothing away. Taller stories than that are told every day in Cyprus.

As I got up to pay, he said, 'Oh dear. I think you have no money.'

'What do you mean? Of course we have money.'

'I don't think you do.' And he gave the slow, broad grin which all Cypriots display when given an opportunity to be hospitable. As we were leaving, he put his hand on my shoulder and said, 'Wait. I will show you something. Look up at the mosque.'

I raised my eyes to the gleaming minaret across the street.

'No, not the new mosque. The old mosque.'

He was pointing at the tower of the old church which loomed above us. What do you mean, the old mosque, I wanted to say. It is a church, a Greek church, and the crosses are still on the roof. But I remained silent.

'Look up there. There is a face looking down at us.'

And sure enough there was a worn stone gargoyle, so weathered as to be unrecognisable as anything except a human head, staring implacably down at the coffee shop tables, the street and the shabby town.

'I know it is very old. It has been looking down like that for 800 years, and it has seen everything that has happened here, and all the people that have lived here. It watched the lives of the Greeks here, generation after generation, and now it will watch over our lives too. I often look up and think about that. It makes me feel . . . strange.'

For the first time his confidence had slipped slightly, and he looked at us self-consciously, lest we might think him foolish and whimsical.

★   ★   ★   ★

We left the car a few yards off the road, under the trees of the Karpasia Forest, and, carrying a picnic basket between us, began to walk in the direction of the sea. The pines became stunted and distorted, growing some distance apart. Each of these trees would hardly provide a roof beam. In time, the carpet of pine needles gave way to sand, with clusters of white cyclamen fluttering between the trees. The dunes were tumbled and confused, and we checked our bearings anew as we reached the top of each crest. Half buried in a hollow, we came upon the remains of a public lavatory, signed in Greek: '*Andres*' and '*Yenaikes*'. It seemed incredible that only thirteen years before this place might have been crowded with swimmers on a summer day.

We walked down the last dune to a patch of pure white sand and low shelves of sun-bleached rock washed by a crystalline sea, which gradually coloured through pale green and blue to a violet horizon. Gathering driftwood into a pile, we made a fire to toast our cheese and salami, while we left a bottle of wine to cool in a rockpool. The flames, almost invisible in the bright light, licked around sea-sculpted branches and twisted roots, gradually blackening the clean skeletal wood. A thin plume of fragrant smoke rose almost vertically. The boys began to construct an enormous sand castle at the water's edge. Modelled on old Famagusta, it grew throughout the afternoon, walls, towers and bastions spreading along the beach. To either side, nothing could be seen but water, rock and sand to the horizon. Half a mile behind us, through the dull green of the pines, a dusty strip of road was visible. During the three hours we remained there, only two vehicles passed along it: a farmer's tractor and a Land Rover of the Forestry Service. An immense silence reigned, for the sea was calm and even the gulls had deserted this coast.

Before leaving Rizokarpaso, we had stopped to talk to the sergeant at the police station, who appeared strangely smart in a shining black uniform among the dilapidated surroundings. He was dubious about the chances of obtaining a pass to visit the Cape, but he wrote down an address in Nicosia where we might apply. He then went on to warn us that we might not visit any of the sites around Rizokarpaso, or indeed leave the centre of the town at all, but must return before nightfall by the road back along the peninsula.

In fact, as I later discovered, there were probably several hundred Greeks in the Rizokarpaso district at that time and a smaller number at Yialousa.* But short of knocking on doors at random and asking the occupants their nationality, there appeared to be no quick method of making contact. Moreover, the authorities were obviously very sensitive on the subject and the attempts to head us off left a nasty taste in the mouth. The restriction on visiting the last 15 miles of the Cape was a real disappointment. We might have seen the place to the north of the town where the ancient city of Karpasia stood, which Demetrios Poliorcetes sacked when he landed nearby in 306 BC, and whose harbour mole still stretches beside the sea, the stones clamped together by rivets of iron. The Arabs finally destroyed Karpasia a thousand years later, though near the Church of Ayios Philon is a mosaic floor from a fifth-century basilica. Further up the coast is Aphendrika, once one of the greatest cities of the island. This too was

*The Association of Rizokarpaso in Britain estimates about 900 in the Karpas District as a whole; mostly older people. Almost all those with young families found it impossible to remain.

sacked by the war-like Antigonid, and only a silted harbour and the citadel can be clearly seen. Byzantine churches are scattered over the whole district, more than there is space to list. Travellers in earlier centuries found a land of ruins and desolation. In 1738 Pococke had identified the site of Urania – yet another city destroyed by Poliorcetes – found talc in the hills and remarked on the number of ruined chapels. Of the far portion of the peninsula he wrote:

All this country to the east of Carpass for about twelve miles is almost uninhabited, except that there are a few Turkish herdsmen on the south side, where there is a fine narrow plain. The desolate condition of this part of the island is occasioned by the constant depredations of the Maltese privateers, who land more frequently here than in any other part. From the eastern point I saw very plainly Mount Cassius near Antioch, and the mountain of Rhossus, now called Cape Hog, which is between Kepsé and Scanderoon.

(Trs. C.D. Cobham, *Excerpta Cypria*)

The monastery of Apostolos Andreas is a modern building on an ancient site, including the wells which are said to have refreshed the saint when he landed on this hazardous cape. Until 1974 the monastery was the most popular place of pilgrimage in Cyprus, for the waters are said to have miraculous properties. So many people made the long journey up the peninsula by bus and by car that a hostel had to be built to accommodate them. Indeed such a holiday atmosphere prevailed at the monastery that the Church became quite concerned, and ruled that pilgrims and monks should not indulge in dancing, music or drinking. Thereafter the monastery's famous hospitality took a slightly more subdued form.

The pilgrimage was not an ancient tradition, but followed a modern miracle, that of Maria Giorgiou, a Greek woman from Cilicia in Asia Minor. In 1895 her small son was abducted by Turkish brigands, and, as time passed without news, she gave him up for dead. But seventeen years later she had a dream in which St Andrew appeared, telling her to go to Cyprus and pray in his monastery for the return of her son. As she crossed the straits in a crowded boat, she found herself next to a dervish – a Muslim holy man – and for some reason told him the story of her dream and the reason for her pilgrimage. The dervish became extremely disturbed as he heard the story, and asked whether her son's body had borne any identifiable mark. When he was told, he pulled away his robe to show her the birthmarks on his chest – he was her son, Panteli, whom the brigands had sold in Constantinople to be brought up as a Muslim. They embraced each other in tears, the boat landed at Larnaca amidst great jubilation, and the dervish shaved his head to be baptised by the Bishop of Kitium.

On the summit of the Cape, very aptly, is a temple to Aphrodite, Cyprus' own goddess. This is the place from which Richard Pococke claimed to see Turkey, Syria and the snows of Lebanon. Beyond the cliffs are the rocky islets known as the Klidhes, the Keys of Cyprus, and on one of these stands a lighthouse, for since the beginning of recorded history this dangerous cape has been feared by seafarers. Dr Sibthorp claimed that 'untameable' wild assess could be found on the hillside, but a hundred years later Sir Samuel Baker allowed himself some amusement at that notion. The donkeys were quite tame, he said, and belonged to the monastery. One legend attaching to the spot is that Isaac Comnenus had retreated to the 'Abbey-fortress' here, before surrendering to the forces of Richard the Lionheart. One might imagine the desperate Emperor, with his back to the sea, submitting to the silver chains, but there is nothing to support the story, and the same is claimed for Kantara and other places.

We swam and lay on the sand through the long afternoon, until the sun began to fall behind the trees in the west and the forest became dark and mysterious. We were a long way from home, and so reluctantly we retraced our steps, found our car, half-hidden by the scrub of myrtle and wild olive, and continued our journey. The day was dying in a blaze of crimson fire over the empty road as we crossed an open moor of thorny scrub and stunted cypress trees, blurred in outline by the soft glowing light. It was Joan who caught sight of a building some distance inland. It was plainly a church, and very old. Our map identified it as Ayios Photios tis Selinias, dating from the tenth century and abandoned more than 50 years ago. We took our torch from the glove box and walked up towards it in a warmth and stillness like the end of a perfect English midsummer day. The church stood foursquare, the epitome of calm repose and harmony with the landscape, the honey-coloured stone mellowed by age and the evening light. It had stood for a thousand years, and such was the enduring strength of its massive walls and roof that it appeared ready to survive for another millenium, as if waiting for the Second Coming. Inside, the torch picked out ancient pillars and capitals; scraps of fresco clung to the wall, but time had almost obliterated these.

We stood outside the door amidst a magical stillness of the kind that has one holding one's breath without understanding why. The only sounds were from far, far away; the distant, sleepy tinkling of bells and the cries of sheep. Bats silently cleaved the air about the walls, their black silhouettes showing momentarily against the light left in the sky. The ghostly white blooms of the asphodel, the graveyard flower, brushed against us as we made our way silently back to the car, no one wishing to break the enchantment. We drove on, with the windows and roof opened to the perfumed night air.

The thousand winding turns of the north coast road would have made an arduous business of the drive home in the dark, and so after Yialousa we continued to follow the south-western road towards Famagusta and the Mesaoria. It was a pleasant surprise to find that our way lay through villages with electric lighting in the streets, and at Bogaz, an old Turkish fishing port on Famagusta Bay, we found a brightly lit restaurant by the roadside, with red and white checked tablecloths and a chalked-up menu. Feeling a little travel-stained among its smartly dressed customers, we dined excellently on a dish of fish cooked with onions and coriander. Then across the Mesaoria, through the darkened villages of Trikomo and Lefkoniko, with brief impressions of the harshly lit interiors of the coffee shops, hazy with blue tobacco smoke and crammed with men in their working clothes, before the night closed in again. A Turkish crescent moon arose and silvered the vast plain, the sleepy soldiers were nodding at the check-points, and a heady scent of wild flowers and dew blew in through the open windows.

CHAPTER NINE

MARONITES AND KANTARA

'Hi, how're you doing?'

The man stood in the kiosk doorway of the London Boy Filling Station, hands thrust in his pockets.

'You must be the man from London.'

'That's right.' He gave me a card: Mahmut Uslucan. The young assistant finished filling the tank and handed me the keys. Mahmut was quite happy to be back in Cyprus after many years working in London garages. Now he grappled with the problems of finding parts for the Turkish sector's ageing population of mainly British vehicles, some of them 30 years old. Here, standing in the sunshine, his little business by the main road surrounded by acres of yellow turban buttercups, he had a wave for every passing truck driver. He looked up at the cloudless sky.

'I know you won't believe this,' he remarked, 'but we get sick and tired of this weather. There hasn't been enough rain this winter.'

'But we had quite a storm a few nights ago.'

'Sure. But it's too little, too late. We'll probably have one more like that, maybe next month. Then that'll be it for the year. Nothing till December. Don't talk to me about the sun.'

'At least the rain brought the flowers out.'

He cast a jaded eye around at the magnificent carpet of yellow waving in the breeze. 'Yeah, I suppose so.' And he turned the conversation back to the problems of shipping second-hand lorries from England.

★　★　★　★

We approached the south flank of the Kyrenia range over the track which runs through the Korphi Forest around the side of Mount Kornos, between verges clustered with mauve cyclamens and pink anemones. The villages of the southern slopes enjoy considerably more sunshine than those on the coastal side, and at any given time seem to be several degrees warmer. All of them command magnificent

135

views over the forested foothills towards the Mesaoria. On the debit side, the communities are remote and the roads are bad, the soil is poor, and most of the rain falls on the northern flanks. Even the moist dew which is derived from the sea does not cross the mountain barrier.

The pine trees in this forest are tall, close-ranked and heavily laden with cones. The limestone rock of the cliffs above gives rise to strange, rugged formations and pinnacles. We stopped the car at the entrance to a steep gorge, filled with tumbled rocks, just outside the village of Larnaca tis Lapithou. The boys led the way up the staircase of boulders grown with oleanders and tamarisks, soon leaving me behind and out of breath. Joan more sensibly propped herself in the corner of a wall and basked in the sunshine, idly watching a large dragonfly hovering over the juniper bushes. The air was filled with the raucous cries of the black Cyprus crows, very like English rooks in their behaviour, which dwell in enormous numbers on the south side of the Kyrenia range. They presumably choose the south side because the crops of the Mesaoria are so handy. These birds are the curse of the Cypriot farmer, who spends much of his spare time waging war on them, without any visible effect on their numbers, or their audacity. In British days, a Cypriot who wanted a game-shooting licence was obliged to bring six dead crows or magpies with him. Someone was shooting close by on the mountain above, and the regular reports of the shotgun came echoing down the gorge. Lest there should be an accident, we retraced our steps and made our way into the village.

The Greeks of Larnaca tis Lapithou, the Graveyard of Lapithos, now renamed Kozan by the Turks, were once famous for their skill in working silver and gold. On this day the women at least were busy, sitting out of doors, knitting, crocheting and making lace. The men were also sitting, in chairs outside the coffee shop, and quite content for their hands to remain idle as they gossiped.

The next village, Agridhaki, or Alemdag, was memorable for the spectacular shower of almond blossom hanging down into the narrow street. An old man, white-haired and leathery-skinned, thin as a rake and remarkably tall for a Cypriot, well over 6 feet, was loping down from the mountain. His legs were encased in long, shiny boots and he carried an ancient hammer shotgun across his shoulder, holding it near the muzzle, a bandolier of cartridges encircling his waist. A group of small children in bright woollen sweaters raced at his heels, shouting excitedly. Leaning against a wall was a venerable Ariel Red Hunter motorcycle, dripping oil quietly into the dust.

We wandered into the church, which stood open to the winds, and watched the birds flying in and out through the broken windows. The cross remained on the roof, but the bell had gone. A few of the older children followed us inside and stood watching us curiously, obviously mystified as to why the foreigners should be interested in this ruinous building. There came a time when we ourselves reached the conclusion that one stripped and desecrated church is very like another, and resolved to confine ourselves to those of historical interest.

The Mesaoria below these slopes is not absolutely flat, but consists of gently rolling undulations and pleasant green meadows through which the road from Myrtou runs to Nicosia. Two of the villages set in this attractive landscape, Karpasha and Asomatos, were traditionally Maronite. When we reached the latter, however, just to the south of the main road, we found that the Turkish army were in possession, the population having apparently abandoned it. The new name of Ozhan was displayed on the sign by the road, and the houses and church were wired off and surrounded by the usual parade grounds and assault course. The next (Greek) village of Kondemenos had shared the same fate. Some civilian traffic was passing through the gate, but we were turned back for lack of a police pass.

Karpasha, which had no identifying signs at all, proved more difficult to find as we threaded our way through the intersecting lanes on the outskirts of Myrtou, before reaching the edge of the Karpasha Forest. The village was largely deserted, with the exception of a few pretty little bungalows which stood beside the road before the grassy, cobbled square. A geriatric old man had been propped up in an invalid chair, warmly wrapped in blankets and shawls. His eyes stared without recognition, and saliva dribbled from his open mouth. A lean dog trotted past the crumbling walls of empty houses.

The Church of Stavros, a reconstructed medieval building, was locked, but seemed in good repair. In the churchyard, at the back, lay an iron frame, with the shrivelled remains of last year's Easter flowers still clinging to it. It looked very like the Orthodox *epitaphios*, the bier of Christ, which is carried through the streets on Good Friday. I knew that, on that day, the Maronites of the Lebanon hold the service of 'Jennaz', in which a statue of the dead Christ is laid on the bier, surrounded with flowers, to be mourned and adored, and symbolically buried in a tomb beneath the church in preparation for the Resurrection.

An old lady wrapped in black came walking slowly down the grassy street, leaning heavily on her stick. She seemed not to be aware of our presence until we greeted her. I asked if there was a coffee shop, but she did not understand my Greek. At that moment a tractor came roaring around the corner, and the driver pulled up to see what was afoot. He was a powerfully built man in his middle years, with thick black hair and moustache.

'I am sorry,' he said, 'there is no coffee shop in this village now. But I would be honoured if you would like to drink a coffee in my house. My name is ——.'

We followed the clattering, smoky tractor to park outside one of the little bungalows, where the man, whom I shall call Peter, ushered us through the garden gate. A 25-year-old MG Magnette stood under the carport at the side of the house, freshly washed and polished, while the garden was bright with geraniums and bougainvillaea. Anne, his wife, after her initial surprise, welcomed us into a spotless room laid with colourful Turkish rugs. All the furniture was modern, and a large television set, video-recorder and cassette-player stood prominently displayed. A hand-embroidered tapestry of Chinese pheasants hung from one wall, while a painting of the Last Supper was placed above the sideboard by their wedding photograph. The colours were a little bright for the English taste, but it was a very comfortable home.

Their two little daughters sat down to play a children's board game with our sons, while Anne went to the kitchen, to return presently with coffee, lemonade and home-made cake on a tray. Peter explained that the girls, his youngest children, together with the few others remaining in the village, were taught every morning by a Maronite teacher who came from Kormakiti. His older daughter and son went into Kormakiti every day by bus, to attend the senior school.

'You know about the Maronites, my people?' he asked. 'We came from Syria many, many years ago. We were here long before the Franks or Turks. We built most of the old churches in Cyprus. Now, there are only 43 of us left in this village. The others have left; gone to the Greek sector or the Lebanon.

'There is nothing for my children here. When they are eighteen and go to college, they will have to go to Lebanon, or perhaps Israel or the United States. Here we live day by day. We still have our own church – you saw that? The priest comes from Kormakiti. Listen, do you write? I mean are you a writer?'

'I try.'

'You should write about the things which happen here. We have tried to live with the Turks, not to take one side or the other. Now they have brought settlers from Turkey, here, into my own village!'

His eyes suddenly blazed with anger.

'Look there, across the road.' He pointed at a rather dilapidated house with a dusty yard full of chickens. 'They brought Turks from the mainland to live in that house. When they came, we tried to be good neighbours. We asked them to visit our home, but they are primitive people. They came in here and sat on the floor! Can you believe it? There is not a table or a chair in that house. They live like animals. How can they expect us to live with such filthy people?'

'How many settlers have come from the mainland, would you say?' I asked, always interested in an opinion on this much-argued statistic.

'A hundred and ninety thousand,' Peter answered without hesitation. (If this were really true, the immigrants would considerably outnumber the Turkish Cypriots.)

'And how many soldiers?'

'Forty-five thousand, fifty thousand.'

'How are your relationships with the army and the authorities? Have they imposed any unreasonable restrictions on you? I mean why are Maronites finding it so difficult to live in the Turkish sector?'

He thought for a moment before replying.

'If you write this, don't put my right name. I come from a large family, one of eleven children. But we had land and enough money. I used to own a house in Lapithos as well as this one. I lost that in 1974, and besides, it wouldn't be safe for us there now; we must live with our own people. On my land here I grow tomatoes and vegetables as before and, as you know, we can travel on either side of the Attila Line. But the soldiers are always causing trouble, making it difficult to work in the fields. Five years ago, we found one of my brothers lying dead on our land; he had been shot. We went to the authorities and they said, "This is disgraceful, there must be an investigation, leave the matter in our hands", but then nothing happened. So we went to see them again and they said, "Unfortunately, nothing can be done, there's no evidence against anyone." When I protested, someone said to me, "Why don't you go away and stop making trouble?"

'I am the only one of my family left here now. One brother is a priest, Father A——; he comes to see us from the Greek sector sometimes. Will you be here on the first of next month? He is coming on that day; for three months they have not given him a pass, but he will be here then. I would like you to meet him because he can tell you more about these matters than I can. I have another brother who is a teacher in the South, and another in England, in Birmingham. We hope to go to England to visit him in April.'

We watched the children playing at catching little cardboard fish with hooks and string, seemingly uninhibited by the language barrier. An army convoy was roaring along the road as we left, rows of steel helmets visible above the sides of the heavy trucks. It is surely no coincidence that the Turkish army's presence is so strong around these Maronite enclaves. They waved a farewell and we promised to return on the first of the month. In the event, Father A——'s pass remained revoked and we never saw him, although we did meet Peter and Anne's older children, who were most charming and had learned excellent English in the school at Kormakiti.

*   *   *   *

The only restaurant in the district was on the forecourt of a disused filling station outside Myrtou. It had a slightly kitsch style, full of lacquered wooden panelling and sheepskin rugs, with a huge enamelled stove. We sat outside in the sun with a beer before going in to eat home-made yoghurt and little *keftedes*. There were no other customers and hardly any traffic on the road, but the young proprietress told us that most of their custom came in the evenings from army officers. Her husband watched his sheep during the day and helped her with the restaurant later.

Ayios Pantaleimon was opposite, behind its fence of barbed wire. Were people ever allowed to visit the monastery?

'What monastery?'

'There. Across the road.'

'Oh. That is an army place. I think it might have been a church once.'

*   *   *   *

The slaughter of the crows continued unabated during the afternoon. Occasionally we passed a car full of farmers, the barrels of the guns protruding from the side windows ready for action. I watched one man pull up, fire and miss from the driving seat of a Triumph Toledo.

Skylloura, or Yilmazkoy, well on the way to Nicosia, was another army camp, although some vines were growing nearby and a farmer was stretched out asleep on the top of his tractor. From here we turned back towards the mountains, to the village of Ayios Ermolaos, named after an obscure saint who was once Bishop of ancient Karpasia. The Turks have renamed it Sirinevle, and there were signs that hard fighting had taken place here in 1974, many buildings being damaged by shelling. The Greeks' cemetery, behind locked gates of corroded wrought iron, had been emptied and the headstones broken up. Even the mosque was covered with Turkish graffiti. There was a village shop whose proprietor was sitting outside in the sun, a tiny school and a shabby square with the usual imposing statue of Kemal Ataturk. A few new houses were occupied, and appeared relatively prosperous in comparison with the older buildings of crumbling mudbrick. Many of the latter, hardly intended to withstand high explosive, were in a ruinous condition.

Sisklipos, or Akcicek, close under the mountains and surrounded by almond trees, was in an even more depressing state. So many houses were damaged or empty that it was almost a village of ghosts, although the occasional figure might be seen in its decaying streets.

The church on the top of the hill retained its cross, but no bell, and stepping over the rubble inside we saw, on either side of the door facing the altar, the red Turkish flag painted on the wall. The soldiers had proudly added the name of their unit – 'PRS KOMANDO' – and again and again someone had painted the name of Bulent Ecevit, without succeeding in hiding the forlorn and faded 'ENOSIS' below.

On a rough dirt road beyond the village we bought an *oka* each of apples and oranges from a pedlar's van, before finding our way back to Agridhaki and Larnaca tis Lapithou. Here, at the place by the gorge where we had walked in the morning, a shepherdess was sitting overlooking the old Greek cemetery with its cypress trees in the valley below. Her flock was grazing the slope, while a mule waited patiently nearby. She was a pleasant woman, who chatted without undue curiosity while sorting through the bundles of wild herbs she had collected in her basket. From here, there was a fine view over the foothills and the Mesaoria, but later, as the sun was setting, we stopped the car again, high in the Korphi Forest. By clambering over the rocks through the trees we emerged on a limestone pinnacle, from where we could look over all the hills and plains as far as the distant snows of Troodos. The crags below were alive with the agile forms of goats, fleeing at the sound of our voices. Hundreds of crows, come to roost in the forest after a good day's feeding on the crop-lands below, wheeled and cawed in the golden light.

But the farmers were not finished yet. As if at a signal, three or four guns opened up from the mountainside, until the detonations reverberated almost continuously from one cliff to another. I walked through the trees to find one hunter, a youth of about twenty, standing over a smoking pile of empty cartridge cases.

'Three Turkish pounds each,' he said (he meant 300 lire), and he had already emptied one bandolier and half of a second. A number of crumpled black corpses were scattered over the thorny scrub nearby, and a couple of winged birds floundered about in the hollow beneath our feet. The sky was nevertheless still filled with the raucous creatures.

'Don't miss,' I told him as we left, and drove on across the mountains to Guzelyali and Hamit Ucok's restaurant, where a great octopus had just arrived from Famagusta. Some of this, together with red mullet, we proceeded to consume, washed down with a straw-coloured wine which was almost good.

★　★　★　★

Those who have read Lawrence Durrell's book *Bitter Lemons* will remember his description of the great house, 'Fortuna', which his

141

friend was having built by the sea, close to the Tekke of Hazireti Omer. We set off one morning to find this tomb, where seven Muslim saints are reputed to be buried, and began to search for a turning down to the sea beyond Kyrenia, in the region of Ayios Epiktitos. Our first attempt led us down an imposing driveway to reach a set of high iron gates, guarded by two sentries. A large house could just be made out beyond, surrounded by beautiful gardens.

'Hazireti Omer?' repeated one of the soldiers. He smiled encouragingly and pointed down a muddy track to the right. We bumped along beside a high wall crowned with barbed wire and emerged on to a marvellous little bay, half enclosed by a crescent of stony land, almost devoid of vegetation. On the far side, the low white dome of the tomb crouched by the sea, shining in the sunlight. It was a scene of great simplicity and purity. But I happened to look behind me, where the grounds of 'Fortuna' ran to the sea, and found that two pillboxes with machine guns and barbed wire had been erected there, and that sentries were guarding the house from the sea as well as the land.

We left the car and walked around the bay on the rocky track. The *hodja* came into view, scuttling and hopping over the stones and thorny tussocks, until he disappeared inside a little domed building behind the tomb (his lavatory). It all seemed just as Durrell had described it, although, 30 years later, this could not be the same old man. As we approached, we were surprised to notice a new Ford with English number plates, parked close by. An elegantly dressed young couple were sitting in it, whom we gathered, as they talked to us, had spent much of their lives in London.

'We come here often,' the woman said, 'to pray.'

We never did find out who was being guarded so closely in 'Fortuna'. A weekend residence for Mr Denktash perhaps, or possibly the famous General? This General was becoming almost as mysterious a figure as the legendary Queen of the Kyrenia range, although I did once catch sight of him in the flesh on the outskirts of Nicosia, riding in a flag-bedecked limousine, flanked by outriders.

On we drove, in the sun of that glorious north coast, past the army camp with its minefield, past the power station where a battered Triumph Spitfire was always parked by the gate, and past the well with a four-bar windlass, where the shepherds watered their flocks. Sir Samuel Baker had described the same curious, handleless winding mechanism, which looks so awkward and inefficient. Past the bald shepherd on the beach, the young one with earphones, and the old one with a duffle bag and water bottle who liked to shake hands and pass the time of day before allowing us to go on our way. Only one or two families were living in the ruined hamlets of Troulli and Alakati, where some of the houses had been turned into pens for the enormous flocks. The scarred walls were covered with slogans: 'Denktash', 'No Surrender'. Occasionally a red-legged partridge bolted across the road ahead.

Akanthou, or Tatlisu, dominated by the huge grey dome of the church, spread itself luxuriantly at the head of a green valley. The wooded slopes of Mount Olympus (Cyprus has two, the other being the highest peak of the Troodos range) crowded close behind the town, while the mists of morning, still undispersed by the sun, stretched out in front of the houses, penetrated by occasional cypress trees. Tatlisu is a name taken from a Turkish village in the south, on the coast midway between Larnaca and Limassol. But many of the people working in the orchards and carob groves below the town were from the mainland, as were a group of girls near an artesian well in a potato field, who pointed out the way. Two tractors preceded us up the road, each with a group of field workers clinging to it, brightly coloured scarves wrapped around their heads. There are ancient sites all through this valley, the fields and groves being ridged and terraced with antique walls and pavements beneath the grass. The present town dates from the seventh century and is full of elegant arches, ornate stone lintels and beautifully carved doors. The Greeks of Akanthou had a reputation for woodwork and embroidery, and their carved dowry chests are famous all over Cyprus.

We parked our car by the church, which is not a building of any historical interest, having been built in the early years of this century, but is impressive by virtue of its sheer size, with nine domes picked out in yellow and grey. A small crowd rapidly gathered around us, and we gained the impression that foreigners had not set foot in Akanthou for a very long time. We found that the door of the church was locked. Then a man spoke in Turkish to someone at the back of the crowd and a girl aged about sixteen pushed forward and said shyly, 'Would you like to see the church? If you wish, this man will get the key for you. And he says "Welcome to our village." '

We expressed our thanks, and the man went down the street for the keys while the girl explained that her name was Nursel and that she had learned her English at school in Famagusta. Her stock had plainly risen among her neighbours at this demonstration of her facility in a foreign tongue, and a number of matrons beamed approvingly at her. People walked up to shake hands with us, and an elderly woman in the dress of the mainland embraced Joan warmly and kissed her on both cheeks. The men smiled and went on down to the coffee shop, but more women continued to gather until the keys arrived and the heavy door was pushed ajar. Everybody followed us curiously inside.

'You understand that the church is now our mosque?' Nursel asked, with a trace of anxiety in her voice.

'Of course. It is good to see that it is being cared for. Shouldn't we take off our shoes?'

'Not necessary. It is not the time for prayer.'

The huge building had been whitewashed, and all was plain except for an elaborate chandelier and Turkish carpets against one wall, where green tapestries indicated the direction of Mecca. An open Koran stood on a wooden rest. In truth, as in most mosques, bare as the Prophet would have wished, there was not a great deal to see. But the women enthusiastically led us everywhere, even up into the gallery under the cupola where once the Pantocrator, Christ in Majesty, doubtless glared down at the world of men. Some broken windows had permitted sparrows to enter, and they flew noisily from one side to another, creating a considerable amount of mess. No one seemed concerned. I pushed a few notes into the collection box to general approval before the door was locked once more.

We asked Nursel if she would join us for a coffee before we left, and she looked embarrassed. It would, we realised, be breaking a taboo. Young, unmarried girls in Cypriot villages, Greek or Turkish, do not drink coffee in the café.

'Perhaps,' I suggested, 'as you are with my family, it might be proper.'

She thought for a moment and came to the conclusion that this was a special case. She was, after all, our interpreter and guide. We were soon seated round a table in the smoky little room; the boy of Nursel's age who served us raised his eyebrows, but she soon recovered her composure and began to talk. She was darkly pretty, though with a faintly pockmarked face. It seemed unlikely that Akanthou, where she had grown up, would hold her for long. She enjoyed her school in Famagusta and planned to train as a nurse. She had really learned to speak English very well, quaintly interposing such colloquialisms as 'a moment only' and 'but of course'. Did she find Akanthou rather quiet? A little, but her father, a shepherd, would not permit his children to go to the cinema in Famagusta. One sensed that this forbidden pleasure would be first on her list of priorities as soon as she reached her nursing college. She liked English pop music: Duran Duran and Shakin' Stevens.

Akanthou may be a remote and ancient village, but its agriculture is modern and thriving, and there was a sense of energy which contrasted with the depressed condition of many communities in Turkish Cyprus. The western European all too easily makes an assumption that Turkish rule results in indolence and decay. The Venetian Ioannis Cotovicus had this to say when he visited Cyprus, 30 years after the Turks first captured it:

> The present condition and appearance of the island is far different, oppressed by barbarian rule and stripped of its old grace and glory; much of it is uncultivated, neglected, deserted. Cities once famous and populous, and full of stately buildings, are now ruinous, squalid and thinly peopled: towns and villages lie desolate and forsaken, for it is the way of the Turks to lay waste city and field, to destroy ancient splendour.

> (Trs. C.D. Cobham, *Excerpta Cypria*)

Some of these accusations might be reiterated when examining the Turkish sector today, but it would not be true of everywhere. And Dr Cotovicus, as a Venetian, can be assumed to have been biased. Akanthou, or Tatlisu, has a large teenaged population, too young to remember much of 1974 and full of fresh hopes and cherished ambitions. One could only wish them well. Nursel waved goodbye to us from the square, standing with her friends beneath the new statue of Ataturk.

★ ★ ★ ★

When the irrigated fields of Akanthou lay behind us, and once more we were among the drier lands by the coast, we caught sight of the Church of Panayia Pergaminiotissa. Half a mile away from the road, standing among the wild rocks and bushes, it radiated the calm and stability amidst the confusion of nature which is so peculiar to Byzantine architecture. Some say that the city of Pergamon stood on this site, others that this lay further west, near Ayios Amvrosios. Certainly something had once been here, for as we pushed our way through tall growths of asphodel, that concomitant to man's disturbance of the soil, our feet slipped on the rubble of ancient walls and felt the solidity of level pavement under the thin top soil. Loose masonry and pieces of column lay half buried in the thorny thickets.

Panayia Pergaminiotissa was one of those churches built as a fortress, with massive walls and arrow-slit windows. Beneath the single dome was a rudimentary cross-in-square design, enlarged by the addition of an apse and side chapels to the nave. The roof tiles had disappeared long before, leaving the bare stone and cement of the barrel-vaulted roofs exposed to the sky. In the dry climate of Cyprus, where they make the roofs of houses from mud, it would be a long time before the elements found their way inside. The churchyard, with its sycamore trees, was grown waist-high with asphodel and thistles, among which could be seen the crumbled stone of several tombs. The walls were haunted by lizards, which vanished into deep crevices as we approached. We found the church door locked – perhaps a good sign – but by shining a torch through a window we could see the drums of the great columns which supported the dome, and the remains of frescos clinging with the rotting plaster to the walls. Among the ruins nearby, we found the coping of a well cut into the rock, which the shepherds still used, and two square doors to a tomb or sunken chapel, barred with stout timbers and padlocked, although ancient paintings could again be made out on the wall inside.

At the junction where the side turning leads up to Dhavlos, someone had built a strange modern house of iron and concrete, quite circular like a lighthouse and several storeys high with balconies. This someone was doubtless a Greek, for the building had obviously been used as a sheep-pen for the last twelve years and was covered with graffiti: 'Long live Denktash'. The road into the village led through a long tunnelled avenue of pines, thick with cones, to the place where workmen were building a new mosque: a very elegant building whose tall white minaret was finely marked with vertical green lines, already a landmark for miles along the coast. A gnarled and venerable almond tree leaned over the road near the steps of the mosque, the youthful cascade of sugar-pink blossom contrasting with the age of the scarred trunk.

The Turks of Dhavlos, which has now been renamed Kaplica, the Hot Spring, might of course have considered converting the Christian church into a mosque, as most villages have done. Yet when we reached it, attracted by a distant view of the cupola, we could see that it had been sacked and was almost beyond repair. Those hopeless Greek words– 'ENOSIS', 'EOKA' – still stand in nationalist blue paint over a village now implacably hostile to Greek aspirations. There was nothing but rubble inside and an incredibly claustrophobic staircase spiralling up into the campanile which retained its bell. I had to back down without being able to turn my shoulders around; surely only a child could have made the ascent? Yet again we reminded ourselves of our decision not to look inside churches – it was becoming altogether too depressing.

A group of curious children were waiting for us as we emerged into the light and pushed the broken gate shut. A woman came around the corner carrying her baby slung papoose-fashion on her back. All these people wore the dress of the mainland: loose silken trousers of red, blue or purple and Turkish slippers. Finally, we were shocked to see an old woman coming in from the fields, bent double and gasping under a load of fodder larger than herself, perhaps 50 or 60 kilos, which she carried with the aid of a band around her forehead. Doubtless someone's grandmother, old enough to have been drawing her pension for years in Britain, she was still carrying loads more suitable for a donkey.

The great forest of Kantara above Dhavlos is a wild place where deciduous woods are mixed with the pines. The trees cover the mountain thickly, and reach a height more normally associated with the forests of northern Europe. The red-barked trunks of the arbutus are unusually prominent, and the pines on the skyline are twisted and distorted into the eccentric silhouettes of a Japanese print. We found the road very steep but well made, climbing beneath a tall radio mast on the heights of Mount Sinai. The hillside had been terraced in places; the marks of tracked vehicles were visible, and areas had recently been felled and replanted. Yet in all this district, indeed until we descended to the coast in the evening, we never saw another human soul.

The British tended to use the forests as a summer resort and, much as the Lusignans before them, retreated to these green mountains from the heat of the plain. Perhaps that is why Kantara village, with its log cabins and corrugated-iron roofs, reminded me of the hill stations of India or Ceylon. Some of the chalets among the pines were in good repair, with modern solar heating panels fitted, but none was occupied; the hostel was ruined and the restaurant locked. Grateful that we had thought to bring a rudimentary picnic, we drove on through the village and emerged briefly into the open on the crest of the ridge, before beginning to climb towards the next peak on which we could see the encrusting towers and walls of Kantara Castle. At this point, approaching the neck of the Karpas peninsula, the island is so narrow that we could simultaneously overlook the Bay of Famagusta and the Caramanian Straits.

Kantara is the easternmost of the three castles of the Kyrenia mountains, balanced on a knife edge from which both the Taurus mountains and the Lebanon, a full 100 miles distant, can sometimes be seen, although we scanned the haze in vain. The Arabic name (Al Kantara, the Bridge, so common in Moorish–Spanish place names) indicates that the Saracens may have been the first to fortify the peak. A majority of authorities claim that it was here that Isaac Comnenus surrendered to King Richard's Crusaders. In Lusignan times the castle shared the stormy history of the other fortresses of this range, which the Turks call Besparmak, but there is no account of Kantara ever having been successfully stormed. Thirteen Orthodox monks were once put to death in Kantara for their defiance of Latin doctrine. The Venetians slighted the defences, since when it has stood empty, still threatening and forceful in its domination of the landscape despite the breached and crumbling walls. In the last century, a hermit haunted the castle: a lonely monk named Simeon.

147

We found a strong iron gate mounted in the entrance to the barbican, but the lock was broken and we pushed it aside to climb up past vaulted chambers where men-at-arms once lodged, past a deep and dangerous cistern and a sallyport – a narrow barred passageway through which brave men might creep to fall upon a besieging enemy from above. That is assuming that they did not succumb to vertigo and literally fall upon their enemy from above, for to me the descent seemed extremely hazardous.

High above the curtain wall, on the flat roof of a tower, we sat and ate a dull lunch of crispbread and apples, surprised to be pestered by midges in this eyrie, 2,000 feet above the Mesaoria. The splintered summits of the mountains lanced their way towards the distant mists of the Karpas like the uncomfortable back of some prehistoric saurian. The same tortured barrier disappeared into the west, behind the slashed black shape of a cypress growing from the walls. We found a Gothic window, standing alone as if intended to be nothing more than a frame for the wilderness beyond. A raven swung overhead and uttered its solitary, blood-curdling croak.

Philip de Novare, the Lusignan poet, had been here with the force besieging Sir Aimery Barlais, who had annexed Kantara on behalf of his master, the Emperor Frederick II. He had spent a night lying under the walls, hoping to learn the mood of the defenders:

> Yes 'reen I watched until the break of day,
> Hard by the walls, alone with no one near;
> High in a tower I heard their woes portray
> Those of Kantara, sorrowful and drear.

(Trs. Patrick Balfour, *The Orphaned Realm*)

It was not long before the garrison surrendered.

Kantara held out for the King during the Genoese invasion Leontios Makhairas described how the young King's uncle, Prince John of Antioch, whom the Genoese had imprisoned in chains in the castle of Famagusta, was helped by a cook to disguise himself and escape here:

And he put a copper pot on his head and a little copper pot in his hand, and said to him, in case he were questioned by anyone: 'Tell him that you are taking the pots to be tinned.' And he brought him out of the castle, and out of the gate of Famagusta, and took him to his country estate at Kolota, and there he mounted him on the mare belonging to the captain of the castle and took him to Kantara.

(Trs. R.M. Dawkins, *Recital Concerning the Sweet Land of Cyprus*)

Now, these stones had been deserted by men for so long that they seemed to be part of the mountain itself, as if the citadel had not been planned and constructed, but had simply grown out of the rocks like some twisted fig tree. Pococke had called Kantara the 'Castle of the Hundred and One Chambers', for he too had been told the story of the Queen and her enchanted treasure.

We followed the forest road back under the ridge to the west. In places, the road builders had constructed grand viewing platforms where one might survey the coast through the tortuous branches of the pines, a reminder of more leisured, peaceful times, when the Kantara Forest had been a popular resort. After a long descent on a very bad road, we emerged from the forest at Phlamoudi, now Mersinlik, a village of very old houses. Many of these were entered from large porches with an archway giving on to the yard, a feature we did not see elsewhere on the island. There was a wrecked graveyard, strewn with broken fragments of white marble, while the church was stripped bare and stank of human ordure. But a friendly woman called up to us from her yard, where she was feeding her bantam chickens, and a happy little boy waved frantically as we drove out of the village, his dog barking and jumping beside him. '*Ne Mutlu Turkum Digene*' was written on a wall, 'He is a lucky man who can call himself a Turk', a quotation from Mustapha Kemal.

On the coast, near a place once known as Peristeria, 'the doves', we came upon deserted boathouses in a cove. They were massively walled buildings, strong enough to resist any storm, partly incorporated into the rock. One was provided with six great arches where the boats must once have been dragged into safety, but only one craft now lay on the strand. The ribs of one side were stove in and the engine was a solid mass of corroded components. The shreds of a red Turkish flag hung from the stern.

'Nobody fishes on this coast now,' Salih had said. The other boathouse had been converted into a sheepfold by piling thorn bushes across the entrance, and the anxious eyes and huddled forms of the flock could be made out through the gloom within.

Near Akanthou someone had once built a modern farm unit – the type of highly mechanised operation where batteries of chickens or pigs are fed with proteins and hormones in order to grow at a prodigious rate. I have no idea whether this proved successful in Cyprus, for the owner must have been a Greek and the sheds were empty, with broken windows and drunken shutters. Then, in the fields near the village, we fell in behind a tractor taking a Turkish family back home at the end of the day. Two men, two headscarfed women, one nursing a baby, and several children had somehow squeezed themselves into the space over the back axle and were driving along as fast as the great whirling tyres would take them, laughing and shouting above the roar of the diesel. The scene made me think of one of those eastern European postage stamps, extolling the idealised virtues of the collective farm and family unity. Soon similar groups on other tractors joined the road from fields on either side, the men with cigarettes lit and their head cloths blowing in the wind, heroic Stakhanovites every one, before the whole merry convoy turned up the hill to the village. We were left alone by the coast, near the place the Greeks called the Nereides. Some say that the ruins scattered near here are those of ancient Aphrodision, the city of the Hittites in Cyprus.

Darkness fell during the long drive back to Kyrenia. We passed a solitary cottage whose open door gave a view of the single room, which seemed more like a Yuruk nomad's tent than a house. An iron stove stood by a large bed covered with bright *kilims*. There was no other furniture, but a great cooking pan of glowing charcoal lay on the floor amidst a confusion of patterned rugs. On the controlled section of road by the army camp the brake fluid warning light suddenly flashed up red on the dashboard. Slowly we crawled in second gear past the checkpoints (was brake failure a valid reason for stopping in a forbidden area?). Finally I stopped and looked beneath the bonnet with a torch, wondering why this kind of thing always happens to the cars I rent. Sure enough, the reservoir was half empty. But then had it been full when we started? There was no sign of any leak. So at the end of a long day, we spent a pleasant hour searching out the last garage open in Kyrenia (thank heavens for Mediterranean opening hours), having the fluid replenished and the system checked. The mechanic could not find a leak either.

Rather grimy and dishevelled, we repaired to the soldiers' restaurant, which we found empty except for the band which was practising for a concert in Nicosia the following night. The main room was being painted by a detail of young soldiers, so Ibrahim, in uniform this evening, opened up the General's room again for us. The night had turned chilly and he dragged a heavy electric heater up to the table, thrusting two bare wires into the wall socket. The sergeant fed cassettes into the stereo, which persistently dragged its spools, elongating the vowels of the singers. Eventually, in disgust, he switched the television on instead, twiddling the dials to find first the Greek side, then the last of the Turkish Cypriot broadcast.

'Six o'clock to eight is our broadcast. Then we switch over to Ankara.'

After dinner we all pulled chairs around the heater, although I, for one, took care not to touch it.

'Ninety days left,' said Ibrahim thoughtfully, puffing away at one of my cigars.

'Doesn't sound too long. How much leave do you get?'

'Forty days on, one day off.'

'My God! What about pay?'

'Fifteen hundred liras a month.'

At that time, this would have bought a cheap lunch in a snack bar or a couple of gallons of petrol. We made sympathetic noises. But I was interested in Ibrahim's family background as an immigrant from the mainland. I asked him if he had any idea how many settlers had come to Cyprus altogether. The sergeant's ears pricked up almost visibly.

'Very few,' Ibrahim replied guardedly.

'But how many would you say?'

'Maybe ten thousand.'

'Do you remember anything of Mersin?'

'Not very much. Sheep. There are very many sheep near there.'

'Is that what your family did? I mean was your father a shepherd?'

Ibrahim looked shocked. He shook his head emphatically.

'He's a receptionist in the hospital at Famagusta!'

I did my best to repair the damage.

'Oh, we met a nice young girl this morning at Tatlisu. She's going to Famagusta hospital to train as a nurse.'

'She's very charming.' Joan added wickedly. 'Have you got a girlfriend? Would you like us to introduce you?'

Poor Ibrahim, the well-brought up Turkish boy, could only shake his head again, speechless with embarrassment. The English, one could see him thinking, would take some getting used to.

Mudbrick and straw houses of Old Nicosia

CHAPTER TEN

TURKISH NICOSIA

Nicosia is not seen at its best when approached from the north, although the route over the mountains from Kyrenia is attractive enough until Geunyeli, an old Turkish fiefdom on the Mesaoria, is reached. From the 1950s, Geunyeli was a stronghold of Rauf Denktash's underground organisation, Volkan (the Volcano), later to become TMT. A sordid incident occurred on 12 June 1958, when a number of Greeks suspected by the British police of planning a racist attack themselves, but against whom nothing could be proved, were released from custody here. Miles from the nearest Greek village, they were left to make their way home as best they could. The Turks of Geunyeli, predictably, killed eight of them, hacking them to death with knives, although direct complicity between the British authorities and the Turkish community was never proved.

Geunyeli, with its narrow street and new mosque, merges into Ortakeuy, an ugly suburb of building sites and smoking factory chimneys, again a traditionally Turkish district, until finally the *muraglia*, the walls of the old city, are reached. Examining the map of old Nicosia, one is immediately struck by the exact symmetry of the Venetian city wall: a perfect circle with eleven projecting bastions, like an engineer's drawing of a cogged gear wheel. Beyond the circle, the city has overflowed in all directions as an uncoordinated muddle of modern blocks and streets, which finally resolve themselves into arterial routes spreading to all corners of Cyprus. Nicosia sits in the centre of the Mesaoria, dominating the communications with the other lowland towns of the island. Only Paphos, beyond the southern mountains, is remote. This central situation was the securest position that could be found, far from the coastal raids of Saracen pirates. I can conceive of no other reason for locating the capital in the sweltering heat of the plain, where the summer temperature has been recorded at 44 °C.

To the west of the walls, through the outer suburbs, the river Pedhieos flows sluggishly and uncertainly on its long journey over the plain to the Bay of Famagusta, having risen high on the Troodos mountains by the Monastery of Makheras. The Pedhieos was directed into its present channel during the nineteenth century. The river once ran through the city, but the occasional floods did great damage. In 1542 Jodicus de Meggen wrote:

> The river flows through the town, as is shown by the stone bridges. Sometimes it is a powerful and violent stream though when we were there, we saw but a dried-up channel as the result of the great heat . . .

A modern map will also show the Line, that tracing confusingly known as the Green Line in the old city, the Red Line in the suburbs, and the Attila or Sahin Line in the countryside. The colours refer to nothing more than the original crayon marks on a military map. Nicosia forms a salient into Greek territory, so that the Line dips down on each side to take perhaps a third of the suburbs into the Turkish sector, while the walled city is approximately cut in half. As a result, the Turks are in control of most of their traditional areas and much of the older, historic part of the city, while the Greeks hold the modern commercial district to the south. There is only one crossing point, in the west of the city, by the famous Ledra Palace Hotel, where the Line leaves the city wall and runs along the moat for a distance.

It was not far from the crossing point that we found a parking place on what was once Marcos Dracos Avenue, named after the EOKA fighter martyred by the British in 1957. But we wanted to enter the city by the Kyrenia Gate, and so we walked around the crowded section of ring road, past the impressive new Turkish Embassy built on the site of an old Muslim graveyard, and came to the great breach which was made through the wall in 1931. This allowed motor traffic to flow freely on either side of the original gate which now stands isolated, a domed tower above a stout portcullis. The Venetians knew this as the Proveditore Gate, but it was the Turks who added its wonderful inscription: 'O, Mohammed, give these tidings to the Faithful: Victory is from God and triumph is very near. O opener of doors, open for us the best of doors!'

Once inside the wall, which has had steps added to the sloping inner flank so that one can stroll on the parapet, we found ourselves in a city crowded not only with cars, but with pedlars, street hawkers and stall-holders. In Ismet Inonu Square, a vegetable market clustered close beneath the wall. Ahead lay Kyrenia Street, its narrow pavements unable to accommodate the groups of citizens and soldiers edging past the truckloads of produce on their way to the main market. Beyond, a huge hoarding showing the head of Ataturk could be seen in the square named after the Turkish leader.

The Turks, as already mentioned, refer to the city as Lefkosa; to the Greeks it has always been Lefkosia. Nicosia is a Latinised version of the original Greek name, which may be associated with Lefkon, the Ptolemaic founder of the ancient city of Ledra which once stood on this ground. On the other hand, the name may simply derive from the Greek *lefka*, a 'poplar tree'. There are a few Roman remains in the area, but it was the destruction of Constantia by the Saracens in the seventh century which brought the city to prominence as one of the few in Cyprus which might be regarded as secure from the sea-raiders. Nicosia was the seat of an Orthodox bishop, and also the site of a Byzantine fortress of which no trace now remains. The Knights Templar, having purchased Cyprus from Richard the Lionheart in 1191 for 10,000 gold bezants, ruled the island from Nicosia. Within a year they had managed to provoke an uprising by their attempts to recover this huge purchase price by taxing the population. On Easter Sunday of 1192, a number of the Knights were forced to lock themselves into the castle of Nicosia in order to escape the fury of the taxpayers. The Templars never did manage to scrape the money together, and were forced to return the island to Richard.

When Guy de Lusignan added the Crown of Cyprus to those of Jerusalem and Armenia, he settled here in the company of 300 French nobles and a large force of soldiers, presumably hardened Crusaders. Much as the Lusignans loved the castles and hunting forests of the Kyrenia mountains, they built their palace here on the plain, although again barely anything remains. The old Latin churches of Nicosia are the main surviving monuments to these Catholic Frenchmen who grew so rich on the trades of the East. Von Suchen wrote of them that: 'An annual income of three thousand florins is of no more account than an income of three marks to us', for in time the nobility of Nicosia grew almost as wealthy as the merchants of Famagusta. They were truly an exotic breed, living in Arabic luxury rather than in the spartan fashion of medieval Europe. And despite the chivalry of Peter I, in time they gained a reputation among their bluffer, northern fellow Christians for the cunning and intrigue normally associated with the Arab mind.

Lusignan Nicosia was said to have been 7 miles around, full of secret walled gardens, courtyards and fountains. King Peter II built the original walls, which rambled over a much greater distance than the 2 miles circumference of the present Venetian circle. But the old Lusignan walls were not so strong. The Egyptian Mamelukes, following their capture of King Janus in 1426, had little difficulty in taking Nicosia, which they then pillaged, slighting the fortifications.

The Venetian defences were constructed rapidly in preparation for the expected Turkish attack. During these works, much of the old

Lusignan architecture was destroyed, churches and palaces outside the new *muraglia* being flattened to give the Venetian guns a clear field of fire. Thus the Royal Abbey of St Dominic, apparently full of fine marble and cloisters of orange trees, where most of the Kings of Cyprus and Jerusalem had been buried, together with the Princes of Antioch, Caesarea and Galilee, was completely razed to the ground. Nothing was to stand in the way of the cannon mounted on these massive ramparts, although interestingly Pococke, who was here in 1738, claimed that he could still make out the remains of the Lusignan wall, which must now be obscured by the modern suburbs. The *muraglia* are as broad as they are high, with the Italian names of the reinforced bastions sounding as a roll call of Venetian soldiers and empire builders: Barbaro, Loredano, Flatro, Caraffa, Podocataro, Costanza, d'Avila, Tripoli, Roccas, Mula and Quirini. Originally, the waters of the river Pedhieos were led into the outer moat.

Many Armenians once had businesses in Kyrenia Street alongside the Turks. When the final divison came, they threw in their lot with the Greeks and moved across the Line. The Archduke Louis Salvator had written: 'Turks, Greeks and Armenians dwell together intermingled, bitter enemies at heart, and united solely by their love for the land of their birth.' This prescient statement had given me a start when I came across it. Every other traveller of the period had written of the amity in which the races apparently lived together. The Archduke's visit in 1873 had been of brief duration, but it seems that with more insight than most he had discerned something of the true relationship between the peoples of the island.

The oldest building in the street is the Mevlevi Tekke, the monastery of the Whirling Dervishes and mausoleum of their Sheiks. In Turkey, Kemal Ataturk outlawed this extraordinary sect in 1925 as something primitive and archaic. Kemal, an atheist himself, who believed in nothing in this world or the next except his own remarkable abilities, forced his new Turkish Republic as far along the road to secularism as he was able. 'Religion is like a heavy blanket,' he once said, 'that keeps the people of Turkey from waking up, from moving forward.' The new Turkey was turning its back on mysticism, and all those sects which would now be described as fundamentalist were made illegal. In 1947 the authorities relented, and in Konya, the ancient capital of the Seljuk Turks, the famous dances were allowed to continue as they still do today, but purely as a cultural event for tourists. Here in Cyprus the tradition of the Dervish monks lived on unhindered, until the death of the last Sheik, Selim Debe, in 1954.

We found that the *tekke* had been turned into a museum. Still prominent in the centre was the wooden dancing floor, and the flutes and drums of the musicians lay nearby in the gallery, as if the dance had only just finished. A group of monks in long black robes and conical hats, symbolising earth and the tomb, once sat on this floor, heads bowed in prayer as the hypnotic chanting and music began. Gradually they would rise, shedding the black cloaks to reveal white garments beneath, and slowly rotate, always anti-clockwise and on their left foot, sometimes for hours on end. The right hand would be held palm up; the left palm down, so receiving God's grace from heaven and transmitting it through their bodies to earth. 'We are spinning,' they would say 'on mystical air.'

In a cold stone chamber, we examined the tombs of their Sheiks, who came from Turkey and Syria, laid chronologically in a row and painted in the holy green of Islam, each surmounted by a Mevlevi hat in stone. The sect once had great power in the Empire. At Eyup on the Golden Horn, the chief Sheik of the Mevlevi Dervishes traditionally girded each new Sultan with the sword of Osman, the first of the Ottoman line.

The founder of the Dervishes was the thirteenth-century Persian mystic and poet Mevlana Jalal-ad-din-Rumi, born far to the east, in the city of Balkh in Afghanistan. Rumi, who was famous for his tolerance in an age of fierce religious antagonism, wrote:

> The lamps are different, but the light
> is the same: it comes from Beyond.
> O Thou who art the Kernel of
> existence, the discord between
> Mohamedan, Zoroastrian and Jew
> is but a thing of private prejudice.

(J.K. Birge, *The Bektashi Order of Dervishes*)

It is said that the Prophet himself, in moments of great vision and inspiration, would jump up in a frenzy and 'gyrate many times'. Poor Rumi, inconsolable after the death of a close friend, wrapped himself in a cloak and abandoned himself to God's love. After a time, it is said, he was inspired to begin the whirling dance, forgetting his sorrow as he was 'consumed in burning ecstasy'. He died on 17 December 1273, later known to the Dervishes as the 'Wedding Night', when their founder achieved the goal of his whole life by merging with God:

> You say the sea and its waves, but in so saying you do not mean two
> different things, for the sea, in its rising and falling, makes waves, and the
> waves, when they have fallen, return to the sea. So it is with men, who are
> the waves of God; they are absorbed after death into him.

(H.V. Morton, *In the Steps of St. Paul*)

The Dervishes, though long defunct, are still causing embarrassment to modern Turkey. There was recently a diplomatic rumpus when Hossein Moussari, the Prime Minister of Iran, paid an official visit to the Republic and breached protocol by declining to pay his respects at the grave of the atheist Kemal Ataturk. Instead he was concerned to visit the tomb of his fellow Persian, Mevlana Jalal-ad-din-Rumi. One has to know the Turks and their sentiments towards the monolithic figure of Ataturk to appreciate the offence which this caused.

Apart from the Mevlevi sect, the museum was a treasure house of information on the Turks in Cyprus. Prayer mats, carved wooden rests for the Koran, marvellously ornate carpets, silver-handled yataghans, Ottoman coins and especially the clothes engaged our attention. The old photographs indicated that the traditional and spectacular Turkish male dress (oh, the magnificence of their embroidered socks!) continued to be worn well into the 1930s. Here too was the craftwork common to both the Greeks and Turks of the island: bridal chests and embroidery. Lala Mustapha's own Koran was preserved, but the most wonderful of all were the firmans and letters of appointment from the Sublime Porte. Every village *muktar* (mayor) and the *hodja* of every mosque had his appointment personally from the Sultan in Constantinople, even until 1914 in the days when the British leased the island. Each letter was a work of art, a magnificent piece of calligraphy in curling Arabic script, marked with the royal peacock seal.

In Turkey itself, this complex written language came to an end when Kemal had a Latin phonetic alphabet drawn up in six weeks, and produced a new official language purged of foreign words. Civil servants were given three months to learn the new Turkish or lose their jobs. Kemal himself toured the country with a blackboard, teaching and haranguing his bewildered people. The fez was abolished; Kemal regarded it as yet another symbol of the past. He himself always dressed in western clothes, and he had the police tear turbans and kerchiefs from the heads of peasants until, in time, they adopted the ubiquitous European cloth cap. When the Egyptian Ambassador arrived at an offical reception wearing a fez, Kemal shouted at him furiously, 'Tell your King I don't like his uniform.' The veil for women was abolished, although in the countryside the tradition of female modesty ran so deep that even Kemal could not force total obedience to this rule. The Turkish passion for altering names began at this time. Both Mustapha Kemal's own names were Arabic, and so he determined to discard them in favour of Ataturk, the Father of the Turks.

Ataturk Square, where we stopped to buy Malcolm a new pair of trainer shoes, was once Konak Square and the site of the Seray, the seat of the Turkish Governor. It was an old Venetian palace by all accounts, with traces of an earlier, Gothic building and still decorated with the lion of St Mark when the Archduke came to visit the governor and inspect the prison next door. He described the meeting:

> After a while the Pasha entered, a middle-aged man, wrapped up in a fur caftan or long coat. Mehemed Veiss is a native of Constantinople, a thorough Turk of the old breed, with mild friendly manners, and speaking nothing but Turkish. He made me sit down on one of the leather armchairs, occupying the other one himself. The conversation was carried on with the help of the dragoman in Italian, and turned principally on matters connected with the island. When I asked for permission to visit the prisons and other public institutions, he anwered, smiling: 'You will find nothing but bad things here, but I know it is the duty of travellers to see bad things as well as good.' He then talked about his Governorships at Beyruth, Bagdad, and other places. After coffee we took hearty leave of each other. The same evening he sent me his carte de visite photograph, and also the citrons and fresh dates I admired so much in his room.

(Archduke Louis Salvator of Austria, *Lefkosia*)

On 12 July 1878 Vice-Admiral Lord John Hay, who had arrived off Larnaca in HMS *Minotaur* from Suda Bay in Crete, and a party incuding Sami Pasha, the representative of the Sublime Porte, came to the Seray to present the Sultan's firman to Bessim Pasha, confirming that the administration of Cyprus was now in the hands of the British. A crowd of Greeks rapidly gathered as the news went round that Queen Victoria was now to rule, and tremendous applause rang out as the Union Jack was hoisted. This association with a Christian empire seemed to the Greeks of Cyprus to be the first step to *enosis*, union with Greece. Great Britain was regarded as a friendly power, sympathetic to Hellenic aspirations, and moreover the nation which had freely ceded the Ionian islands to Greece fourteen years before. Later, as disillusion set in, the agreement between Britain and Turkey was to become known as the 'Thieves' Deal'.

Why did Great Britain desire to control Cyprus? As early as 1814, John MacDonald Kinneir of the East India Company had made a strong case for attaching the island to the Empire:

> The possession of Cyprus would give to England a preponderating influence in the Mediterranean, and place at her disposal the future destinies of the Levant. Egypt and Syria would soon become her tributaries, and she would acquire an overawing position in respect to Asia Minor, by which the Porte might at all times be kept in check, and the encroachments of Russia, in this quarter, retarded, if not prevented. It would increase her

commerce in a very considerable degree; give her the distribution of the rich wines, silks and other produce of that fine island; the rice and sugar of Egypt, and the cotton, opium and tobacco of Anatolia. It is of easy defence; and under a liberal government would, in a very short space of time, amply repay the charge of its own establishment, and afford the most abundant supplies to our fleets at a trifling expense.

(Trs. C.D. Cobham, *Excerpta Cypria*)

The politicians of 1878 were less ambitious. At the simplest, strategic level there was concern for the route to India through the Suez Canal, and the possession of three naval bases – Gibraltar, Malta and Cyprus – would effectively guarantee British domination of the Mediterranean. The Foreign Minister, Lord Salisbury, further argued that should the Ottoman Empire finally collapse under Russian pressure, so that the Tsar controlled Asia Minor, then a new line of defence would be called for, 'another dyke behind the shattered Turkish breakwater'.

It has been suggested that Disraeli, enchanted by Cyprus as a young man, saw the island as a possible home for the Jews of the Diaspora and the idea was certainly discussed in Zionist circles at the time.

Gladstone, however, argued that, if it was intended to assist the Turks against Russia, Cyprus was further from the Dardanelles than Malta, and facilities at Constantinople would be of greater value for putting British warships into the Black Sea. A station on the Persian Gulf, effectively a British lake at that time, would be more useful, both as a check to Russian influence and to protect India. Moreover, the philhellene Gladstone, who was later to gain the gratitude of Greek Cypriots by consistently arguing for *enosis*, objected on principle to the idea of Britain administering a territory belonging to Turkey. But with the exception perhaps of Gladstone, there was little thought for the feelings of the Cypriots, it being assumed that they would happily welcome a benign British government, particularly if the anomaly of Turkish sovereignty might be removed. Thus Sir Samuel Baker considered that:

. . . when Cyprus shall belong absolutely to Great Britain, so that the Cypriotes shall feel that they are British subjects, they will become the most amenable and contented people in the Empire.

(Samuel Baker, *Cyprus as I Saw It in 1879*)

The first High Commissioner, Sir Garnet Wolseley, was concerned to find some 300 convicted criminals on Cyprus, and complained that the island 'under Turkish rule was made the receptacle for the worst criminals in the Sultan's empire.' The Turkish administrators – the *kaimakans* who governed the six districts of Cyprus and the *cadis* or judges – were hopelessly corrupt. The bribery and nepotism were eventually purged, but nevertheless the British continued to govern the Greek majority under not English law, but Turkish.

For some reason it is often assumed that after 1878 the British adminstration achieved some kind of revolution in Cypriot affairs, rapidly correcting centuries of Turkish neglect. The facts do not bear this out, for Cyprus had after all been leased from the Sultan in return for British support against Russia. No one, least of all the foreign investor, was sure how long the British would stay and this factor alone tended to prolong the state of poverty in which most Cypriots lived. Moreover, in the early years British officials were very concerned with collecting the rent. This had been set at the average difference between revenue and expenditure in Cyprus during the last five years in Turkish hands. The Turks had spent virtually nothing on Cyprus and squeezed the maximum possible amount of taxation from its people, the average difference, and thus the specified rent, being £99,799.11s.3d. In fact the Porte never received any of this money from Britain, it being used to pay off interest on a loan made to Turkey in 1855. Nevertheless, despite a certain amount of aid from the British Government, the new administration tried hard to provide most of the rent from taxes on Cypriots, usually raising a contribution of about £60,000 a year. In order to achieve this, the budget for public works was drastically pared and much ill feeling was caused. Winston Churchill was one of those who spoke in condemnation of the tribute in the early years of this century, contending that taxes raised in Cyprus should be used solely to benefit Cypriots:

> . . . the fact stares me none the less in the face that we have no right whatever, except by 'force majeure', to take a penny of the Cyprus tribute to relieve us from our own just obligations, however unfortunately contracted. There is scarcely any spectacle more detestable than the oppression of a small community by a Great Power for the purposes of pecuniary profit; and that is, in fact, the spectacle which our financial treatment indisputably presents. . . . an improvement upon Turkish standards is not a sufficient or suitable defence for British policy.

The tribute ceased in 1914 when Turkey entered the Great War on the side of the Central Powers and Britain annexed Cyprus, thus giving the inhabitants British citizenship for the first time. Turkey formally renounced her rights to the island at the Treaty of Sevres on 10 August 1920, further ratified by the Treaty of Lausanne in July 1923, although two more years passed before Cyprus became a Crown Colony.

A grey column in Ataturk Square, which the Venetians probably took from the ruins of Salamis, was once surmounted by a lion of St Mark. Venetian coats of arms adorn the base. The Turks overturned it in 1570, although the Archduke found it standing under a plum tree clustered with crows. In 1915 it was set up in its present position, surmounted by a ball of marble in place of the lion. The square is now dominated by a modern hotel, the Seray Palace, which is the only building of any great height in the entire Turkish sector of the city. Behind lies an old mosque, the Seray Onou, and the post office, once the telegraph office at the terminal of the cable to Syria and Constantinople.

We turned off to the east, into the maze of narrow streets which form the market, past a row of cobbler's shops where the calf-length Cypriot hunting boots were sold for five or six pounds, past barrows of artichokes, cauliflowers and apples. The streets were crowded with shoppers, while the occasional army jeep forced its way through on the horn. In the covered market we bought spicy sausages, cheese, herbs for cooking, and *loukoumi*. The butchers' stalls were running with gore from the morning's dismembering of goats. A pile of blood-stained skulls, complete with horns, were left, such as are nailed up over the doorways in the villages for good luck. From an old man in a dark, fragrant shop where a hundred different kinds of coffee were stored, I bought a little bag of the finely ground powder, carefully measured out on ancient scales. He smiled warmly, expressed his pleasure at seeing an Englishman, and overcharged.

In this quarter there are two ancient caravanserais, for men came from distant parts of the island to the bazaars of Nicosia. The Kumarjilar Khan, the Inn of the Gamblers, is now the home of the Antiquities Department. The Beuyuk Khan, the Great Inn, opened for business the year after the Turkish conquest, and continued to care for travellers and their animals until the British took it over in the nineteenth century and made it into Nicosia's central prison. (The Turks had used two courtyards of the Seray as a prison, where chained criminals from many of the Sultan's provinces were kept and used for public works as needed.)

We found the Great Inn in the throes of restoration, but through the rubble and scaffolding the bones of a remarkable building could be seen. On entering through an arched gateway, high and wide enough for a loaded camel, we found ourselves in a paved courtyard, surrounded by colonnades supporting two storeys of shaded ambulatories. The rooms which give off these pleasant arcades are each large enough to house a merchant, his goods and his servants. In winter they were heated by a fireplace in the corner, each with its own curious octagonal chimney. Part of the lower cloister had been walled up during the building's use as a prison, leaving only heavily barred windows and doors, but the builders were now in the process of removing these modern additions, and all would soon be restored to the condition of the sixteenth century. In the centre of the courtyard stands a *mesdjid*, a little domed and pillared chapel with a fountain, where travellers might wash and pray. The Khan is altogether a tribute to the refined and civilised life to which the Ottoman Turks at their best aspired, a building kind to both body and spirit.

Close by in Mousa Orfan Bey Street stands the medieval Church of St George of the Latins, now sunk below the level of the pavement and used as a Turkish bath for centuries. It is known as the Beuyuk Hamam, the Great Bath, and according to the Archduke Louis was one of two in Nicosia belonging to the government (there were also six privately owned baths). Men used the bath in the morning; on Monday and Thursday afternoons it was reserved for Turkish women, on Tuesdays and Saturdays for Greeks. Membership cost two Turkish pounds a month, and by prior arrangement with the manager one might arrange to reserve the whole bath for one's own family on certain days. The main hot-air room of this pleasantly civilised establishment had an octagonal water tank with divans along the walls; there were other chambers with marble seats, cupolas and tanks of fresh water, while light was admitted by bell-shaped glass skylights. Undoubtedly the Turks acquired their passion for bathing from the Byzantines when they captured Constantinople, and so the tradition of the Roman bath lives on.

But our eyes were constantly drawn by the sight, over the rooftops, of the twin minarets of the Selimye Mosque, the greatest building in old Nicosia. Its history is very like that of the Latin Cathedral of Famagusta. Building commenced in 1209 under the Parisian Archbishop Thierry, at the instigation of Henry I's wife, Queen Alice of Champagne. The services of the finest French masons were obtained to shape the soaring pillars and arches and the fretted traceries of the windows above the parvis, so that it has been compared to the cathedrals at Chartres and Rheims. Here the Lusignan kings received the Crown of Cyprus, before going on to Famagusta to be consecrated as Kings of Jerusalem and Armenia. The Cathedral of St Sophia was plundered by the Genoese in 1373, and again by the Mamelukes in 1426, and on several occasions it was repaired after severe earthquake damage. But its use as a place of Catholic Christian worship came to an end with the Turkish capture of Nicosia in 1570.

Selim II's decision to invade Cyprus, on the face of it a logical enough project for the son of the conquering Suleiman the Magnificent, was undertaken in curious circumstances. Selim, known as the Sot or the Drunkard, was the first of the degenerate Sultans. It is a remarkable but irrefutable fact that the first ten Ottoman Sultans, those who built the great Empire, were without exception competent and energetic rulers. They led their armies personally, combined military prowess with skilled statesmanship and manifested a love for the arts. All these qualities were combined in Suleiman, who loved hunting and gardens, wrote poetry, devised new laws and built mosques, aqueducts and castles. He engaged the pirate Barbarossa to terrorise the seas with the Imperial Fleet, led his warriors to take Belgrade and Rhodes, and narrowly failed to capture Vienna. The decline which set in towards the end of his life has been variously ascribed to the influence of his Russian wife, Roxelana, the first of a number of powerful Sultanas to wield enormous power from the harem, his dangerous practice of allowing subordinates freedom to enrich themselves at the expense of the state, and the cumulatively corrupting effect of the luxuries of Constantinople on the hardy and ascetic Turkish race. Whatever the reason, the death of Suleiman represented the closing of a chapter, and of the 26 Sultans who followed until the twentieth century and the foundation of the Republic, scarcely one possessed the strength of character required of a ruler. Their vices ranged from indolence, through dissoluteness and extravagance to capricious cruelty and morbid paranoia. Several were actually dangerous madmen. The change is so remarkable that it has been suggested that Suleiman's line was broken, and that Selim was in fact the son of Ibrahim, a Greek slave who became Suleiman's boon companion and Grand Vizier of the Empire.

Selim the Drunkard was undoubtedly fond of Cyprus wine, the sweet Commandaria which had been exported since the time of the Crusaders. It is recorded that he was constantly in a drunken state; the Sultan's example so corrupted the rest of Constantinople that even the *Mufti* felt unable to condemn this breach of Koranic Law, and the habit of drinking alcohol became widespread. It is often said that Selim was persuaded to the expedition against Cyprus with the idea that he might own the source of his favourite tipple; also that he was fond of the island's falcons, which, like those of Candia, were famous.

But another influence was at work on the Sultan. Selim took little personal interest in the administration of the world's greatest empire; this was the beginning of the age of the Grand Viziers, who, provided they could indulge the whims of their Sultans, wielded almost limitless power on their own account. Mahemet Sokolli, who had been Suleiman's last Grand Vizier, had served Selim well, leading the armies and fulfilling all the roles which an earlier Sultan would have undertaken for himself. Selim, who cared nothing for war or any other thing except self-indulgence, was quite content for this state of affairs to continue. Sokolli, however, had a rival for the Sultan's ear.

Joao Miques, or Joseph Nasi as he was later known, was born in Portugal of a rich Jewish family which had been expelled from Spain in 1492 by Ferdinand and Isabella. Rather than accept enforced conversion to Christianity, he fled from Portugal with his beloved aunt, Gracia de Mendesia, first to the Low Countries and then to Lyons, where they founded a bank, only to have it confiscated by their Christian persecutors. They fared no better in Venice, where Gracia was insulted and imprisoned for her faith. A final refuge was found in Constantinople, where a large colony of Spanish Jews had been established, refugees from Christian intolerance who were kindly treated by the Turks. Many had risen to positions of influence within the court.

Nasi was introduced to Selim some years before he ascended the throne. Selim was Suleiman's second son and only became the heir to the throne due to the machinations of Roxelana, his mother. She poisoned Suleiman's mind against Mustapha, his first-born, with suggestions of treachery, so the Sultan had Mustapha strangled in his royal tent. At this time Nasi espoused Selim's cause and worked as a faithful agent to advance his master's chances of obtaining the throne. When Selim became Sultan in 1566, Nasi was rewarded with a series of honours and high offices and was eventually created Duke of Naxos and Prince of the Cyclades in recognition of his efforts.

Nasi had sworn to take vengeance against Venice for the injury done to his aunt. To deprive the Serene Republic of one of its most prized colonies seemed to him to be fitting justice, and it was he who planned the attack on Cyprus and solicited the Sultan's support for the scheme. He also told Selim that he had just received information that Venice's great powder magazine had been destroyed in an accidental explosion. Mahemet Sokolli, the Grand Vizier, was opposed to the idea, but Selim – whether for the wine, or for the hawks, or simply in a mood of spitefulness – overruled him for once, and an army and invasion fleet were prepared.

Lala Mustapha Pasha landed unopposed at Limassol and burned that city, together with the villages of the surrounding countryside. There were a number of 'Rumelians' (Greeks) with his army, and indeed it is said that a Greek Cypriot priest guided him to Nicosia, which he was to take with much less difficulty than he later experienced at Famagusta. Within the walls of the city were 76,000, of whom only 11,000 were fighting men. These included 1,500 Italian mercenaries, many of them sick, 3,000 Cypriot militia, 2,600 armed citizens, 2,100 Cypriots paid to fight by the state, or the retainers of private persons, 1,000 'gentlemen adventurers', 500 Albanian cavalry, 200 Albanian infantry, 200 Cypriot artillerymen and 60 Italian artillerymen. Against these were ranged Mustapha Pasha's experienced army of 100,000 of whom half were professionals.

According to Giacomo Diedo, amidst the doom-laden atmosphere of the siege by this huge army, the Latin Bishop of Paphos, truly a courageous man:

> . . . preached at length to the nobles and a large concourse of people assembled in the Church of S. Sophia, pointing out the greatness of their danger, but also the confidence, which each one should repose in the omnipotent hand of God, of being able to resist the fury of the barbarians, who sought in the conquest of their strongholds to profane their altars, trample down their religion and turn their churches into foul dens of a false faith. He assured them of the earnest resolve of the Senate to give the island efficient help: he pictured to them the preparation which the princes of Christendom were making for the common cause, and finally exhorting all to be constant, he offered himself as the companion of their dangers, and joined his prayers to theirs, that God might bless their arms with victory, and spread weakness and confusion among their enemies.
>
> All were moved by the bishop's discourse, and there was not a man who did not promise to fight to the death.

> (Trs. C.D. Cobham, *Excerpta Cypria*)

Courageous sorties were made by the Venetian captains Podocataro and Andrea Speglio, and also by the Albanian Andrea Cortese, who gained the admiration of the Turks for his fearlessness before they captured and beheaded him. There were even moments of light relief, such as the day the Turks drove a donkey up to the ramparts, shouting, 'Don't hurt the poor ass, it can do you no harm.' In the south of the city, within the Costanza Bastion, stands the Mosque of Bayraktar, the Standard-Bearer, marking the spot where this Turkish hero died on the wall. It was at the next bastion, Podocatoro in the southeast, that the Turks finally gained entry after seven weeks, the sentries having fallen asleep with exhaustion. From here they flooded into the streets of the city.

The sack which followed lasted for six days. According to the Venetian Paolo Paruta:

> The Turks ran without any order or discipline all over the city, plundering the houses, destroying the churches, dishonouring matrons, violating virgins, and putting all to the sword, without any distinction either of sex, age or condition. So as the Turks slew that day above 20,000 persons; and those whose lives were spared by the cruel army, rather for their greater punishment, than out of any charity, were tied in chains, dragged over the dead carcases of their parents and friends, and carried away prisoners.

> (Trs. C.D. Cobham, *Excerpta Cypria*)

The Superior of the Dominican Convent, Angelo Calepio, also lived through the slaughter to tell his harrowing story:

> And now indeed that terrible roar of artillery and musketry ceased to thunder in our ears, but the change was a sad and mournful one, for on every side we heard nothing but the ceaseless wailing of poor women parted from their husbands, the shrieks of children torn from their mothers' arms . . . The victors kept cutting off the heads of old women; many of them as they marched along to prove their swords split open the heads of men who had already surrendered. Did a prisoner try to escape, he was caught up and his legs cut off, and as long as any life was left in him every Janissary who passed had a cut at him.
>
> Among the slain were Lodovico Podocatoro, and Lucretia Calepio, my mother, whose head they cut off on her serving maid's lap. They tore infants in swaddling clothes from their mothers' breasts, dashed some down on the ground, others by the feet against a wall: of whom I could baptise only one.

(Trs. C.D. Cobham, Excerpta Cypria)

The siege and subsequent massacre took place during a summer heat wave which must have intensified the horrors. Then came the dividing of the spoil. According to Calepio:

> As they themselves owned, they enriched themselves to such an extent that never since the sack of Constantinople, had they won such a treasure, as well of things sacred, as those of common use . . .
>
> The day after the capture of the city was held a general bazaar or auction of the spoil. First were sold the good-looking youths and pretty girls, the buyers taking no thought or count of their noble birth, but only of the beauty of their faces. The rest of the men were sold at extremely low prices, though something more was paid for those who were fit for work in the galleys. In the same day they made a division of the spoil and I wondered much to see them sell some most precious gem for a very small sum. A thing worth a hundred sequins they gave for four: they knew as little about pearls and precious stones as pigs do: anyone who had some little knowledge bought valuable objects for next to nothing, and made a fortune.

(Trs. C.D. Cobham, Excerpta Cypria)

Fra Calepio, who was born in Nicosia, had lost most of his friends, and his own mother had been beheaded. He himself, a condemned prisoner, would very likely die in the galleys. Yet despite all these woes, his Venetian respect for wealth and the virtues of careful

167

business was plainly outraged by the behaviour of this barbaric race, whose talents lay in war-making rather than trade.

Later, he reported, a ship was filled with the handsomest youths and girls as a personal present for the Sultan. However, as it stood out to sea from the coast of Cyprus, there was a tremendous explosion and it sank with all hands. Maria Sinclitiki, a noble Cypriot lady, preferred death to dishonour and fired the powder magazine, thus depriving Selim of his entire cargo of beauty. Selim himself lived for only three years to enjoy his island prize. Drunk on Cyprus Commandaria, he slipped while entering his bath and broke his skull on the marble floor.

In Nicosia, the Turks had dragged the Christians' very bones from their graves and scattered them in a rage around the streets. Even in St Sophia the tombs were opened, although a few of the stones remain in a side chapel. Then the religious statues and pictures were removed and the two incongruous minarets were added, and for 400 years the great church has been dedicated to Islam.

Removing our shoes, we entered the whitewashed nave. Nearly all the decorations and stained glass have been removed in accordance with Islamic practice, which forbids representation of the human figure. According to Martoni, in the fourteenth century the vault was painted in blue with gold stars. Now, denuded of all superfluous additions, the essential bones of the building were revealed. Parts of the cathedral are older than the whole; the huge drum columns which support the nave have Byzantine capitals, and the pillars in the apse are thought to have come from Salamis. The whole orientation of the building has been changed, for the beautiful carpets were laid diagonally, facing with the prayer platform towards the Holy City. A venerable grandfather clock, its green face marked with Arabic symbols, ticked slowly to Mecca time. The light from the chandeliers illuminated the Koranic inscriptions hung on the walls and picked out, here and there, a kneeling figure on the rich carpet, lips moving silently in prayer.

The beautiful Latin Church of St Nicholas, which stands beside the Selimye Mosque, was locked. The Orthodox Greeks of Nicosia used it as a cathedral during the Venetian period, but under the Turks it gradually fell into ruin, a process accelerated by earthquakes. For many years it became a cloth market and grain store, hence its Persian name: the Bedestan, or Covered Market.

We made our way west, through the alleys around Paphos Street, once a thriving artery but now full of ruined, deserted houses. We were very close to the Green Line, where no one wants to live. The walls began to show the scars of the skirmishes which took place here in years gone by. Once the barrier between the communities was a makeshift one: piles of refuse and rubble, overturned cars, pieces of old furniture. Now it is wired like the Berlin Wall at the height of the cold war. But nevertheless there was life among these tumble-down buildings under the rust-tipped minaret of the Tourounjilou Mosque. These had become the streets of the metal workers and car repairers, all crowded together in oriental fashion. In lock-up garages and cavernous workshops, excavated under the empty houses, oxyacetylene torches flared and sparked, drills shrieked and pneumatic chisels vibrated as the metal of ancient vehicles was twisted and tortured back into shape. In a courtyard shaded by a palm tree, the dust clogged with old sump oil, a man in tattered overalls was respraying the gutted body of a Triumph TR6 sports car.

There were always traders and workshops along the line of Paphos and Hermes Streets. Archduke Louis Salvator listed a total of 23 different bazaars in the city: the Bazaar of Manufactures, which sold all kinds of imported goods; the Tailors' Bazaar; the Bazaar of Calico, Rugs and Hides; three separate Shoemakers' Bazaars, specialising variously in European shoes, Cypriot peasant boots and Turkish slippers; the Bazaar of Yarns; the Cabinet-Makers' Bazaar; the Carriages Bazaar, which developed into the modern car repairers; three bazaars for items made of copper, silver or iron; the bazaars for earthenware and haberdashery; Taverns; Vegetables and Meat; Fish; the Halva Bazaar, which sold sweetmeats; the Women's Bazaar, which sold all kinds of needlework and clothes, jewellery, cakes and sweets; bazaars for the sale of cotton, flour, wheat and barley, and finally mules. In addition there were small groups of shops specialising in blankets, tin plate, tobacco, coffee, saddlery and firearms.

At intervals, above walls whose plaster was pockmarked with bullet holes, the United Nations flag could be seen flying on an observation tower. At one point we could see a church on the skyline (it must have been Ayia Phaneromeni), the bells intact in the campanile. Later we were to hear the eerie sound of the church bells ringing in the Christian part of the city. Near the Paphos Gate the sentries became very apparent, with rolls of barbed wire blocking side steets. The Catholic Church of the Holy Cross, financed at the turn of the century by Queen Maria Christina of Spain, was out of bounds, although we later gained access from the Greek side. Similarly, the ruined Armenian Church of Sourp Asdouadzadzin, the Blessed Virgin, once a Benedictine convent, was out of reach behind the wire. In 1965 the Turks bored a tunnel under the barrier here, which eventually collapsed during a rain storm and was sealed by the UN.

Deflected by the wire, we turned north along Tenzimat Street, the Green Line now on our left, marked by signs warning against photography or attempting to look across. All the houses in the street, with one exception, were empty, crumbled plaster exposing the mud-brick beneath, unpainted wooden shutters, and windows piled with sandbags to protect the militia who once fought from them. Here and there a square hole had been cut for a sniper's periscope. The tiles were beginning to break from the edges of the flat roofs, and the overhanging balconies were sagging. The single, stubborn old lady who remained smiled at us as we walked past, and continued watering the geraniums growing in tins around her front door.

The Line itself consisted of nothing more than a solid row of oil drums, banked up above head height, packed with earth and topped off in some places with French marigolds. Every so often a sniper's loophole had been contrived by driving an open-ended wooden box completely through a drum, so that one could look out across the moat to the huge Ledra Palace Hotel, once a haunt of the journalists who came to report on the troubles, and now occupied by the UN. Here the Turkish sentries stand on the bastions in full view of the Greeks in the streets below, though a wary peace has reigned for some years. Occasionally there is an outburst of slogan shouting through megaphones.

In Mufti Ziya Effendi Street stands the Mosque of Arab Ahmed, built over a Christian church whose Lusignan tombs can still be seen in the pavement of the floor. In the graveyard is the tomb of Mehmed Kiamil, a Turkish Cypriot who rose to be Governor of Cyprus and eventually, as a very old man, the Grand Vizier of the Ottoman Empire. He was unfortunate enough to hold this position during the turbulent time following the Young Turks' deposition of Abdul Hamid and the disasters of the Balkan Wars. On 23 January 1913 he was presiding over the peace conference, about to cede Adrianople to the Balkan Alliance, whose armies had reached the Chatalja Lines outside Constantinople, when gunshots and shouting were heard outside the chamber. The Turkish Minister of War went to the door and was shot on the threshold as the Young Turk, Enver Bey, burst into the chamber with a band of supporters and held a revolver against Kiamil Pasha's chest, forcing him to resign. The armistice thus effectively sabotaged, Enva led a purged army into a renewed attack across the Chatalja Lines and saved Adrianople for Turkey. Poor Kiamil died the same year and was buried in his native Cyprus. He had always been a good friend to Britain, and a memorial was erected in 1927 by Sir Ronald Storrs, who distinguished himself as one of the more enlightened governors of the island. The Mosque of Arab Ahmed possesses a famour relic: a hair from the beard of the Prophet, which is revealed to the faithful with due cermony every year.

We ate a good lunch of egg, onion and meat pilaf with spinach, washed down with Turkish beer. The restaurant was crowded with farmers and their wives, for it was Friday and the country people had come into town for the market. Many, we noticed, wore a paper badge pinned to their lapel, indicating that a donation had been made to charity that day. Once it had been a paper flower, like an English poppy or Alexandra rose, and the badges are still called rosettes, but now they are no more than simple labels with the name of the charity.

In the quiet siesta hours of the mid-afternoon, we found ourselves in a backwater of ancient dusty streets behind the Selimye Mosque. There was no traffic here, and occasional groups of children played hopscotch undisturbed on the corners. In places, the wooden balconies of the old houses almost met overhead. Here stands the little domed library given by the reforming Sultan Mahmud II, the son of Aimée Dubucq de Rivery of Martinique, who was captured by Algerian corsairs and presented by the Bey of Algiers to Abdul Hamid I. The Sultana Aimée, whose beloved cousin Josephine became the wife of Napoleon Bonaparte, spent the rest of her life in the harem but never lost her love of France, which she transmitted to her son. Mahmud, the one possible exception to the long line of 'degenerate' Sultans, brought French doctors to Constantinople and instituted a quarantine system, founded newspapers and discarded the spectacular Turkish costume of kaftans and turbans. He lived the relatively modest life of a French gentleman, although he was overfond of good champagne, and encouraged Turkish students to study in Europe. Perhaps his greatest achievement was the bloody subjugation of the rebellious Janissary corps, while his greatest disappointment was the loss of Greece from the Empire. The little library he endowed in Nicosia contains Turkish, Arabic and Persian manuscripts, and there was once a school where boys studied the Koran. We found the Lapidary Museum, where odd examples of the mason's skill have been saved from demolition, to be locked for the afternoon, and so came to the Mosque of Haydar Pasha. This is another fourteenth-century Gothic church, once dedicated to St Catherine, though little remains of the interior.

On the corner of Haydar Pasha Street I asked some children if they could show us Kitchener's house, but perhaps not surprisingly this meant nothing to them. Captain Horatio Herbert Kitchener of the Royal Engineers, then a young man of 28, came to Cyprus in the first year of British rule, charged with conducting the first trigonometrical survey of the island. His one-inch-to-the-mile map (now a great rarity and very valuable) was published in 1885. He spent much of his time roaming the forests and mountains with mules and a bell tent, but from 1880 to 1883 the man who would later become Field Marshall Lord Kitchener of Khartoum had maintained a small house here on Haydar Pasha Street.

Halfway down the street, I put my head through the open door of a shop to ask for directions. The interior was dark and spacious: a sort of chandlery, filled with open sacks of rice and grain. A middle-aged man, half asleep, was nodding on a chair by the counter.

'Lord Kitchener's house? Of course. I can show you, but you cannot go very close. Come outside.'

He led the way out into the sunlight, and stood with his hands in his pockets looking down the road. I noticed for the first time that two armed sentries stood at the far end. We had not realised that the Green Line was so close.

'I don't want to point, not with the soldiers there. But do you see the steps on the right near where they are standing? That is the house. Before you go, you can walk a little further down to look from the outside. But come into my shop first; I speak English so rarely now. My name is Hizber Hikmet. Welcome. I have nothing to offer you . . . but here, have some of these.' He virtually forced a handful of boiled sweets on each of us.

'I am very sorry,' I said, aware of the Mediterranean etiquette which forbids social calls during the early afternoon. 'We are disturbing your rest.'

'Not at all, my dear; I am a little tired today, but my shop is open. I have had my lunch and my coffee, praise be to God. This is relaxation, this is pleasure. You must forgive me, my English is a little out of practice, although I was educated at the English school here. I was in Kitchener House in fact. Let's see, I left in 1952, when Mr Jackson was the headmaster. And I have many relatives in England. My elder son went to Loughborough University; I came to see him invested with his degree. I have a niece who is married to a Member of Parliament, for . . .' He scratched his head trying to remember the London constituency, before giving the name of a Conservative backbencher.

'Is it difficult for you, with your business so close to the Line?'

'Not a shot been fired since 1974. My great-grandfather founded this business, in what is now the Greek sector. We moved here in 1964, in my father's time, for safety. Now my brother and I are partners.'

Above the counter we could see portraits of the father, the grandfather and the venerable founder. It really was a remarkable shop. Apart from the grain and pulses, there were sacks of all kinds of herbs and spices, coriander, cumin and cinnamon, in such quantities that it seemed that a further generation would be required to sell the present stock. On the walls were hung coils of rope and twine, cowbells and mule harness. There were shelves of cigarettes, tinned tomatoes and candles. A man came in to buy rat traps.

'We have terrible trouble with rats here,' confided Mr Hikmet. 'I can't tell you the damage they cause.'

172

An old lady came through the door and wished us good day, gossiping with Mr Hikmet as he weighed out cannelloni beans and dried maize for her. I asked about the *tespi*, the Turkish rosaries hanging from hooks along one shelf. He reached up with a long rod and brought one down to show us.

'There are 99 beads, for the 99 names of God, three little stops – can you see? 33 beads between each. We use the Arabic word, *souphan*, to greet Allah.' His eyes suddenly sparkled with mischief. 'Of course you call Him God, but the true name, the international name, is Allah.'

'The international name?'

'Of course, my dear. Every man, woman and child on this earth sounds His name with every breath. All-ah. All-ah.' He chuckled at his little joke. 'Isn't this nice? It is so pleasant for me to speak English. I listen each day to the BBC World Service. That is a wonderful thing.'

'Yes, but did you know that the British Government is proposing to cut the service down? They say it is costing too much.'

Mr Hikmet looked scandalised.

'My goodness, it's worth any price. How terrible. Now tell me where you have been in Cyprus; what are your plans?'

We spread the maps on the counter and discussed routes and projects. He was determined that we should miss nothing, and soon we had taken down pages of notes and suggestions. I began to think of a hundred and one questions to ask him. For instance, what was the origin of the TMT symbol, the wolf howling at a crescent moon, which we saw in the square of many villages?

'When we formed our organisation of fighters, for defence you understand, and to oppose the Greeks fighting for *enosis*, the grey wolf was chosen because of an old legend of our people. They say that when the Turks first came out of Central Asia, an old grey wolf pointed out the way to the new lands of the West. It's only a story.' Mr Hikmet was plainly embarrassed by the association with the fascist Grey Wolf Party of the mainland. 'I don't believe in it myself. I sometimes think that such things are best forgotten in times like these.'

At the back of his shop, Mr Hikmet owned an enclosed yard, as parking space for a dozen or so of the village buses which came daily into the city.

'They come very early,' he said. 'Some of them leave at five or six o'clock in the morning. The drivers pay me a small rent for parking here during the day. Most of them work in the market. Then they will drive their passengers back to the village this afternoon. This one is being repaired. The owner is looking for another axle.'

The bus looked like a stranded leviathan, propped up on baulks of timber, with the rear springs hanging forlornly. Mr Hikmet showed us his pride and joy, an Austin Metro newly shipped from England.

'But we don't use it on the bad roads over the mountains. When we go for a picnic, we take our old Morris Minor.

'I wish my wife could meet you, but she is out this afternoon with my younger son. He goes to school in France, at Grenoble, but he is visiting us at the moment.'

I bought the rosary. Mr Hikmet wished to make it a present, but we told him that he had been more than generous with his time already, and after all, business was business. He noticed some Greek bank notes in my wallet.

'What do you have there?'

'Drachmas. We go to Greece sometimes.'

'Of course. What is the exchange rate now?'

I told him to the best of my knowledge.

'I too have been to Greece,' he said quietly, 'to see some friends.'

'Does the present situation make you feel cut off?' I asked him. 'I mean with the Line just at the bottom of the street.'

'Oh no, *taksim*, partition, was the only way in which we could live in peace. One could wish it otherwise; I had friends among the Greeks once. But as things were – what else could we do? To tell the truth, I often forget that the Line is there now . . . Well, my dears, come and see me again soon. You are always welcome at my shop.'

The Beuyuk Khan, the 'Great Inn' or caravanserai of
Turkish Nicosia

CHAPTER ELEVEN

BARBARISM

A pair of cheerful boys were washing their feet in the ritual fountain outside the Yeni Jami, once a medieval church and now known as the New Mosque because it was rebuilt during the eighteenth century. According to the Archduke Louis Salvator, this was made necessary because a Pasha dreamed that treasure was buried beneath the floor, and subsequently tore the old mosque almost to pieces in searching for it. The devout Turks of Nicosia complained to the Sultan about this impious behaviour, and the Pasha was sentenced to death. All the surrounding area was once a graveyard and one or two tombs are still visible. It appeared that prayers were about to begin, and as we hovered uncertainly on the threshold one of the priests caught sight of us. He came forward with a warm smile and shook our hands, patting the boys on the head. He was a youngish man, charming and cultured.

'My dear sir and madam, please come in to see us.'

'My wife does not offend?'

'Of course not. Please come inside.'

We slipped off our shoes and followed him.

'Ladies are welcome in the mosque. They come to worship on Fridays. Only they pray here, on this dais with the curtains drawn so that ladies and gentlemen cannot see one another. The reason is very simple; when one is praying one must have total concentration, total devotion to Allah. There must be no distraction and . . . well, we are all human, are we not?' He beamed over his spectacles.

The custom of separating the sexes by a screen was by no means confined to the mosque; nineteenth-century travellers remarked that the Greek women prayed in a latticed gallery with a separate entrance to the church, and the same practice was followed in Crete and other Orthodox lands within the Ottoman Empire.

'Let me introduce you to the *hodja*.' A wizened little man with one gold tooth smiled, and pumped my hand vigorously. 'You must excuse him, he doesn't speak English and he's rather deaf. And this is the *muezzin*. What you call a singer, a chr . . . chor . . .'

175

'A chorister?'

'Ah yes, that is what I meaned to say. In a few minutes he will give the call to prayer.'

'If I may ask, a *hodja* is a village priest, a parish priest?'

'Yes, there is a *hodja* for every mosque.'

'And an *imam*. Is that position perhaps equivalent to a bishop?'

'Yes, you could say so. Or a Catholic monsignor would be a better example. I myself am actually an *imam*,' he added modestly.

The days of climbing the minaret are over; the *muezzin* switched on his microphone in preparation. We walked to the door and looked up at the speakers, high in the tower.

'It's new,' said the *imam*. 'The old minaret was destroyed by a bomb in 1974. Come and visit us again. God be with you.'

* * * *

We collected our car from the Ledra Palace checkpoint. A black Mercedes had just arrived at the barrier from the Greek sector. Turkish police officers were checking documents and talking to the occupants. We turned around and drove north into the suburb of Kumsal. Here and there, around the perimeter of the city, we had seen rusty yellow signs, pointing to the 'Museum of Barbarism'. Some sort of Chamber of Horrors, I wondered idly, thinking of Madame Tussaud's. No, of course not; it must be political propaganda of some kind – Greek atrocities, no doubt. But we felt that we should go and look.

In a leafy suburban avenue, not far from the Ministry of Tourism and Culture, we came to an ordinary bungalow, with a drive and a little fenced garden, exactly like every other in the road. A discreet notice announced it to be the Museum of Barbarism. The front door of the house was open and the guardian, a grey-haired, elderly man with a strangely distant look about his eyes, was sauntering in the garden. He glanced at us with a certain curiosity, but said nothing. No one else was there.

A row of photographs was displayed on each wall of the little hall. The first showed the disembowelled corpse of a small child. We hurriedly bundled the boys back to the car to read their books before returning. Pictures of mass exhumations: tangled bodies of massacred Turks being taken from the ground by men in disinfected masks. Dimly remembered pictures from the newspapers of 22 years before were once more brought forcibly into focus. The ungainly, dummy-like appearance of murdered men, midriffs bare, laid on the concrete for the harsh black and white photographs of newspapermen. The intolerable squalor and hopelessness of the refugee camps, concentrating on the suffering of the very young and the very old.

The uneasy truce between the two races in Cyprus which the imposed constitution of 1960 had brought lasted for a little over three years. This constitution has been endlessly argued over by both factions ever since, but the essential problem of the new Republic was that the Turkish Vice-President, elected by and representing only 20 per cent of the population, held a power of veto on defence, foreign affairs and security. This the Greeks found intolerable, and Makarios attempted to revise the constitution by abandoning the powers of veto, providing for the election of the Greek President and Turkish Vice-President by all the members of the House of Representatives rather than by the separate races, together with the withdrawal of certain advantages which Turkish Cypriots enjoyed in the civil service and armed forces. (The National Guard, for instance, had been recruited on a basis of 60:40 in favour of the Greeks; this was now to be changed to 80:20, in accordance with the true ratio of the populations.) The Greek proposals produced an atmosphere of great tension, which may have been heightened by the fact that both Greece and Turkey, two of the original three guarantors of the constitution, were undergoing their own political crises at the time.

The feared explosion of violence occurred at 2.15 a.m. on 21 December 1963, in the centre of the old city. Two cars containing Turks were stopped in Hermes Street by Greek police who asked for the occupants' identity cards. (According to the Turkish version, the cars were stopped illegally by armed Greek youths, the police arriving shortly afterwards.) The Turks resisted and the Greek police opened fire, killing two and wounding others. Firing began all over the city, intermittently at first, then becoming heavier as both sides occupied strategic positions and barricaded themselves into their respective quarters. According to the Turks, automatic weapons were issued to the Greek police, though not to the Turkish contingent. Certainly policemen and ex-EOKA members were in the forefront of the fighting. By 23 December there was also shooting in Larnaca, while in Nicosia the Greek church bells were tolling continuously, and automatic fire could be heard from all quarters. The Turks claim that their wounded were refused transfusions by the Government Hospital. On the 24th, Christmas Eve, Makarios and Dr Fazil Kutchuk, the Turkish Vice-President, met for the last time in an atmosphere of despair. It seemed that forces were unleashed which neither man had the power to control.

The Museum of Barbarism exposed every Greek atrocity to maximum effect; no Turkish atrocity was mentioned. Yet such evidence as was given would be hard to refute. Particular prominence was given to the family of a major in the Turkish contingent of the National Guard, murdered while he was away on duty on Christmas Eve 1963.

Family photographs were displayed above cases of blood-stained clothing and towels, together with the account of Hasan Yusuf Gudum, an eyewitness:

On the night of the 24th December, 1963, my wife Feride Hasan and I were paying a visit to the family of Major Dr Nihat Ilhan. Our neighbours Mrs Ayshe of Mora, her daughter Ishin and Mrs Ayshe's sister Norber were also with us. We were all sitting having supper. All of a sudden bullets from the Pedieos River direction started to riddle the house, sounding like heavy rain. Thinking that the dining room where we were sitting was dangerous, we ran to the bathroom and toilet which we thought would be safer. Altogether we were nine persons. We all hid in the bathroom except my wife who took refuge in the toilet. We waited in fear. Mrs Ilhan, the wife of Major Doctor, was standing in the bath with her three children Murat, Kutsi and Hakan in her arms. Suddenly with a great noise we heard the front door open. Greeks had come in and were combing every corner of the house with their machine gun bullets. During these moments I heard voices saying, in Greek, 'You want Taksim eh!' and then bullets started flying in the bathroom. Mrs Ilhan and her children fell into the bath. They were shot. At this moment the Greeks, who broke into the bathroom, emptied their guns on us again. I heard one of the Major's children moan, then I fainted.

When I came to myself 2 or 3 hours later, I saw Mrs Ilhan and her three children lying dead in the bath. I and the rest of the neighbours in the bathroom were all seriously wounded. But what had happened to my wife? Then I remembered and immediately ran to the toilet, where, in the doorway, I saw her body. She was brutally murdered.

In the street amidst the sound of shots I heard voices crying 'Help, help. Is there no-one to save us.' I became terrified. I thought that if the Greeks came again and found that I was not dead they would kill me. So I ran to the bed-room and hid myself under the double-bed.

An hour passed by. In the distance I could still hear shots. My mouth was dry, so I came out from under the bed and drank some water. Then I put some sweets in my pocket and went back to the bathroom, which was exactly as I had left it an hour ago. There I offered sweets to Mrs Ayshe, her daughter and Mrs Norber who were all wounded.

We waited in the bathroom until 5 o'clock in the morning. I thought morning would never come. We were all wounded and needed to be taken to hospital. Finally, as we could walk, Mrs Norber and I went out into the street hoping to find help, and walked as far as Koshkla Chiftlik.

There, we met some people who took us to hospital where we were operated on. When I regained consciousness I said that there were more wounded in the house and they went and brought Mrs Ayshe and her daughter.

After staying three days in the hospital I was sent by plane to Ankara for further treatment. There I have had four months treatment but still I cannot use my arm. On my return to Cyprus Greeks arrested me at the Airport.

All I have related to you above I told the Greeks during my detention. They then released me.

It has the ring of truth. But the international press provided confirmation:

. . . I saw in a bathroom the bodies of a mother and three infant children murdered because their father was a Turkish officer . . .

(Max Clos, *Le Figaro*, 25–6 January 1964)

We went tonight into the sealed-off Turkish quarter of Nicosia in which 200 to 300 people have been slaughtered in the last five days.

We were the first Western reporters there, and we saw some terrible sights.

In the Kumsal quarter at No. 2 Irfan Bey Sokagi, we made our way into a house whose floors were covered with broken glass. A child's bicycle lay in a corner.

In the bathroom, looking like a group of waxworks, were three children piled on top of their murdered mother.

In a room next to it we glimpsed the body of a woman shot in the head.

This, we were told, was the house of a Turkish Army major whose family had been killed by the mob in the first violence.

Today was five days later, and still they lay there.

The house was one of a row surrounded by gardens and garages not unlike a tidy English suburb.

Now there was an intense and brooding air.

Silence hung over the street, and apart from a few dogs the only living things were two or three unshaven, scowling Turkish policemen carrying rifles.

(Rene MacColl and Daniel McGeachie, *Daily Express*, 28th December 1963)

The Turkish Cypriot army contingent left its barracks and established itself in the north of the city, dominating this district and the road to Kyrenia. Jets from the Turkish mainland made a series of low passes over Nicosia, while the Greek army contingent was similarly deployed in defensive positions. At this stage Britain, the third guaranteeing power, brought troops out from the Sovereign Base Areas ready to intervene between the combatants. On 30 December 1963 the 'Green Line' was established in Nicosia, with the agreement of both Greek and Turkish commanders, patrolled by British soldiers. Attempts to find a political solution continued, but with

179

little result. A conference at Marlborough House the following month, with Duncan Sandys in the chair, ended in deadlock. The Americans suggested a NATO solution, in which the island would be policed by 1,200 American troops and a mixed NATO force of 10,000, while the island remained effectively partitioned. The USSR came out strongly in support of Makarios, claiming that the American scheme was an unwarranted interference with a small nation's sovereignty. Makarios appealed to the United Nations, where Turkey had fewer friends, and at the end of March 1964 a UN force under Lieutenant-General Gyani, an Indian, was sent to the island. Greece began to make arrangements to increase its military contingent to 10,000, which was achieved by mid-summer. Grivas, the EOKA leader, was back on the island to lead the Greek National Guard. The fighting continued, around St Hilarion in April, at the Kokkina enclave in August, while murders and shooting incidents all over the island strained the resources of UNFICYP. At the time of writing, 23 years later, the United Nations peace-keeping force is still fully deployed in Cyprus.

Joan had seen enough. She went outside to join the boys in the car. It had only just dawned on me that this stuffy little house was No. 2 Irfan Bey Street. And here was the dreadful bathroom, the bath stained brown with dried blood and cracked by the bullets, the ceiling still splattered with brain and pieces of scalp. In all that time, nothing had been moved or changed. On the door, visitors had scratched a graffiti of hatred. Did the Turkish Cypriots bring their young people here to see this, or was it only intended for foreigners? Surely such things should be decently covered up, if not forgotten? The atmosphere suddenly seemed unbearably oppressive, and I could have sworn that the whole house smelled of blood.

I walked outside, looking preoccupied without doubt. Just beyond the fence, in the next drive, a man was polishing his car. How could he bear to live next to such a house? The guardian with the strange eyes still said nothing, but he had picked a small bunch of violets from a flower bed, which he now handed to me, whether in thanks for having listened to their story, or in consolation, I could not tell. It was a welcome gesture.

CHAPTER TWELVE

THE MOUNTAINS OF KYRENIA

One evening, in the foothills under Profitis Elias, we rambled among the small villages which look out from the protection of the mountains towards Nicosia. Both Greeks and Turks had once lived in close proximity here. At Krini the sentry boxes which guarded the village until 1974 were deserted, as were those of Pileri, with its ancient aqueduct, cobbled road and new mosque. At Keumurju, where there is a *kephalovryson*, the boys of the village were playing on the grassless football field. All were quiet, rural backwaters set above rich, green pastures, restful after the dust of Nicosia. Towering eucalyptus and plane trees stood against a golden sunset. Our wheels slipping on the muddy track, we climbed up to Aghirda, above the main road to Kyrenia, where it enters the mountain pass under St Hilarion.

The men of this old Turkish stronghold once had a reputation for brigandage, taking advantage of their position to descend on travellers in the pass. But this was most unusual in Cyprus. As early as the seventeenth century, Cornelis Van Bruyn wrote that:

> To all of these advantages you may add that of being able to travel where you will in the island without fear . . . The Greeks of the country are naturally polite and good natured.

(Trs. C.D. Cobham, *Excerpta Cypria*)

This was certainly not true of most of the Levant at that date. Sir Samuel Baker was relieved to find that the revolvers he had brought with him were quite unnecessary. There was a lonely bandit during the British period, one Midas, who used to haunt the forests of the Troodos mountains with an old rifle. He was caught and executed when he came down to Limassol to have a wound dressed by a doctor there. But Midas, it seems, was of Italian origin . . .

★　★　★　★

On the road from Kyrenia to Lapithos, near the London Boy Filling Station, stood a tiny kiosk, a little wooden cabin crammed with sweets, soft drinks, beer, ballpoint pens, cigarettes, cheese, cheap watches, torch batteries and every kind of vegetable. Seven days a week, day or night, it always seemed to be open. We formed the habit of stopping whenever we passed, to buy a bar of chocolate or a packet of biscuits, but mainly to talk to Sadiq Gemayel, who ran the shop with the aid of his wife and various members of his family. Indeed, Sadiq was such a likeable man that hardly a driver passed down the road without at least waving and hooting, if not pulling into the kerb for a gossip.

Sadiq's kiosk did a brisk trade, and he would probably have been a wealthy man if he had not become seriously infected by the insane Cypriot generosity (he was, I believe, originally from the mainland).

'Welcome, welcome! My shop is your shop,' he would invariably say, shaking our hands before filling our arms with oranges and lemons which he would pull from the stall behind him.

'Do you like these? Here, have an aubergine; we grow them here. No, please, accept this from me, it is my pleasure. When you want more lemons, come and pick them from my garden.'

Only once did Sadiq's stock fail us. Steven wanted a rosary like mine, but Sadiq did not keep these. Instead he thrust his hand into his own pocket and brought out a string of the amber-coloured beads, which he poured into Steven's palm.

'Here, you take this; I can get another. My brother has come from Istanbul today and brought this *tespi* with him.'

'Oh but we can't possible accept. A present from your brother!'

'Of course you must. There is no question – look, here he is. You must meet my brother, Mr Gemayel from Istanbul . . . and his wife . . . a lady and gentleman from England, my good friends . . .'

We all shook hands, and as we left they pushed more oranges in through the window of the car, standing in a row to wave to us as we pulled away from the kerb.

'Come again soon,' said Sadiq. 'My shop is your shop.'

$\star$ $\star$ $\star$ $\star$

Corporal Ibrahim Yakar was celebrating.

'It is a very happy day for my family,' he said. 'I have a new cousin, a girl, born this morning. I have just heard.'

'Will there be a party?'

'Oh yes. Tomorrow night. And I think I can get leave. It is a very good day.'

Ibrahim was always a cheerful lad, but on this evening his overflowing high spirits had even the sergeant grinning. (This last individual was always rather suspicious of us, probably because we asked too many questions. I was once tempted into provoking him by asking whether his was a unit of the Turkish NATO army, or of the Turkish Aegean army. He was no doubt preparing a long dossier on our activities.)

Ibrahim told us about Turkish marriage customs on the mainland; how a girl wears one or two bangles on her wrist when engaged. Even today, the women of the Yuruks, the pastoral nomads of Anatolia, are much sought after as brides by men from the settled villages and towns, partly for their beauty and spirit, and partly for their skill in weaving. Of course marriages in the secularised Turkish state no longer take place in the mosque.

Ibrahim planned to come to England next year, to improve his English, and perhaps his prospects.

'Come and stay with us,' we said, and tried to explain what it would be like. We warned that he would find things expensive.

'What, for example, would be the cost of one *oka* of beef?' he wondered, looking at the extensive remains of the *kebabs* he had served to us earlier. Joan gave him an estimated price for 3 pounds of steak in England. I don't think he believed her.

'But there are many things you would like to see. There is even a mosque near our house. One of the first in England, I believe, quite old.'

'Are there so many Muslims among the English?'

'No, but there are many people from Pakistan in our town.'

Ibrahim made a wry face.

'Don't you like Pakistanis? We get on very well with them.'

'Noisy people, noisy people.' And he shook his head.

'But look, Ibrahim, have you actually met anybody from Pakistan?'

'No, but I have heard this. Everyone knows it is true.'

There was no persuading him. It struck me just how rarely one manages to change a Turk's opinion on any subject, by rational argument or any other means – not that they lose their tempers; they are too polite. They simply know best. The same, for that matter, might be said of the Greeks, or even the English.

★   ★   ★   ★

Sometimes, by way of a change, we would leave the car in the shade of the forest under Mount Kornos and walk off up the track, in the general direction of St Hilarion, along the ridge. After the shepherd's hut, with the thornbush enclosure for the animals, we would climb higher, and rarely met another human being all through the day. There would be a tintinnabulation of sheep bells from the lower slopes. Although we seldom saw the shepherds themselves, there would sometimes be signs of their presence: perhaps a bottle of water left strategically by the trunk of a pine tree, or the remains of a fire. For some reason, the paths which they used with their animals had been marked out with borders of stones among the cyclamens, perhaps years before. In one place there was a circular water cistern, donated by the UN in 1969, with a metal ladder for inspecting the top. Then higher up, close under the peak of Kornos, we would leave even the flocks behind, walking through carpets of anemones: pink, violet and white.

In the sunlight of the very early morning, the villages of the southern slopes dreamed far below us. Sometimes the cry of a *muezzin* would penetrate the thin, cool air from the slender pencil of a minaret:

> Arise to prayer,
> Arise to salvation,
> Prayer is better than sleep,
> Arise and praise God.

Once, an army helicopter came nosing along the ridge, flying low and turning its shiny bluebottle windshield to inspect us momentarily, before disappearing round the corner of the mountain. On that day, we scrambled close under a cave in the southern face, staring into the sunlight at the haze hanging over the Mesaoria and the Troodos mountains. The forest road was heavily eroded in the steep places; it would take a tough car to climb up so far. As the sun rose higher in the sky, we took off our jackets and swung along in our shirtsleeves. Occasionally we saw a partridge. The trees gradually became more stunted, spaced further apart, until they gave way to *phrygana* and bare patches of karstic limestone. Then the track switched between two peaks and over to the north side, away from the sun, and we found ourselves walking in a cold mist which swirled among trees which were larger and covered in moss and ivy. Tall hyacinths grew in their shade. The plantations of these higher slopes had been protected from goats by wire fences. The shapes of the trees came and went as a chill breeze tugged fitfully at the edge of the cloud. Everything was covered in droplets of moisture. Then, in the space of a few minutes, the sun burned through, the cloud evaporated and we found ourselves looking down on Lapithos and Karavas, dwarfed by the height. Half-way to the horizon, the gunboat from Kyrenia was patrolling the Straits, ploughing a lonely white furrow parallel with the coast.

We came to a long strip of metal and rubber links lying on the ground; it was the sheared-off track of a light tank. A few yards further on, the olive-painted body of the tank itself came into view; it had slewed and run off the path out of control, and was now irretrievably jammed among the rocks and cypress trees, the turret pointing downhill towards the coast road. The Turks had left it as a monument, and a small plaque explained – assuming that I translated correctly – that the crew of the tank (one of whom had a Kurdish name) were charged with carrying out an outflanking movement above Lapithos, during the later stages of the invasion of 1974. When their vehicle was accidentally disabled 'in this precipitous place, instead of surrendering, they remained here and carried out their duty by engaging the enemy, firing on the flank and inflicting heavy damage.' Everything was as it had been left in 1974, the hatchway thrown open and the paint barely scarred. Most of the equipment appeared to be American.

In time, we came to a crossroads where the path from the Lapithos *kephalovryson* came up the mountain. A line of telegraph poles marched over the ridge and down again to the south. Sometimes, when we craved for a break from motoring and the noise of the villages and towns, we would walk up on this track from the apartment, making our way along the ridge until we had explored most of the road to St Hilarion. But on this day we were feeling less energetic, and so retraced our steps to the forest below Mount Kornos, to collect our picnic from the car, and the beer and soft drinks I had left to cool in a little stream. We strolled through the trees to a meadow surrounded by olives and carobs, where a donkey stood tethered by a stone well and water tub. Although the bells of the flock sounded all around us, the shepherd was nowhere to be seen. Little paths were marked with stones through the pine needles of the surrounding woods, leading to ruined stone huts and sheepfolds. On the ground beneath the trees, strange clumps of brown caterpillars writhed, entwined with gossamer webbing.

In the late afternoon we drove out of the forest and down into Larnaca tis Lapithou, where the same shepherdess was stationed with her mule in the usual place by the gorge, her distaff twirling as she strolled on the verge. In the fields below the village, men with tractors were spraying the green crops, while the youths had gathered to play football on the pitch near the road. Sheep had been turned into a vineyard to graze, which seemed strange as the early shoots were beginning to appear.

At Myrtou, on the road to Cape Kormakiti, the sentry at the barrier waved us down to a halt. Had we a police pass? He showed one as an example. No? He shrugged his shoulders and looked perplexed. I showed him Kormakiti village on the map and after a moment's thought he smiled 'OK' and waved us through. There seemed to be no logic to these decisions. The sentry at the next barrier stared at us open-mouthed, but made no attempt to stop us.

At dusk, the Maronite church of Kormakiti was locked. They remembered us in the *kafeneion*, and made room for us to sit and drink coffee with them. They were watching the Greek sector's news broadcast on television, repeated in Greek, English, Turkish and Armenian. Greece had made new moves towards talks on the Cyprus problem, and President Kyprianou had made a speech condemning settlement from the Turkish mainland. 'Turkish Cypriots will become second-class citizens,' he warned. The Maronites listened impassively; they had heard all this before. The volume was courteously turned up during the English broadcast.

It was a warm evening and the street door had been left open. A group of children ran in to buy sweets, bantering with their fathers and uncles at the tables. A nun walked by outside, a most strange sight here in the Turkish sector. The army's lorries rumbled past at intervals on their way to and from the Cape. We felt comfortable and relaxed, a little tired after our walk, and time drifted past. The men next to us, I realised, were no longer speaking in Greek which I can understand a little, but had lapsed into the archaic Arabic dialect which their ancestors had brought from the Lebanon. Many of the words, it is said, are from Aramaic: words which Christ and his disciples would have used in everyday speech.

I asked the proprietor what we owed him, and he named a modest figure. 'Turkish liras, Turkish money,' he said with an air of infinite disgust. Outside the moon had risen, and a steady chorus of croaking sounded from the frogs in a nearby tank.

On the outskirts of Myrtou, I took a wrong turn which led into a prohibited zone. I screeched to a halt a soon as I realised, and began to reverse back towards the main road. But a sentry materialised from the shadows and signed for us to stop. He walked round to my open window. He's bound to ask for the police pass, I thought. But no, had we got any cigarettes? Thankfully, we gave him a handful and we were on our way. In the town, the police were checking the papers of bus passengers, but no one troubled us and soon we were running through the Gecitkoy gorge, where moonlight glinted on the swift waters of the stream, and on to Mr Ucok's restaurant at Guzelyali.

★   ★   ★   ★

The traffic lights in Kyrenia are still marked 'STOP' in English, and the pillar boxes, although now painted bright yellow, still show the names of George VI and Elizabeth II. On the eastern road out of town, a discreet sign points to the English cemetery. One day we went to look at the graves of these expatriates, which are in fact contained within a larger, Greek cemetery, the only one we saw which had not been vandalised. The Turks' football club lies beyond the cemetery wall, the pitch being an area of red dust totally devoid of grass. A few young men were practising penalties on the morning of our visit.

The inscriptions on some of the graves among the irises indicated a certain mild eccentricity: 'Doc. E.M. Fraser, Poet, Philosopher, Potter'; 'I did it my way'. One or two were quite recent. A few stubborn English stayed on after 1974, and the numbers are increasing once more.

On the road towards Ayios Epiktitos, a stooped and aged gentleman standing by the side of the road hailed us. He was dressed in a turban, a long European jacket and waistcoat of antique cut, and pinstriped baggy trousers. A heavy watch chain hung across his chest, and he sported the most wonderful moustache and whiskers.

'Good morning, sir and madam. I wonder if you would oblige me with a ride in your *araba*?'

Once we had him comfortably settled in the front seat with his ornately carved walking stick between his knees, he shook hands very formally with all four of us and we exchanged names. He was from Limassol originally, he told us, and now lived all alone, though he had sons in London and Birmingham. A few hundred yards down the road he stopped me. This, it seemed, was his destination. We assisted the old man to emerge and handed him the stick. He made a courteous bow, so low that I feared he would topple altogether.

'A thousand thanks, sir and madam. I am coming to England in three months to visit my sons, so perhaps we may meet again.' He turned and, infinitely slowly, began to make his way towards a nearby coffee shop.

Our route to the Halevga Forest Station lay over Mount Pentadactylos and the past the side turning to Kythrea, or Degirmenlik. In that district, we knew that we were unwelcome. But we came to a roadblock even before the Degirmenlik turning was reached. The sentry called an NCO and I pointed on the map to the Forest Station. There was a long conference in Turkish.

'What nationality are you?'

'English.'

'Very sorry. You must go back.'

There were genuinely regretful smiles and salutes as I turned the car round to cross the Pentadactylos pass once again. We dawdled on a side road down through Klepini on the north side, now renamed Arapkoy, Arabs' Town, and settled from the mainland. Just as in Durrell's time, there were fields of anemones above the village. A shepherd was herding his flock on muleback through the narrow street, holding his little daughter on the saddle in front of him, a lean wolf-like dog following behind. The bells had been removed from the main church, Ayios Loukas, which had been turned into a mosque. The second, smaller church stood in a little graveyard full of blue flowers and upturned tombstones. We pushed open the squeaking iron gate in the wall, watched curiously by a woman in bright blue trousers and shawl. As we approached, a large lizard scuttled away from a sunny patch on the heavy wood of the door. Some of the *iconostasis* was intact, but the church was being used as a sheepfold, and the floor was littered with straw and dung. This was the Byzantine Church of the Panayia.

The Greeks who once lived in Klepini used to believe that the population of the village was mysteriously limited to 40 families and that, if this number was exceeded, death would soon effect a reduction. I have no idea whether the new inhabitants have paid any attention to this legend.

The hamlet of Vourkaris, further along the coast, had become so ruined that the Turks had not troubled to find it a new name, indeed it was not even on their map. We left the car to look at the remains of an olive oil mill: huge circular stones which once rotated in a shaped trough about a heavy beam. The walls and roofs of the ancient houses had nearly all fallen, and we took the place to be deserted until we came to a penful of sheep and a washing line strung between two walls. A tiny, ruinous house was occupied, and a tall, ungainly woman, heavily pregnant, limped stiffly down to talk to us, holding a half-smoked cigarette between her fingers. Behind her, through the open doorway, we could see a motley collection of children climbing out of a large bed to gaze curiously at us. A ragged child, two or three years old, came trotting down the weed-grown steps after his mother, who began to chat to us amicably. They had come from the mainland and lived by their sheep.

The little boy came up behind her and pulled at the leg of her *shalvar* trousers. Taken by surprise, she stepped backwards and staggered, almost falling over him. Something seemed to be wrong with her sense of balance. Recovering herself, embarrassed and angry, she leaned down and struck the child three or four times heavily about the head with her clenched fist. They were hard, thudding blows of the kind normally given to a dog or a recalcitrant mule, and their force drove the infant into a crouching position at her feet. A thin keening wail arose for a few seconds. The woman turned back to us and smiled brightly. The crying stopped almost as soon as it began, and the little chap wiped the tears into the dirt of his face and sniffed into his sleeve. His round, crew-cut head was covered with callouses and scars, and he would grow up, it was plain, as hard as nails.

Further inland, at the head of the narrow road, lies the little Turkish village of Trapeza, surrounded by vegetable gardens in the foothills of the mountains. It has been renamed Besparmak, the Turkish equivalent of Pentadactylos, and was abandoned for a period during the bloodshed of the 1960s. Now some of the little houses were occupied again, and a white-haired, elderly man digging potatoes hailed us as we stepped out of the car.

'Mustapha,' he introduced himself, shaking hands over the fence. 'Welcome.' He seemed both surprised and delighted to see us, and shouldered his spade: 'If you would like to come to my house for coffee, I would be honoured.'

We thanked him and asked what he was growing. Mustapha did not have all the English words, but he pointed out asparagus, lettuces, spring onions, spinach, celery and coriander. It was a wonderful garden, with a fine view of the mountains and the sea, and he made his living from it without any mechanical aids: no tractor, or even a rotivator. Did his back ache? Sometimes. The important thing was that he had a little water; the British brought the water.

Mustapha's wife, a good-natured, motherly woman in a red headscarf, was sitting in the yard of their tiny home slicing beans. A domed clay oven with a large stock of firewood stood against one wall. A vine had been trained over wires to provide shade in summer. The house consisted of two small rooms: a general-purpose kitchen and living room downstairs, and a bedroom above, reached by steps from a yard. On the flagstoned floor of the kitchen stood a single armchair, which Mustapha insisted that Joan take, and three old rush-bottomed chairs around a heavy wooden table. Boxes of freshly picked vegtables were stacked against the wall, which was hung with mule harness, sickles and gin traps. Spades, forks and mattocks stood in a corner, together with a pile of decorated reed baskets. A corn dolly hung from a nail. On the other side of the room, which was about 12 feet square, stood a cooker, worked by bottled gas, and a refrigerator. A single electric light bulb hung from the ceiling, the wire having been tacked up from a new junction box on the wall. There were no windows.

The electricity had come in ten years ago, said Mustapha as his wife made the coffee and Joan handed round cigarettes. There were five families now in Trapeza. In this house, they had somehow brought up five sons and four daughters. The younger children were at school in Nicosia, and the older ones in England: Birmingham, Ilford, Hackney, the Mile End Road. The sons were all doing well, owning a chain of steakhouses and fish and chip shops between them. One had married an English girl. As we drank the coffee, Mustapha's wife proudly brought out a pile of photographs of children and attractive grandchildren, self-conscious family groups in the living rooms of modern English houses, and a dark-haired young man grinning by the door of his brand new Ford.

★   ★   ★   ★

All Cypriots adore picnics, which in this climate can be enjoyed at almost any time of the year. Nevertheless, there is a season for this pleasant activity, which traditionally opens on a Sunday in late March, prompted perhaps by the Greek holiday of *Kathara Deftera*. Thus one Sunday morning we found that the normally deserted coast road to the east of Kyrenia was disturbed by the occasional car, the occupants heading for a favoured spot, to build a fire, grill *kebabs* and drink wine. We had similar plans but, as we crested the brow of one of the little ridges against which the restless sea frets and worries, we found a group standing disconsolately around a Renault with its bonnet propped up, the same model as our own car.

After a brief struggle with my conscience, I pulled over. After all, I thought, I would not wish to be left stranded with a broken car in such a lonely place. The man, with his head in the engine compartment and a look of baffled fury on his face, spoke only Turkish. But his wife had good English, and while I looked at the engine, something I know a little about because of the garage business my family operates, she translated, and he sorted out the screwdrivers I needed from his tool kit. A pretty little girl, their daughter, and another woman, the wife's sister, accompanied them. The engine had just died, they said, and would not restart. This on their first picnic of the year!

The engine had died due to lack of maintenance; the contact breaker pivot had not been lubricated for years, if ever, and the spring had broken. Without a replacement, the engine could not be made to run at all. I explained this to the wife, who translated to her husband. He looked unconvinced. Would we help him try to push-start the car down the hill? I tried to explain that without a contact breaker we might as well push it all the way back to Kyrenia. Another car stopped and two men jumped out, prodding hopefully at ignition leads and battery terminals in their turn. But in time the true situation became apparent.

It was the wife who came to a decision. If we would be so kind as to drive her back to Kyrenia, we could go to see her husband's cousin, who would open his garage up for us and no doubt find this little thing which was so important to make the car go. With an inward groan at the thought of our lost picnic in the sunshine, we smiled encouragingly and said, 'Of course, no problem.' The woman and the little girl climbed into the back of our Renault, while the husband and sister sat down to wait by the stranded car. He did his best to look grateful, but I could sense his irritation and general feeling of inadequacy at the whole situation.

As I turned round and began to drive back to Kyrenia, the woman, in her early thirties, attractive and vivacious, introduced herself as Sevinc Bayraktar.

'Sevinc means joy,' she told us.

The little girl's name was Nursel.

'You are very, very kind to stop and help us. I don't know what we would have done.'

She sniffed disapprovingly at the sentry on the checkpoint by the main road.

'I don't like so many soldiers in the countryside. It is not very nice for tourists, people like you, to see them everywhere. They should stay in the mountains.'

'We rather like the mountains ourselves.'

'Whatever for? There's nothing there.'

'Perhaps that's why. But don't worry, the soldiers don't bother us, and we understand why they're here.'

'I still don't like them down here near the town,' Sevinc insisted. 'No wonder the tourists don't come. I haven't practised my English for years.'

'Where did you learn to speak it so well?'

'I come from Limassol, and I went to an international school there, St Mary's. My father spent much time in England on business, and I once hoped to live in England too. But of course the war made it impossible.'

'What happened to you then?'

'My mother had died a little before. When the war broke out, my father was in England, and my brothers and I were alone in the house. Greek soldiers came and took my brothers away. I had to remain indoors, alone, for more than two months. It wasn't safe for a Turk to be seen in the streets, you see. But my Greek friends came, my friends from school, and they brought me food and money, and told me to try not to worry. You can imagine how I was feeling then. I didn't know if my brothers were alive or dead, and I couldn't contact my father. I miss those friends now. We cried when we parted. I haven't seen them for twelve years, not to write or to telephone or to visit. I would like to see them again, but I think I never can now. They were Greeks of Cyprus, not the soldiers from Greece who imprisoned my brothers.'

'And when did you hear about them?' we asked.

'They were released from prison at the end of two months. My elder brother has told me he would commit suicide rather than face it again. Every day the Greeks beat them with the butts of their guns. Then we came here, and my father could join us. He had been terribly worried with no news all that time.'

'You have Greek friends, but you support partition?'

'I want *taksim*, but not union with Turkey. We don't have enough jobs for our own Cypriots. Fewer people come from the mainland now, and this pleases me. They are different people from us. I want two separate states in Cyprus, just as it is now. Greek friends or not, only *taksim* can make us safe. Also, Turks were not given good positions in the Republic,' she added.

'And your husband. Is he also from Limassol?'

'No, he is from Kyrenia. I met him here, and we live in Ozankoy, near Bellapais. He's a chartered accountant and works for the Ministry of Finance. But my husband is also very interested in politics, and he stood for election just recently, as a member of our Legislative Assembly. He lost, but not by very much. I think perhaps he will succeed next time.'

Sevinc's cousin Oscar (the relationship was actually more obscure), owned the big garage opposite the British cemetery. Indeed, I eventually discovered that Oscar had a finger in a remarkable number of pies for a man not yet 30. He also owned a car rental business with an office in the town centre. This young entrepreneur, displaying the dogged determination never to miss a business opportunity which was doubtless the mainspring of his success, was spending his Sunday minding the petrol forecourt. But nothing was too much trouble for a relative, and he insisted on locking up and coming back with us, after raiding the workshop for tools, and the stores for a set of contact breakers.

'I will ride back with you,' said Sevinc. 'Oscar's driving frightens me.' We saw her point as he streaked past us in a fuel-injected hatchback, tyres smoking on the bends.   Joan wanted to ask Sevinc about school attendance, for, in spite of the smart new schools built since 1974, we had been surprised at the number of school-aged children minding flocks in remote areas. But Sevinc considered that truancy, among Turkish Cypriots at least, was unusual.

'All the childen must go to nursery school first, at five or six. It's only for about three hours a day, mostly play. Then there is serious schooling for about six or seven years, but after that, for my own children, I am concerned for their education. When they are older, I would like them to go to relatives in England for schooling. I also have a son, who is ten now, and I think a great deal about this.'

I made my hands thoroughly grimy fitting the new contact breakers, and guessed the gap because neither Oscar nor I had thought to bring feeler gauges. No one was more relieved than I when the engine finally spluttered into life.

'My husband is very grateful,' said Sevinc. He nodded his head vigorously. 'I wonder if you would like to visit us one evening for dinner. It would be a great pleasure for us. When can you come?

Tuesday? Look, I will write my name for you, and the name of the village, Ozankoy. Just ask anyone there for Sevinc Bayraktar, and they will show you the house. I have a big fireplace and we can cook *kebabs* on the open fire. You will like it.'

Suddenly we found ourselves alone again, the Bayraktars' Renault making its way over the crest of the hill, while the exhaust note of Oscar's Volkswagen had already faded to a distant hum.

'I hope to God that car makes it back to Ozankoy,' I remarked to Joan, 'or we may find ourselves less than welcome on Tuesday night.'

This very spot seemed as good a place as any for our belated picnic, and Steven and Malcolm disappeared towards the sea, rolling down the sand dunes and chasing the lizards which scampered off to hide in the patches of yellow gorse. But the countryside was not quite as lonely as we had at first thought. While Joan and I were unloading the picnic basket from the boot, two cars came past with shotguns protruding from the windows. Then an old man carrying a fishing rod and bag stumped up from the sea, erected a camp stool and sat down to wait by the side of the road, about 50 yards away. He paid no attention to us. It was like a scene in one of Jacques Tati's M. Hulot films. I strolled up for a word, just as one angler to another.

'Any luck then?'

He looked up, adjusted the brim of his hat against the sun and registered my presence. His tackle was very primitive; no more than a line tied directly to a stem of giant reed.

'Only one fish. Not enough wind today. How much are you paying for that car?'

'Six pounds a day.'

'You were robbed.'

'Really?' I said. 'It seemed very cheap to me.'

'They tricked you because you are a foreigner and don't know the right price. You should have come to me. I would have arranged a better deal for you.'

'Ah.'

'I have a new Mercedes,' he remarked conversationally. 'It cost fourteen million liras.'

'Very nice.'

At this juncture, a battered pick-up truck hove into view and stopped level with us.

'This is my son. He's come to collect me.' The old man began to gather up his equipment and pile it into the back.

'Where's the Mercedes then?'

'We don't use that out here.'

I imagined that his house might look as scruffy and utilitarian as the pick-up. But I quite believed in the Mercedes. Many Turks, we came

193

to realise, are great savers and hoarders, living almost in poverty and then splashing out on some spectacular symbol of affluence.

We ate among the sand dunes, which the builders of Kyrenia raid for materials. The boys never tired of sliding down the crests. Occasionally a whiff of roasting *kebab* meat would drift past on the breeze and mingle with the sweet scent of the gorse flowers. Someone nearby was playing Turkish music on a transistor radio, and the blast of shotguns sounded intermittently from near and far.

Later in the afternoon we packed away the remains of our meal and drove as far as the Panayia Melandryna Monastery, which is visible from the road near Ayios Amvrosios. We parked beneath an olive tree, not far from a merry picnic party where three cars surrounded a smoking barbecue, and walked towards the distant walls of the monastery. The building itself was not of much interest, being a long barracks block of square cells, whose barred windows gave straight out on to the mountainside. The roof had fallen in, and it might have been abandoned 20 or even 50 years before. But the nearby church of the monastery, another Panayia Pergaminiotissa, was a delightful building of white limestone, with the bell still hanging in the campanile, although the tiles were gone from the barrel roof and the creepers and thorns had established themselves in their place. The original Byzantine walls had been reinforced in 1731 with great buttresses on either side. Between the church and the monastery lay a shelf covered with ancient pavements and grown with asphodel, perhaps the site of the original monastery. This terrace, with its single blossoming almond tree, came almost level with the roof of the church which snuggled beneath the protection of its wall. A nearby sunken well was still used by the shepherds. We clambered over some corrugated iron blocking the open doorway of the church, to find it full of penned sheep. The beautiful carving of the *iconostasis* was all that remained of the interior decoration.

As we regained our car and were about to leave, a little girl from the group around the barbecue appeared and offered us a skewer of lamb through the open window. Before we knew it, we were surrounded.

'Come, stay with us for a moment. Have a drink with us at least.'

'You're very kind. But just for a little; I'm afraid we have to go.'

'Come for a little then.'

It would have been useless to resist. I am quite sure they would have taken the ignition keys away. In a moment we were escorted to the scene of revelry, where the ground around the fire was greasy with mutton fat and strewn with orange peel, pieces of bread and empty cartridge cases. A number of folding chairs were standing about, and in these we were made to sit.

'Hey, Englishman — do you drink wine?'

'Of course.'

'Well then, try this.' And I was handed an enormous tumbler, filled not with wine, but with the sweetish Cyprus brandy. There were three men in the party: one tall, dark and quiet; a second lean, wiry-looking character with a thin moustache, and wearing army combat jacket and trousers with unlaced boots, who constantly played with a new shotgun; and a short, smiling, bald-headed man who replenished our glasses with every mouthful we took. They were all pleasantly drunk to a greater or lesser extent, and a surprising number of empty brandy bottles lay around the fire.

The thin man put down his gun and insisted on toasting cheese, tomatoes and olives for us, while more gobbets of lamb were roasted on the spit. There was yoghurt from a communal pot and huge radishes. After the food came cigarettes and more brandy. Joan managed to escape to join the wives, who were placidly sitting in a circle, cheerfully knitting as always, with the wool laid in hanks on their shoulders. Our boys had wandered away to play with their children, of whom there were five or six, ranging in age from a small toddler to a lad of about sixteen.

'Look here,' I remonstrated eventually, feeling somewhat dizzy, 'I'd better go easy with this stuff. I'm driving.'

They stared at me in genuine amazement: 'So you're driving? So what? We're driving. What's that got to do with anything?' And round went the bottle again. Not the same one, a new one. Someone suggested group photographs. I have the one which Joan took before me as I write. The women and children smile brightly, while the men stand arm in arm, for support as much as in friendship, and look faintly dazed. It emerged that they were all retired policemen.

'Rather young to be retired, aren't you?' I remarked to the bald man, whose name I now knew was Nazim. He smiled broadly under his thick black moustache.

'I'm 40, and already living on a pension. Not bad, eh? But that's nothing. Look at this rascal [he nodded at the thin man with the shotgun]; he's only 32 and he's retired also.'

Eventually, he did admit that they worked a little at the offices of a shipping company in Nicosia, where they lived – 'But nothing serious, you understand.'

Someone fired unsteadily at a partridge flying high to the left towards the sea, and missed.

'The hares are out of season,' said Nazim. 'The British brought the partridges to Cyprus. Now that is something to thank you for.' He showed me a large-scale shooting map issued by the government.

'In England,' I said, 'you can only shoot with the permission of the owner of the land.'

'Really? How extraordinary. Hey, you're not drinking. Serefe! Skol!'
'Skol?'

'Where we come from there were too many Danes. And Irish. Men from Austria. My job was liaison with the UN.'

'Where are you from? From the South?'

'No, from Kokkina.'

'Well, well. We had a long talk with a fellow villager of yours the other day. He's a forester in Rizokarpaso.'

'We know him, we know him. There are several of our people there. So you understand how we lived in Kokkina? There is only the military there now. Listen, have you been to the Greek side? Do the British only listen to the Greeks? What do they tell you about Cyprus?'

'Obviously they tell their side of it.'

Through the fumes of the brandy, deep-felt convictions and passions were rising to the surface of Nazim's mind. The words began to tumble over each other to escape.

'In Europe, everyone is anti-Turkish. Whenever we are in conflict, you take the opposite side. Armenians, Kurds – look at the trouble we have with those people But always you say that we are in the wrong. Look what is happening in Iran and Iraq, how they treat their Kurds. Do you criticise them?'

'To be fair, we do.'

But Nazim was unconvinced.

'And what is this thing between you British and the Greeks? I have never understood it'

'We owe a lot to their culture, I suppose.' To be truthful, this was a question I often asked myself. What is it, in the Greek spirit, which attracts the English so much? 'Perhaps,' I added, 'we admire their love of freedom.'

'Culture!' exploded Nazim. 'The Greeks of Cyprus aren't Aristotle or Socrates. In that sense they're no more Greek than I am. They're a mixture of people. Freedom! I'll show you what freedom means to the Greeks.'

He unrolled the map again, and began to point out the names of the lost Turkish villages south of the Line: Sogucak, Zeytinlik, Gecitkele, Camlibel, until he ran out of breath.

'Do you think we wanted *taksim* if our people could only have lived safely in those places? We were forced into it; we had no other choice.

'The British mean well, but they don't understand the Greeks. Greeks are all dreamers. You know they have their *Megali Idea*, their Great Idea? They want Istanbul – yes, even today. In 1922 Venizelos sent them to war for it, although Ataturk defeated them. For that, they lost Izmir, the city they called Smyrna, but still they did not learn their lesson. And they still want Cyprus; it is all part of their plan.'

'They were offered Cyprus in 1915 as an inducement to join the Allies, but they turned it down.'

'It is true, but only because they believed it would fall into their hands later. Listen carefully to what I say Englishman.' He gripped my arm and shook it gently in emphasis, his face close to mine. 'This is important, listen, and tell them in England. Whatever the Greeks say, we only want peace in Cyprus. It was the Greeks who began the troubles in 1955. All we want now is peace. But if they ever attack us again, we Turks will fight – any time. I was a soldier before I was a policeman. I fought in 1974, and I am ready to fight again. Never forget this.'

I asked the question I so often felt obliged to ask, with a vague sense of guilt: 'If you had been in our place in 1960, what would you have done? What arrangements would you have made for the new Republic?'

'Republic? Arrangements? Why do anything at all? You should have stayed for a hundred years.'

'But the days of empires are over. How could we have stayed with the world as it is today, when the majority wanted us out? It would have been 25 years more bloodshed.'

'You stayed in Ireland.'

There was a tremendous explosion by my right ear. One of the little boys and the toddler had managed to discharge the shotgun and had blown a branch out of an olive tree just above our car. Nazim, calmer now, smiled benignly at them and went on.

'The trouble of course is that Cyprus, Greece, Turkey, they are all little countries. The British bases, NATO and American policy; these are the really important things. The Americans are half responsible for the situation. Didn't they support the Colonels in Greece? Weren't they behind the coup against Makarios?'

Didn't Kissinger sit on his hands and watch the Turkish army's invasion, I thought, though I said nothing. The Americans made a convenient scapegoat, and we ended by blaming them for the whole mess, and thus remained friends.

'Stop talking politics, Papa,' said Nazim's son, bringing us coffee. His family had heard all this before, many times. I was invited to try the gun, a Spanish over and under job, and dutifully shot another branch off the olive tree. (I felt a pang of guilt after this, but no one bothers to pick the olives here now.)

'We come out for a picnic every Sunday in summer,' said Nazim, packing the chairs away in the back of his Triumph Dolomite. We exchanged addresses. 'Look, see this place in London. Is that near to you? That is my cousin's address; he has a dry-cleaning business. We hope to visit him next year, so maybe we'll meet again then?'

We drove in convoy as far as Ayios Amvrosios, delayed by the tractors crawling back from the fields. Here, we pulled up in the village square by the Ataturk statue, while their three cars roared past in a blaze of klaxons and shouted farewells towards the mountain road to Nicosia. The people of Ayios Amvrosios came out of their houses and the coffee shop to see what all the noise was about.

The Turks had renamed Ayios Amvrosis as Esentepe, after a village in the Troodos mountains, and the signs of the population exchange remained in the form of the numerals painted by the doors of houses to identify them for allocation. A6, A7 and A8 were scrawled along a row of modern apartments. The houses on the outskirts of the village were very old and falling into ruin. A few of them were said to have tessellated floors from earlier, Byzantine dwellings. The Greeks of Ayios Amvrosios were famous wood carvers and, even by the standards of Cyprus, a land of skilled carpenters, the doors and window frames were very fine.

The church in the centre of the square was one of those grand nineteenth-century Orthodox buildings, converted to a mosque. As we stood by the locked door, the elderly *hodja* shuffled up: a little gnome of a man with thick spectacles and a woollen hat.

'Welcome to Cyprus,' he said, shaking hands. Then he pulled an old fob watch, made in Constantinople, from his waistcoat pocket. He opened its cover and peered at the face dubiously. The men had already left the coffee shop and were waiting expectantly in the square for evening prayers. Did I have the correct time? I showed the *hodja* my digital watch and he stared at the unfamiliar figures in dismay. These meant nothing to him, it was plain. Then he came to a decision, took a large key from his pocket and went into the mosque. In a minute the speakers crackled, and the high, undulating cry rang out over the village and its surrounding pastures.

It was warm enough, that night, to sit outside by the swimming pool, writing first by lamplight, then dreaming by moonlight until the early hours.

CHAPTER THIRTEEN

NEVER SLEEP UNDER A FIG TREE

It had rained a little just before dawn, which pleased Salih, who was relieved of his normal watering chores. I found him examining the first sprouting leaves of a fig tree in the garden, a bougainvillaea flower tucked behind his ear, and handed him his coffee.

'Never sleep under a fig tree,' he said. 'It will make your skin hot and itchy. You'll have bad dreams. Sleep under an olive tree.'

'Are the figs good here?'

'Not like in Paphos. We grow everything there.'

'Day off yesterday, Salih?'

'Afternoon off. I take my wife for picnic by the sea. Near the soldiers' restaurant.'

'We know it. We go there most evenings.'

'Sure. Cheap restaurant.'

'Where's Mr Kemal?' I asked. 'I haven't seen him for days.'

'Kemal finished.'

'Finished?'

'New hotel manager just come. Was Under-Manager of the Heathrow Sheraton before, in England. He is,' said Salih reverently, 'a Bey. From a very noble family.'

In time, we came to know the Bey, a mainland Turk with a shark-like smile full of bad teeth, which always made me feel uneasy. As a very new broom, he was invariably up and about at first light, and late at night he could be seen through the uncurtained window of his great office, his desk covered in open files. For some reason, he and his wife, with whom Joan became friendly, had decided to live in the apartment across the swimming pool from ours, and so our isolated tenancy of the complex came to an end. Now, poor Salih had to watch his step under the critical gaze of his superior, and so our morning coffee and smoke became a somewhat clandestine occasion. The owners of the hotel expected great things, it seemed, from their new manager, and the Bey had been issued with a brand new Mercedes, painted in metallic gold, which stood in the empty car park next to our dusty Renault. Occasionally the luxurious car would fly past us on the

199

road to Nicosia, or we would see it parked by the harbour in Kyrenia, where the hotel owned a restaurant.

Salih brought more flowers for our table as we ate breakfast. The radio was broadcasting in English from the Greek sector; *Dallas* and *Yes Minister* would be shown on television that evening. Would Cypriots, Greek or Turkish, laugh at *Yes Minister*, I wondered idly. Perhaps they would; they all seemed to believe implicitly in conspiracies in high places. Apart from English, Greek and Turkish, Nicosia broadcasts in Armenian and Arabic for limited periods each day.

On the way to Morphou, we stopped for a while in the little gorge which the Paleomylos river cuts through the forested hills near Panagra, or Gecitkoy. The road follows the river, which runs fast in a bed of smooth rock. A little feeder-stream tumbles down the mountainside, and before joining the main river falls into a series of deep, clear pools worn into the limestone, a secluded bathing place just out of sight of the road. Joan waited here in the sunshine with a book, while the boys and I scrambled up the little watercourse, which had cut its way through hillsides fragrant with gorse and bright with yellow and white anemones. The cypress trees were shedding their pollen in the breeze like puffs of smoke. Occasionally an army truck could be heard grinding along the road, but when we returned it was to the tinkle of goatbells. We found that the herdsman, sitting side-saddle on his mule, had stopped to pass the time of day with Joan while his animals moved on ahead like a brown flood.

We turned towards the sea on the plain beyond Myrtou, through the trees of the Dhirios Forest, whose branches were clustered with white nests of caterpillars. We passed an army camp hidden away amongst the pines before emerging into open, sandy fields guarded by ragged scarecrows. The village of Ayia Irini lies a mile or so from Morphou Bay: an untidy settlement, dozing in the sunshine. The sand was sifting through the streets, encroaching from the coastal dunes. We asked in the village for Paleokastro; a Turkish woman understood the Greek words and directed us along a dirt road through the fields. A pack of lean dogs ran with us, quarrelling and biting at the tyres, until they were finally left behind. But as we came close to the coast, there were tracked military vehicles ploughing through the sand in the distance, and a notice warned us that the area was a forbidden zone. The hillock on which an ancient temple stood, known to the villagers for time out of mind as the Old Castle, was thus inaccessible.

The Ayia Irini site was excavated by a Swedish expedition in 1929. It thrived during the sixth century BC, a time when the whole area of Morphou Bay had grown wealthy from copper. The strange terracotta figures which were recovered from this temple stand ranked in the Cyprus Museum, their beards and helmets pointed in the oriental style, a motley crowd of soldiers, charioteers and minotaurs, staring enigmatically across time.

At Morphou itself we made another attempt to reach the sea, following the sluggish Serrakhis river through plantations of orange trees, until we came to Syrianokhori, a village standing among beds of giant reed, growing two and three times the height of a man. Syrianokhori, the Place of the Syrians, may once have been a refuge for Maronites from the Holy Land, but its new Turkish inhabitants have named it Yayla, after their village in Tillyria. Yayla is the old nomads' word for a summer camp. One of the first houses we saw as we emerged from the orange groves plainly belonged to a staunch supporter of Turkish nationalism, for a magnificent mural had been carefully painted on to the whitewashed wall, depicting a grey wolf howling at a crescent moon, crossed scimitars and the TMT initials. Many of the other houses were very ancient.

We went into the café for a beer, and found it full of orange farmers taking a break from the fields. One of them told us how the oranges were bought up from the producers by five companies, including Sun-Zest, which owned the processing plant outside Morphou.

'What do you think of the price?'

'Between ourselves, it's fair. All these things are controlled by the government and the price is fixed every year. The village owns the trees. Most of the first-class fruit goes to England, a small amount to France and Italy now. Second-class fruit goes to the Arab countries, and for bottling. We can't complain about the prices and we could be worse off. All this is new to us, you understand. All our people moved here together from a village in the Paphos district.'

'You were lucky to get such good land.'

'Well yes, but you know this village is surrounded by drained marshes. It's cold in winter, hot in summer, always damp. It looks pretty but it's an unhealthy place to live. We can use the reeds though. Look over your head.'

The ceiling appeared to consist of split lengths of bamboo, tightly packed together.

'I made that one. There are rafters above made of split trunks and concrete above that. In the old days it would have been dry seaweed, to absorb the moisture, and clay packed on top. It's quite watertight if it's done properly. Our people have always made baskets, furniture and all kinds of things from reeds, as long as anybody can remember. We're the only people in Cyprus who do this.'

'May we ask you about when your people came here from across the Line? How did the authorities allocate the houses? Did they try to give you equivalent property to that which you had owned in the Greek sector?'

This suggestion seemed to cause him much amusement.

'Pot luck! Nothing but pot luck, as you say my dear. It might be good or bad, but you had to take the first house offered. Mine's not too bad. Perhaps these difficult times will end one day, although they have lasted for most of my life. In the fifties I was in the Cypriot detachment of the British army during the fighting against EOKA. I worked as a guide for the Argyll and Sutherlands, the Parachute Regiment, the Lancashire Regiment . . . Do you think my English is good?

'Now that you are here, I can show you a good beach if you like. Do you have a car? Come and follow me as I go home, and I will show you the way. You will find yourself quite alone by the sea. Even now, I'm still guiding the English . . .'

We followed his new Talbot through the muddy lanes, and waved our thanks as we passed his pretty bungalow on the outskirts. The track was more like a canal of shallow water, which led us through thick reeds nearly meeting overhead. There were actually wild ducks paddling about the deeper sections which took flight at our approach. The snipe-shooting on these marshes was once said to be the best on the island. But we had been well directed; the water never became too deep for the car, and we eventually emerged from the thickets on to the open coast and a flat, sandy beach which stretched for miles in either direction.

He was quite right; it was a wonderful beach, with a view of Cape Kormakiti and the distant Kyrenia mountains on one hand, and the copper coast, backed by the blue hills of Tillyria, on the other. A warm wind blew into our faces from the shallow waters of the bay, where we swam before drying ourselves at a smoky driftwood fire. The view, the wind and the sun put us in a carefree mood, but the swim had made us hungry, and so we drove back to Morphou and along the coast through avenues of huge eucalyptus trees. Children, in red and white uniforms, were chattering happily as they poured out of a school, guarded by a soldier at the gate. Near Karavostasi we passed the Danish soldiers from Viking Camp One, strung out along the main road on a training run, while one stout lad puffed away 300 yards behind. We had a closer look at the deserted copper workings and the mounds of ore lying by the road. The railway tracks from Skouriotissa had been torn up where they approached the Line, only a short distance inland.

As the Danes were engaged in their jogging, the restaurant by the police post was empty. The owner and his wife were eating their own lunch at one of the tables.

'What would you like to eat?' he asked disconcertingly. 'Anything at all. You name it.'

Such a remark is not as surprising as it might seem in Cyprus, where the range of traditional dishes, delightful as some of them are, is somewhat limited. We settled for red mullet and a salad remarkable for its superb tomatoes. And of course the wonderful *houmous*, which he had served us before.

'There's no great secret to making *houmous*,' he said, 'but you must use fresh lemons.'

The walls of the restaurant were festooned with all manner of kitsch decoration: travel posters, pin-ups of pop stars, turtle and crab shells, a stingray tail, Christmas cards and crackers, a portrait of Rauf Denktash, postcards from England and Australia, an English survey map of Cyprus, reprinted in 1981 and using Greek names throughout, the new Turkish map, road maps of mainland Turkey (very poor these, because the only accurate maps, particularly of the east, are restricted to the army), two illustrations from Kipling's *Jungle Book*, and a card advertising a Soho nightclub.

The couple sat with us over coffee and a cigarette. The man cast a glance around, and at the sea beyond the open door.

'It's not a bad little place,' he said. 'The Danish boys keep us going. But it's nothing like the bar I had before in Limassol. That really was something. We lived on the Sovereign Base Area in those days, just outside Episkopi.'

'How did that come about?'

'I always worked for the British. I was a soldier from 1955 – I guided the Royal Greenjackets around local areas. After that, I had a civilian job driving for the British army: ambulances, tankers, that kind of thing. So we lived on the SBA. We paid for water, electricity and everything to the Republic of Cyprus, but we were under the jurisdiction of the British Military Police.

'In 1963 I joined TMT like everyone else. Although we were on British sovereign territory, we weren't safe; we still needed to protect ourselves. All the men were expected to guard the village and their homes. At that time I had the bar in Limassol. You should have seen that; it was quite a place. I would have been a rich man by now if I still had that bar. Of course I lost it after 1963. Limassol was only 7 miles away, but it might have been a thousand after that. I had heard some EOKA men were looking for me because I had helped the British, and I knew that they would kill me for sure if they ever caught me in a Greek area. When the invasion came in 1974, all the Turks in that district came into the SBA for protection. There were 10,000 of us trapped there for six months. Then James Callaghan arranged for us to leave for Turkey. I read that he was criticised everywhere for allowing this, but you can imagine how grateful we feel to him. Civilian aircraft came from Greece, strangely enough, to fly us to Turkey. And after some months we came here.'

'How did they allocate homes to refugees from the South?'

'Ha! It was a charter for lazy men and thieves. They received homes as good as anyone else.'

'And TMT today?' we asked him. 'Is it still active?'

'Not in the same way. Now the organisation's aim is to keep up our spirits and remind us of our beliefs, rather than to actually protect us. Since 1974, that job has been done by the Turkish army. But in the years before, well almost every Turk old enough to carry a rifle was a member.

'Make no mistake about it, the Turkish army is our only protection.' He glanced inland, in the direction of the Attila Line. 'If the army left, the Greeks would be down here tomorrow. *Taksim* is the only safe solution; two separate states. I am a poorer man than I was, and I know that I will never have another business like my bar in Limassol . . . but I am still alive, and my family is safe.'

'Do you think that it might end in union with Turkey?'

'God forbid. Most of our problems are caused by the mainland Turks who have settled here. Cypriots are Europeans, and these people are not. Most of them come from forest areas; they are very ignorant, with no education. All they know is how to keep goats.'

'All right, suppose a time comes when Turkey is no longer prepared to support the cost of maintaining an army here. Will you not then be forced into some kind of settlement?'

'I think, in time, we can get a settlement on our own terms which still leave us with *taksim*. The important thing is to improve our economy, and that will bring us strength. You know some of our people have done very well abroad. We should try to persuade all the Turkish Cypriots who settled in England and Australia to come back with their money and invest it in business here. The trouble with Cyprus, you see, is that no one wants to work. No one even wants to own up to working. Life is so pleasant and easy here. Take my own brother, for example. He worked hard at his business in Blackpool, but now he has come back to Cyprus to live cheaply and well on his pension. He has found himself a house at Esentepe – you know it? Well then, you saw what a nice place that is. But what will he do all day? Drink coffee, I suppose.'

'What about the Arab countries? Are they not prepared to help your economy?'

'No, take my word for it, we must look to Europe. The other Muslim countries have nothing in common with us but the religion. Look how the Arabs treat their women; they still make them cover their faces. We are Europeans and we are white. What have we in common with people like that? Besides, the Arabs are all busy trading with the Greeks. I came to London one time, to visit friends, and everywhere there were rich Arabs. One day, in a restaurant, I was almost the only white man there. I found that extraordinary. I did not expect that in England.'

'You have some Negroes here.'

'Ah, but they are Turks, not Africans.'

★　★　★　★

The solitude of Vouni Palace was disturbed by three soldiers who had parked their radio truck and carried a portable transmitter to the summit. Voices distorted by static crackled across the airwaves. Their weapons stood against an ancient wall, and while two fiddled with the equipment, the third scanned the hills of Tillyria with binoculars. I had intended to do the same, but thought better of it and left my binoculars and camera in the car. The soldiers gave us a disinterested glance and carried on with their work, though one of them later startled us when he worked the bolt of his carbine. A UN convoy ran along the road far below: Forward Control Land Rovers converted into ambulances, with fluttering blue flags.

We explored some of the dying villages nearby, positioned on minor roads amputated by the Line. A woman was gutting fish in the courtyard of a little wooden church. At Ambelikou we passed a memorial to two Danish soldiers in a grove of eucalyptus trees: 'Fallen in the Service of Peace 16.8.1974, Sergeant Benth Schultz Christensen, bn 21.9.52, Private Carsten Busk Andersen, bn 12.8.1951'. Twenty-two and twenty-three years old.

So we came, late in the afternoon, to Lefka, a town hidden in the hills a few miles from the coast and within spitting distance of the Line. According to Father Calepio, Lefka sent 300 soldiers under Paolo Vicentino to the siege of Nicosia, but after the conquest it became a Turkish stronghold. On the outskirts we stopped to look at the graves of the fighters who died defending Ghaziveran in 1964, neatly tended in a little enclosure off the main road.

Lefka has always been a fortunate place, for, though surrounded by the dry Troodos foothills, a copious supply of good water passes through this little valley, one of the few perennial rivers of the island. The irrigation channels which run everywhere along the contours have so exploited this water that we found the town to be full of orchards and gardens, and alive with the sound of trickling streams. The houses were hidden by thick groves of palm trees. The oranges of Lefka were famous in medieval times, and are still considered to be the best in Cyprus. Sir Samuel Baker had been equally charmed by the town.

> The houses of Lefka are almost concealed by the luxuriant foliage of the gardens and orangeries. We rode through narrow lanes streaming with water and shaded with the elm, ash, maple and innumerable fruit trees.

(Samuel Baker, Cyprus as I Saw It in 1879)

In ancient times, and until recently, Lefka had another source of wealth in the copper mines of the nearby mountains. The graves of Greek and Roman miners have been found all around. During the heyday of the Cyprus Mines Corporation, many of the men worked in the mines of Skouriotissa and Mavrovouni, and during the great strike of 1948 the Turks of Lefka showed total solidarity with the Greeks of Xeros. This was a bitter and long-drawn-out dispute with an American company whose attitude, even the British Colonial Office admitted on several occasions was 'high-handed and unconciliatory'. It also involved a certain amount of violence, for the police opened fire on a crowd of strikers and, in the famous incident of the 'Train Battle', ten miners' wives stopped the ore train near the coast at Xeros and stoned the strike-breaking crew. The interesting feature was the joint involvement of the Greek Pan-Cyprian Labour Federation and the Pan-Cyprian Committee of Turkish Trade Unions. There is evidence that the administration was disturbed at the emergence of this combination, and only ten years later, when 'divide and rule' had become the watchword, such a pact between the two communities had become inconceivable.

Now the copper mines were on the wrong side of the Line, although some efforts were being made to extract ore from opencast quarries on the outskirts of the town. On a prominent hill, the giant silhouetted figure of a martial Turk had been erected, where the Greeks would be sure to see it too from the other side: 'Turkish youth, it is we who established the Republic, but it is you who will enhance it and give it life!' Kemal Ataturk'.

In the impressive new square, a statue of Ataturk had predictably been erected. A grandiose conception of the type which Franco or Mussolini would have appreciated, it depicted the leader mounted on a prancing and very male stallion. We preferred to follow a maze of lanes through the gardens to emerge on a grassy bank above a little cottage standing near the stream. Friesian calves were grazing under orange trees laden with fruit. Where the water meandered nearby, tall palm trees spread their luxuriant heads. Beyond the palms, further up the valley, where the sun had already sunk behind the misty peaks, lay

Greek territory. The evening was very warm and still, except for the occasional sound made by the calves moving in the grass and the steady croaking of a tankful of frogs, unseen near the stream.

Our voices must have been heard in the cottage, for a sprightly man appeared and clambered up the bank to inspect us. He was remarkably like a frog himself, with large, black, protruding eyes, which mischievously swivelled from side to side in order to gauge the effect of his remarks on us. He might have been 60 years old.

'English? Welcome, welcome. What do you think of my garden?'

We told him, quite truthfully, that it was one of the most beautiful places we had ever seen.

He chuckled with delight. 'Wait, wait. See what I grow.' He seemed literally to hop splayfooted down the slope in the fading light, and returned in a minute or two with an armful of oranges, which he eagerly pushed into our hands. 'Now, try these,' he said, 'and tell me if they are not the best oranges in Cyprus.' They were.

'This is my summer house, my summer garden. I have a larger house in the town, and also a shop.'

'And have you always lived in Lefka?' I asked, hoping for once to hear a happier story than the tales of the refugees.

'My family have always been here. My father and his father. Now I have a brother who lives in London [is there a Cypriot who doesn't, I wondered to myself]; he has a restaurant near King's Cross. Do you ever go near there?'

'Well, yes we do sometimes.'

'Now then, here is the name. We'll play a trick on him. You walk into his restaurant, and just say: "Greetings from your brother Halil in Lefka." Can you imagine his face? Will you do that?' He beamed, his eyes rapidly switching between Joan and myself.

'OK, we will.'

'Ah, that pleases me. As you are an Englishman, I know that you will keep your word. Now I will give you some directions. Go up this little road – it is good enough for a car – until you come to a junction, and there you turn right, back into the town. Right, you understand, it is very important that you don't turn left. Come and see me if you come to Lefka again.' And his rubber boots flapped off into the lush vegetation of his grove.

The moon had risen as we were talking, and silvered the distant peaks. We took the indicated road, which led up the hillside to the scars of the opencast copper mine. At the junction we encountered a shepherd, bringing his flock in late. He gestured firmly to the right. The other road plainly led to the Line. The moon was now bright and full, sailing like a white ship through the palm trees as we drove down into the town.

We stopped in Karavas to buy provisions and drink a coffee with the owner of the store, which was crowded with a few customers and many others who had come to gossip. Salih was right; most of the shopping is done by the men, in the evening when the day's work is finished. Later, coming home from dinner in Kyrenia, we stopped before the lit window of a furniture store. Here, the incredibly ornate nineteenth-century French-styled furniture for which the Turks seem to have such a weakness was displayed, glittering with lacquer and gilt. It seems a shame to waste the skilled Cypriot craftsmen on such tasteless reproductions.

★ ★ ★ ★

Early in the morning we began to climb through the streets of Lapithos towards the mountain. There were empty houses here which I coveted: houses with double wooden doors, carved in a diamond pattern, arched stone lintels embossed with a pomegranate motif, wrought-iron grids and Ionic columns to the windows, and overhanging lemon trees in gardens run wild. These houses had not been needed for the new population in 1974. Spurned in favour of the modern concrete bungalows, their lizard-haunted walls remained innocent of the painted numbers allocated to the others, T5, T6, T7, and the creepers were slowly gaining a hold. But many remained in good order after twelve years, and for the expenditure of a modest sum would make fine and elegant homes.

We traced the stream uphill, past the remains of one of the water mills which once ground the village's corn, and past a coffee shop where old men in traditional Cypriot dress sat in sunshine. At the large church which is now a mosque, built on a shelf halfway up the slope, the *hodja* came to show us round. When we failed to understand his Turkish, he switched to bad French, and so we communicated tolerably well. He was a youngish man, who doubled as the village schoolmaster, dressed in an old-fashioned, double-breasted suit and fingering a rosary of amber beads. His copy of the Koran was spread on a beautifully carved wooden rest.

The café under the plane trees at the *kephalovryson* had been closed for years, although the flat roof of the cistern provided a fine viewing platform over the village and the coast. From here, we went on to the empty mountainside and up towards the forest road. At an isolated spring, a Greek had once built himself a summer house: two rooms and a concrete verandah between a pair of almond trees, facing over the Straits towards Turkey. The view was almost painfully beautiful, high in the clear mountain air. Since 1974 it must have lain derelict, but the almonds still poured their blossom over the balcony, and a shepherd, watering his flock at the nearby spring, had left the remains of many fires in a corner of the terrace.

On the crest, a rusty sign pointed to St Hilarion Castle, and a faded Byzantine eagle was painted on a flat rock, with 'ENOSIS' and 'EOKA' woven around it in authentic sky-blue. Through gaps in the forest we could look down on Nicosia lying in a haze on the plain; if we turned around, the coastal villages were spread below our feet. With binoculars we could pick out the houses we knew, and even imagined that we could see our parked car. The calm surface of the Straits showed strange lines and whorls, evidence of obscure currents or ships long past. Strain our eyes as we might, we could not penetrate the mists to the mountains of Turkey, 40 miles away.

When the outskirts of the village were reached once more, I was tired and hot, having carried Malcolm on my back some of the way. Here we parted, for while Joan and the boys were mindful of their lunch, I wanted no more than a cold beer in a café and would join them later. All the way down the mountain under the hot sun I had been imagining, with fond anticipation, a glass beaded with condensation and the slightly salt taste which would sting my throat with the first swallow. But Lapithos, it seemed, had no *kafeneions* or *tavernas* in the Greek sense, only little coffee shops. Turkish men do not drink beer at midday. I tried first at the top of the village, where the be-whiskered patriarchs sat on their rickety chairs in the sun. They were very ancient men and spoke rarely, smiling vaguely at nothing in particular, gripping their gnarled walking sticks and splaying their booted legs as if afraid of being unseated. Every two or three hours, an old lady brewed each of them a tiny cup of coffee on a gas burner in a dark room which gave on to the street. But she had no beer.

'*Yok*,' she said, throwing her head backwards and smiling regretfully.

Hayir is one Turkish word for 'no'; *yok* is another, meaning more properly 'there isn't any', 'there's none to be had', and always accompanied by that glance to the heavens. There is something very final about *yok*.

In the larger coffee shop by the bus stop, the proprietor offered to look in the refrigerator, the smelly contents of which came as a revelation. There he found a rusty can of Coca-Cola, but it would have taken a brave man indeed to consume anything, even from a sealed tin, which had been stored in that chamber of horrors, so I thanked him and walked on. Finally I washed my face and drank cold water from the fountain by the old mosque: a delightful building with its peeling whitewash and palm trees, surrounded by lush grass and yellow ranunculus flowers. It should be better cared for. The Greeks of Lapithos had insulted their Turkish fellow villagers by painting

'ENOSIS' in blue, high on the brown stones of the minaret, and this no one had managed to expunge in the years since 1974.

I passed the main Greek cemetery, where broken white marble lay tumbled among the flowers, and then the Turkish one, undamaged but equally overgrown with ox-eye daisies, and protected by dull green–black cypresses. The lemon groves below the village were so richly carpeted with ranunculus, exactly the same colour as the fruit above, that the green of the grass had all but disappeared. As I passed beneath a gnarled and ancient tree on a footpath, I heard a slow rustling sound and looked up. There, on a branch, a huge and repulsive lizard had been disturbed by my passing. Its neck was frilled like a dragon's and its open mouth was large enough to engulf a human fist. It stared at me for a moment with basilisk eyes, and then slowly crawled away into the hollow rotting trunk, drawing after it a truncated stump of tail. Cotovicus had written in 1598 of chameleons in Cyprus which had the wonderful property of changing their colour at will. He firmly believed that they lived on nothing but air.

When I returned to the apartment I was relieved to find some lunch left, and beer, after all, in the refrigerator. Joan was talking to the Bey's wife. They had been seven years in London, while her husband was working at Heathrow. I felt a certain sympathy for the pressure the man was under. It was plain that the hotel was far from making a profit.

In Kyrenia, we visited the Fine Arts Museum, once the personal collection of a rich Englishman, housed in the mansion which local craftsmen had built to his order. For some reason, the army had blocked off the streets around the Dome Hotel, and so we made our way round to the harbour at the other end of town, and climbed the hill to the little Anglican church, which stands in grounds clustered with cyclamen. Memorial plaques made interesting reading: four soldiers of the Black Watch who succumbed to fever in 1878 (Baker mentioned these) and an English couple who 'died in the tragic events of 1974', having lived for 24 years in the town.

★　★　★　★

The village of Kazaphani has been home to Turks for time out of mind, but nevertheless they felt the need after 1974 to change its name to Ozankoy, which I translate as 'Poet's Town'. I edged our car through narrow, unlit streets, looking for the Bayraktars' house. Twice I knocked on doors and showed the name written on a piece of paper, only to be given directions in Turkish which I could not follow. At last, the noise and light from the windows led us to a crowded bar. 'Sergeant Osman's Place' was written above the door. The room was filled with tobacco smoke and men playing cards, all talking at the tops for their voices.

'It's close by,' said a young man who spoke English. He led me outside and down the street, where in the dark I stumbled over a great millstone protruding from the wall.

'This was once a water mill?'

'I suppose so. I hadn't noticed. There, that is where the Bayraktars live.'

I drove the car up, and the door opened at the sound, casting light over the stone steps and cobbled road, as Mr Bayraktar came out to shake us warmly by the hand, followed by his wife, Sevinc. Their own car, I learned to my relief, was running perfectly. We were led into a comfortable lounge with an ornate suite in the French style, a large gilt mirror and a heavy sideboard. A log fire was blazing in a stone hearth in the corner, filling the room with its heat and a faint smell of wood smoke. The television had been left on, the volume turned down, and remained so throughout the evening.

Mr Bayraktar looked at me and said something in Turkish. His wife said, 'He wants to know if you will drink beer, wine, Scotch whisky or Turkish *raki*'

'A *raki* would be very pleasant.'

This seemed to meet with his approval, and he turned to the sideboard, while Sevinc asked the same question of Joan and went to find a bottle of white wine to share with her. She brought the boys some juice, squeezed from clementines grown in the garden. Mr Bayraktar brought two tumblers, which he had filled with generous measures of the 'lion's milk' over a few cubes of ice. We all drank a toast.

'What do you think of my fireplace?' asked Sevinc. 'I had it built specially. This is a very old house; my husband inherited it from his parents, but I asked him to have this put in for me. It is very popular with my friends in winter. They like to visit so that we can cook *kebabs* indoors.'

I had noticed the usual large wood-burning stove in the hall, a very elegant one shining with enamel, but open hearths are not so very common or necessary in the warm climate of Cyprus. Indeed the room had already become extremely hot. Mr Bayraktar wiped his brow, poured more *raki* and began to assemble iron grids in the fireplace.

'I will bring the salad,' Sevinc said, 'and my husband will cook the meat. What word do you say to cook meat, barbecue? Well, he can't barbecue unless he has a drink. Don't you find that strange?'

'I'm just the same myself.'

Mr Bayraktar, it seemed, had to put up with a certain amount of teasing from his talkative young wife.

211

'You wait,' she whispered to us. 'He does speak English. After two drinks, maybe three, he will begin to speak. The more he drinks, the better he speaks. Wait and see.'

We watched the *kebabs* and *sheftalia* sizzling and spitting on the hearth, while Sevinc brought salad, *pitta* bread, savoury rice and fried potatoes from the kitchen. I helped Mr Bayraktar carry a huge round table from the next room, which we placed before the fire. Finally, Sevinc set a great dish of yoghurt and a plate of black olives in the centre.

'Olives are expensive in England?'

'They certainly are.'

'These are from my own trees in the garden. If you like them, I will give you a big jar to take back. Just use salted water and change it sometimes and they will keep.'

The meal was huge and we barely did it justice. At the end, with the fruit, Mr Bayraktar began to slice up a highly spiced garlic sausage, which he toasted and offered to us wrapped in *pitta* bread.

'It's very good,' said his wife. 'But your breath will smell terrible in the morning.'

'Can we help you to wash this up?'

'Oh don't worry about that. A woman will come tomorrow to clear up.'

The Bayraktars' children were both staying with relatives. Malcolm had fallen asleep on the sofa. Sevinc stroked his head in a maternal way, while Steven curled up beside him to watch an American film on television. Over coffee, Sevinc began to talk once more about her lost Greek friends.

'Tell me.' Joan asked at last, 'you were very close to so many Greek people. Have Greeks and Turks ever intermarried in Cyprus? Can you think of any cases?'

'Never. Turks marry English, Americans and many others, but I don't believe I have ever heard of a Turk marrying a Greek, even in the old days. But as a foreigner you must understand that things were once much better between our two peoples. I can remember this from when I was a little girl, and from what my parents told me. Makarios, I really believe, was a good man, and wanted peace for everyone in Cyprus. But there were those who would not obey him. When Grivas came back, things were very bad.'

Her husband now began to speak, slowly but quite clearly: 'The Turkish people will never forget what happened in 1963 and 1964. Never. We can never go back.'

'I would rather be poor and live in peace, than rich and live with war again,' said Sevinc. 'I have my children to think of. I want to see them educated, married and happy.'

'You have a dowry to find?'

'Of course. If we don't help the young people, who will? We will have to buy them a house, because the government isn't going to give them one. My husband has a little land which he inherited in the village, so perhaps we can sell that, or find the money to build a house on it. It is a worry.'

I began to repeat the old song which Lawrence Durrell quoted in *Bitter Lemons*:

> If you should come to Kyrenia
> Don't enter the walls.
> If you should enter the walls
> Don't stay long.
> If you should stay long
> Don't get married.
> If you should get married
> Don't have children.

Sevinc was delighted and joined in at the last lines.

'How could you know that?'

'I read it in a book written by an Englishman who once lived near here. And I read another one somewhere; now, how does it go? I remember:

> Whoever has not given birth,
> Whoever has had no house built
> And whoever has not borne the expense of a daughter's wedding,
> Knows not the fear of God.'

I must have drunk more than enough *raki*. But Sevinc clapped her hands, then laughed: 'It's true, it's true. We do say that.'

We asked Sevinc's husband about his politics, but he went to fetch more ice and another bottle before replying.

'He thinks of nothing but political matters,' said Sevinc. 'Every day he reads all the Turkish and foreign newspapers. He keeps them in a big pile on top of the wardrobe, and sits in bed reading them. Sometimes I pinch him, but he just goes on reading.'

'My party is the New People's Democratic Party,' her husband said, pouring out more *raki*. (This movement was then recently formed, but we had seen the YDP initials painted on walls everywhere. The other political forces in the Turkish sector at that time were the Republican Turkish Party, the Communal Liberation Party and, of course, Rauf Denktash's National Unity Party.)

'Would you tell us your political position? What are your policies?'
Sevinc translated this.

'We are concerned to redress injustices which occurred at the trans-
fer of populations in 1974. Some people lost and some gained un-
fairly, and there is much to put right, perhaps by taxation.'

'And settlement from the mainland?'

'We condemn this. But it is a problem which may solve itself. Very
many have gone back of their own accord. If they have any kind of
trouble, they always go back to Turkey.'

'I don't quite understand.'

'Well, they aren't like Cypriot people. They don't trust the authorities. If there is a quarrel amongst themselves, they don't involve
anyone from outside. Sometimes there is a feud, bloodshed even, but
usually one of the parties leaves for the mainland. If they have a
dispute with the authorities, or perhaps with a Cypriot, about land or
grazing rights, they don't hire a lawyer and take the matter to court as
we would. They simply leave. That's the nomads' way.'

'How many settlers would you estimate there to be in the North
now?'

'About 20,000.'

'What about the big issues?' I asked. 'Partition and foreign policy?'

'We broadly support Denktash's position. We would like a settlement, of course, but partition must continue. Two separate states.
And we are concerned to remain independent from Turkey, both
politically and financially. I say this although I am a Turk and a
patriot.'

He was beginning to talk for himself more and more, although his
voice was slightly slurred. He poured more *raki*.

'It is late,' we said, 'and we should go. We can sleep in tomorrow
morning, but you have to drive into Nicosia to work.'

'He takes the bus,' said Sevinc. 'He leaves the car for me. Anyway
this is a pleasure for us. My husband is surprised that as English
people you are interested in these things. Besides, Cyprus is not like
England. If he likes, he can stay at home tomorrow. Or he can go into
the Ministry, and if he feels tired he can say: 'Oh, I don't feel so good.
I'll go home at lunch-time.' And no one will mind. That's the trouble
with Cyprus. Everyone's so relaxed here.'

Sevinc, with her excellent English, had been to stay with friends at
Windsor, enjoyed herself enormously and felt at home. Her husband,
however, was deeply afflicted with that inferiority complex which so
many Turks develop in their relations with Western Europe. At the
Ministry of Finance he had been peripherally concerned with the
affairs of a Turkish consortium which had sought to buy advanced
engine technology from the British motor industry. One might think

214

that this approach would be rather flattering to such a lame duck. But the Turks had been turned down, abruptly and without reason. He felt insulted.

'You must think Turkey very backward. But you won't help our industry, even when we offer to pay. Can you explain that?'

I couldn't. He had once been to London, alone in 1969, and had felt isolated and friendless. In all his story, only one girl, who helped him find an address, had shown him any kindness.

'You don't welcome foreigners,' he said. This, too, I had to admit. But it became worse.

'I went to the wax museum, where all the tourists go. Madame Tussaud's? Yes. There I saw the Queen of England. And next to her they had put Tom Jones, the singer. Nothing but a playboy, and you put him next to your Queen.'

I wrinkled my brow, trying to remember. We had only been once to Madame Tussaud's and so long ago. It might have been so.

'So I look for Kemal,' went on Mr Bayraktar, 'the Father of My Country.'

I began to experience a sinking feeling. Mr Bayraktar's dark face, flushed with liquor, had filled with suppressed rage. 'Bayraktar', an old and honourable Turkish name, means 'the Standard-Bearer'. In that moment, I could picture his war-like ancestor planting the horse-hair standard on the walls of Nicosia, amidst the powder smoke and carnage at the end of the siege.

'For a long time I cannot find him. Then I see that he is next to Hitler. Hitler! The most evil man of this century and the enemy of your country, and you put the founder of our nation beside him. How could you be so unfeeling?

'I am certain no insult was intended,' I began rather feebly, 'although it was certainly very tactless . . .'

'It certainly isn't so now,' said Joan. 'I am quite sure that Hitler is displayed alone, in the Chamber of Horrors.'

(We promised to check when we returned to England. The dreadful thought struck me that Mustapha Kemal might have been melted down. In the event, someone told me that he now stood beside Colonel Gaddafi of Libya, hardly an improvement.)

It is certainly true that very few English people take any interest in the history of Turkey, and the Turks feel this. So as Mr Bayraktar continued to pour the *raki* we engaged him in a long conversation, ranging through the Crimean War, the last Ottoman Sultans, the British leasing of Cyprus in 1878, the Young Turks and the Balkan Wars. By mutual consent, we skirted around Gallipoli, to go on to Venizelos, Kemal Pasha and the Asia Minor War of 1922.

'Our nations should have a great deal in common,' I told him. 'We have both lost great empires, and are learning to make our living without them.'

Perhaps this struck a chord.

'Yes, yes. And we have stood with you in two world wars.'

I began to protest. Sevinc saw that she had mistranslated, and rapidly corrected herself.

'Well of course we were against you in the First War. But in the Second, we were with you. In spirit.'

Well at least they did not join the Axis Powers, I thought. Then I told a story about a cruise ship, docked in Marmaris at a time when a reunion of the veterans of 1922 was being held.

'The British passengers were the only ones who made a point of standing to attention during the Turkish national anthem. We would expect the same from you. People should respect each other's national feelings.'

He stood up, suddenly and unsteadily, to shake me by the hand, speaking emphatically in Turkish. Sevinc translated: 'He says you are a most honourable man. If you wish to do any business in North Cyprus, if you have any problems, anything at all, contact him at the Ministry and the problems will disappear.'

I was somewhat taken aback; moreover I was beginning to feel deeply guilty for my shameless manipulation. But Sevinc continued on a lighter note: 'He also says that you are a good friend and he wishes you could speak better with one another. He would like to take you some day on a trip to Turkey. They have special baths there; have you heard of them? They offer pleasures which he does not want to describe in front of me, or your wife!'

Sevinc's laughter and their warm farewells followed us out into the darkness of the night.

CHAPTER FOURTEEN

SOURP MAGAR AND ANTIPHONITIS

One hot noon we lay on the Pachyammos beach, letting the sun soak into muscles tired by swimming. The smoke from the fire on which we had cooked our lunch trailed lazily downwind along the water margin. Rolling over, I could see the boys' heads appear occasionally among the dunes, where they chased lizards and dragonflies. Behind them, the distinctive purple slope of Pentadactylos thrust against the sky.

'Has it struck you,' I asked Joan, 'that in all the time we have been wandering about Turkish Cyprus, we haven't met a single tourist? Foreigners certainly, but all of them diplomats or United Nations personnel: people with a job to do. Nobody like us: just looking.'

It was quite true. On our visits to this beach we had only ever seen the occasional shepherd on the hills inland, and once a couple of men had come from a building company in Kyrenia to load their lorry with sand from the dunes near the road. No wonder the hotels had problems. Doubtless a few tourists would appear when the summer season began, but I could not believe that Turkish Cyprus would ever seem crowded.

Behind the beach, in the area known as Kokkinospita, the Red Houses, three perennial streams have cut deep gorges through the grazing lands, exposing the light sandy soil to erosion. Here, we came across what appeared to be an eagle, struggling to gain height in the hot, still air and casting a shadow right across the road as it swung over, searching for an updraught. The crows had discovered its predicament and were mobbing it, taking turns to dart in, before backing away to a respectful distance. We stopped and watched through binoculars until the right thermal was found and the circling became regular as the great bird began to rise towards the peaks. One by one its tormentors dropped away.

Several travellers on these mountains claimed to have seen the rare imperial eagle which, though close to extinction in Spain, has an eastern race which might well cross the Straits from Turkey. Such a sighting would have been a treat, but from its larger size I suspect that this was actually a griffon vulture, strayed from its normal range over the Troodos.

On the outskirts of the small village of Kharcha, we broke our rule again and stopped to look at the church. Our guidebook listed only the Church of Arkhangelos, from the nineteenth century, containing a floor of rounded pebbles. But this surely was much older. We walked around the overgrown churchyard, examining the grey walls. Large frilled lizards, of the kind which had seemed so repulsive in the lemon grove, squeezed themselves into fissures in the stone at our approach.

I looked up to see an elderly man watching us, unusually fair-haired, pale and thin, wearing a grey suit and smoking a cigarette. He walked up and shook hands languidly, showing a large gold ring. He had that Turkish quality of watchful repose, the opposite of the Greek's nervous high spirits, which demonstrates itself in an economy of movement and a habit of noticing everything and saying little. It seemed that we interested him.

'Welcome. I am the *muktar* of this village. Would you like to see the church?'

He felt in his pocket for the key and unlocked the padlock on the door. They had been keeping sheep in the church. There was not much to see, but the *iconostasis* had been left, and a wooden gallery.

'It is very old,' said the *muktar*. 'Roman.' Presumably he meant Byzantine.

The road up to the Plataniotissa Forest is made beautiful by the tall trees, which only grow on the moist northern slopes. A stream runs down close by, to fill the cistern provided for the village by the UN in 1967. Higher up, the rock is split by deep gorges and pitted by caves, while deciduous trees are mixed with the green pines. In all this district the arbutus is very common, remarkable for its startling red bark, which can be peeled off to show pure white wood beneath. This is the tree traditionally used by Cypriot carpenters to make the coffee shop chairs which double as foot rests. Indeed, when a Cypriot really relaxes, he uses five of these – one to sit in, one to support each leg, and one to support each arm. Perhaps even a sixth, on which to stand his cup of coffee.

High above is the radio mast of a listening station, and the trees are silhouetted on the skyline above the precipice. The road, marked on the Greek map as a forest road, had now been paved to the top, and was in excellent condition. The Halevga Forest Station at the summit was once the headquarters of the Northern Range Forest Department, with a hotel and café: a place of refreshment for pilgrims on their way to visit the remote monasteries of these mountains. But this station, which the army had so carefully barred us from approaching on the south side, was now totally abandoned.

The forest road which follows the ridge was still drivable with care. Referring frequently to the map, we crawled to the west for some miles in the direction of Pentadactylos, through the most spectacular scenery of all the Kyrenia mountains, with jagged pikes of rock ahead and a huge abyss on our right-hand side. Once or twice, we stopped to look out over the coast from a projecting spur, and found ourselves suffering from vertigo at the sight of the crows moving above the tree tops below.

There is an old story from the time of the Saracen raids that a Christian bishop once ran along this ridge to save his life, with a band of blood-crazed pirates close on his heels. His desperate prayer to heaven was answered at the last moment, and he found that he was miraculously able to leap huge distances from precipice to precipice, while his Saracen enemies fell and were dashed to pieces.

In time, it became clear that we had overrun our objective. With difficulty, I found a place safe enough to turn the car around, and we retraced our steps. It was Steven who first spotted roofs among the trees far below in a kind of alcove in the side of the mountain. The place seemed inaccessible at first, but there was a road leading down a steep moss-grown track, deeply gullied and strewn with rocks and gravel washed down by the winter storms. When halfway down, I became convinced that the car would not be able to climb back up, but we were already past the point of no return. We shortly arrived at a little grassy patch in front of the Armenian Monastery of Sourp Magar, the Virgin Mary.

A monastery was first built in this remote cleft of the mountain in about the year 1000. The first monks, Coptic Christians, dedicated it to the hermit-saint, Markarius of Alexandria. In 1425 the monastery was made over to the Armenian people of Cyprus, for whom it remained a place of pilgrimage until 1974. During the Armenian massacres in Turkey in 1894–6, a time when mutilated corpses are reputed to have drifted across the Straits from the mainland, the monastery became an orphanage to house young survivors of the terror.

By 1974, we knew, the monks no longer lived in Sourp Magar. But there had been a guardian who lived alone here and kept a guesthouse for visitors. And every May the Armenians of Cyprus would make the journey into the mountains in memory of the past. We had therefore expected to find the present building, which is relatively modern, in a reasonably preserved condition. But although the walls stood firm, the whitewash slowly peeling, almost every roof had been pulled in, every window had lost its glass and shutters, and every arched door had been torn from its hinges. The trees in the courtyard had grown wild, and the long, pillared cloisters were strewn with broken roof tiles. Only the church, built in 1811, was still solidly roofed, although

219

the ceramic tiles had been prised from the walls. This was the result not of twelve years of weathering, but of systematic destruction. The Turks seemed to have reserved a peculiar vindictiveness for their old enemies, the Armenians.

Nothing could detract, however, from the fine situation of this large building at the edge of the cliffs, and we spent some time exploring it. A rusting refrigerator lay on it side in what had once been the kitchen. There was a deep well in the courtyard, dangerously unguarded. Beside it stood an orange tree, half a dozen fruits glowing like lamps in the rich, green foliage. I shinned up to pick one – for who would mind? – but, as I should have realised, they were the bitter oranges that are planted in public places to deter such pilfering. Outside the east wall, overlooking a hummocky area of scrub thorn, stood a pillar with an inscription in the strange lettering of the Armenian language – unintelligible to us, but dated 1933.

The Renault groaned and protested, but on full throttle in bottom gear it managed to claw its way up the steepest section of the slope. Joan and the boys had walked up to improve its chances. I switched off at the top to let the engine cool while I waited for them. The empty cartridges by the road proved that hunters still found their way up here occasionally. More difficult map reading followed as we crawled along dirt tracks for miles, somewhere above Ayios Amvrosios. We were searching for the Antiphonitis Monastery, but we entered a maze of intersecting, unsigned tracks, and we knew that the Monastery of Apati also lay in these hills.

We stumbled on Antiphonitis late in the afternoon. Having become well and truly lost, we had taken to climbing every rocky bluff and scanning the countryside with binoculars. Again, it was Steven who spotted the red tiles of a Byzantine dome, half hidden by trees. This time we left the car on the track and walked down through the forest, uncertain as to what we would find. But there, as if it had been hiding in shyness, stood a jewel of a church, remarkable not so much for purity of Byzantine style, but for its position in the wilderness. The air was still, and the forest undisturbed by any sound. Everything about the building appeared perfect, even to the integrity of the graveyard wall.

Christ Antiphonitis, Christ of the Echo, is a twelfth-century church which has outlasted the monastery it once served, and of which no more than ruins remain. The construction is unusual, being octagonal, with a huge central dome supported by eight pillars. Succeeding conquerors had been charmed by this Orthodox church; the Lusignans added a narthex, and the Venetians built the loggia, the row of arches in the churchyard which once supported a wooden roof. They must all have used the same quarry because the warm, honey-coloured stone matches perfectly.

We pushed our way through the thick wild fennel which had erupted in a vivid green froth around the outer wall, and passed through the arched entrance. There were fig trees in the churchyard which had once been carefully pruned, but we could not find the copper bell which travellers had described, and the spring seemed to have run dry. Nor could we identify the liquid amber tree, or the *Xylon Effendi*, the Wood of our Lord, whose hacked trunk Dr Sibthorp was shown by the *Hegumenos*, or Abbot, in 1787. This may no doubt be blamed on our botanical ignorance, but the early travellers reported such a confusion of inaccurate Latin names and species that perhaps we may be forgiven. If the tree that they were shown was *Liquidambar orientalis*, it was the source of the sweet-smelling resin known as storax, once used by apothecaries as an expectorant.

The door of the church stood open, and the windows were smashed, allowing birds to fly in and out of the great dome as they pleased. The Turkish soldiers had broken away part of the *iconostasis* in 1974, though what remained was beautiful. The afternoon was well advanced, and the small windows allowed little light into the interior. Malcolm shone up his torch, but it barely dispelled the gloom. We were looking for frescos which had been famous: the *Baptism of Christ* from the twelfth century, the *Tree of Jesse* and the *Last Judgement* from the fifteenth, with a Pantokrator, *Christ in Majesty*, in the dome. Whether the vandalism of 1974 or the subsequent effect of the weather through the open windows was responsible, I could not say, but very little appeared to be left of these, and the remaining paint adhered patchily to the wall. Only the figures of martyrs and apostles on the curve of the massive pillars could be made out with any clarity. Before the invasion, although the church had been disused, a guardian from Ayios Amvrosios had been in regular attendance. Now, the state of the undergrowth made it clear that no one had been here for months, or possibly years. We should, by this time, have become inured to such callous neglect, but we were appalled that no effort was being made to prevent this building falling into ruin.

We found the sixteenth-century Church of Apati by chance in the dusk as we drove home, a small tiled building on a hill, apparently to the wrong side of the track. But careful map reading convinced us that the church was in the right place and that it was we who had become lost again. By climbing a steep bank, grown with orchids and clematis, we found a simple, rustic chapel, once restored and now undamaged in its peaceful churchyard.

We came down to Ayios Amvrosios on one of the old cobbled roads of Cyprus, thinly overlaid with modern asphalt. The setting sun was misty over the countless indentations of the coast to the west; the evening was warm and the boys rode with their heads and shoulders out of the sun roof. A startled hare bolted along the road in front of us, the long ears flashing white in the beam of the headlamps. It is said that Cypriot hunters shoot them in the moonlight, by the light of their eyes. Sir Samuel Baker enjoyed his shooting in Cyprus, though he lost one of his English spaniels from snake-bite:

> I have never tasted any game so delicious as the Cyprian hares. They are not quite so red or curly as the European species, but the flesh is exceedingly rich and possesses a peculiarly gamey flavour, owing to the aromatic herbs on which they live.

> (Samuel Baker, *Cyprus as I Saw It in 1879*)

CHAPTER FIFTEEN

THE MESAORIA

The next morning found us on the Mesaoria, at the old Turkish village of Bey Keuy near Kythrea. There we knew ourselves, as foreigners, to be unwelcome. But we hoped that we would be permitted to continue east over the plain, along the quiet back roads. The Turkish sector's prestigious new airport, soon to be officially opened, was not far away, and broad new highways were in the final stages of construction. The tower of the water drilling rig on the plain punctured the horizon abruptly. No one seemed concerned at our presence in the village, where we stopped to ask our way, but on the road leading across the fields to Petra tou Dhigeni (the Rocks of Dhigenis), now known simply as Yenice Koy, or New Town, two armed sentries stepped out to wave us down. Once again, we were forced to make a detour by the main road. The whole district was under close military surveillance and a light aircraft made regular circuits overhead.

At Epikho, once a village of camel drivers, an old woman was painting her front door, and a new school had been built. Pigeons were nesting in old clay pots and buckets wired to the walls of the houses. In time, we passed out of the sensitive area and found our route unhindered through Exometokhi and Kourou Monastir, across undulating open land. There were few villages, and the road, bordered with waxy white asphodels, ran straight between fields of anemones. There were old, neglected vineyards, and occasionally a grove of eucalyptus trees or a humpbacked stone bridge showed where water sometimes flowed in an irrigation channel. Orchards of blossoming almond trees stood above yellow ranunculus, the distant mountains around Kantara visible between the branches. The day was already becoming hot, and when we stopped we could hear the larks singing their hearts out. A few palm trees clustered where the ground was moist enough to sustain them, and in places the smooth swell of the land was interrupted by a tumulus, or scarred by ruins. Time had stood still here, perhaps even moved backwards. The women were spinning as they watched their flocks of sheep, and many still wore a white veil.

All this fertile land once suffered from dreadful plagues of locusts. The Italian Villani wrote in 1355 that:

> At that time the locusts were so abundant in the isle of Cyprus that they covered all the fields to the height of one quarter braccio and ate everything green on the earth and so destroyed [the farmer's] labour that there was no fruit to be had in that year.

(Trs. C.D. Cobham, *Excerpta Cypria*)

The poor Cypriots had no defence, beyond a faith in the efficacy of certain locust-dispelling icons. Once a priest was despatched to Syria to fetch a certain holy water, and sometimes migrating flocks of a particular small bird would appear to feed on the voracious insects. But in the main, the locusts brought starvation in their train. The Turks instituted a locust tax, which obliged every adult male to collect and hand in 30 *okas* of locust eggs for destruction. In the parts of the island affected by the pest, this involved between two and ten days' labour, while peasants from other districts were obliged to buy their quota at the market price of two piastres an *oka*.

At Psilatos, renamed Sutluce, attempts had been made to impress with a new mosque, a statue of Ataturk and a monument to TMT: all rather overpowering when crammed into the square of such a small village. The Greeks of Lefkoniko, now Gecitkale, apart from being recognised as skilful lace-makers, were once teased for eating donkeys, a taunt arising from some half-forgotten story. This is a larger town, where we tried unsuccessfully to buy film and walked around the Church of the Archangel Michael, surrounded by rubbish and litter, the initials of TMT painted in red over the walls. Gypsos, named by the Greeks for the gypsum mined nearby, is now Turkish Akova, and the women, for some reason, wear black as the Greeks do.

At Syngrasis, an area full of old churches and antiquities, our map showed a large dam, an impressive and definitive patch of blue near the Chapel of Tris Pedhes. But there was no water to be seen, only a shallow depression in the ground with an area of caked mud in the centre. A shepherd was grazing his animals nearby, warmly dressed in a pullover and thick jacket, despite the heat of the day, a knapsack slung over his shoulder and a long stick in his hand.

'It was full last year,' he said, 'but we had no proper rain this winter. Even in a good year the dam can be too low and dirty to water the beasts.'

Once there were proud signs outside Trikomo, welcoming the visitor to the 'Birthplace of Grivas Dighenis'. The famous guerrilla leader of EOKA, revered almost as a saint by Greek enosists, was born here in 1898. Whatever one's opinion of George Grivas' role in the troubled politics of his homeland, one cannot help but feel that the pugnacious old warrior was fortunate to die in January 1974. By that time, EOKA B was fully engaged in the plot to destabilise the government of Makarios, in collusion with the Colonels' junta in Athens. The coup and assassination attempt against Archbishop Makarios, the installation of Nikos Sampson as president and the invasion by Turkey followed each other almost as night follows day. Grivas would surely turn in his grave if he knew that the Turks held his home town, which has been renamed Iskele.

Trikomo is a quiet place, with a reputation for fine pomegranates. Baker was surprised to find a steam engine here, puffing away as it drove a cotton gin. This frantic industrial activity is no more, and the enervating midday heat had driven most of the inhabitants indoors. A dog lay outside the twelfth-century Church of Panayia Theotokas, snapping tetchily at the flies which buzzed around its head. The church was locked, sealed off from the town by a stone wall and shaded by great cypress trees. By peering through a broken window we could see the *iconostasis* covered with fine paintings, chandeliers and carved wooden pews thrown around in confusion, all thickly coated with dust.

The other church of Trikomo, the miniature Chapel of Ayios Iakovas (St James) in the central square, was similarly locked. A dozen or so people could probably hold hands in a ring around this delightful little domed building, which so enchanted Queen Maria of Romania that she had a copy built on her estate by the Black Sea. I sat down in the small patch of shade it provided, while Joan and the boys went into a shop to buy soft drinks. The idlers outside the café looked up for barely a moment before continuing their desultory conversation. I was all but asleep when the others returned.

Windmills were turning on the plain near Bogaz, clanking as they pumped the water to the surface from deep beneath the ground. Bogaz means 'the Throat', or 'the Straits', after the Turkish name for the Dardanelles, and is one of the few fishing ports in Northern Cyprus. We sat at a table by the edge of the sea, drinking beer and waiting for the little restaurant to cook our red mullet. The sun was burning high in the sky, glaring harshly over the sand and water, so that it was painful to look at the line of ancient, rusty caiques which rolled at the jetty where the boys played. A container ship was moving out from Famagusta, feeling her way slowly through the water and towering above the coastlands as if an apartment block had decided to go for a very sedate stroll. A fisherman started up the single-cylinder diesel engine of one of the caiques and set off north, in the direction of the Karpas peninsula, the detonations of the exhaust sounding flat across the water.

★ ★ ★ ★

In Famagusta, on behalf of my family business, I visited the founder of a company engaged in reconditioning lorry engines and importing motor components. Nothing resulted from our negotiations, but, as a product of both English and Cypriot cultures, I found him interesting.

'Please come and join me for a coffee. Excuse my hands, but we have a problem with a reboring machine.'

He was dressed in white overalls, and was wiping his greasy hands with cotton waste. His hands-on style contrasted with those Turks who ran their companies the old-fashioned way – from a seat in their favourite café. His lieutenants had insisted that he would wish to talk to me – and it was plain that this he would do, politely, for ten minutes and no longer. He had learned his English working as a mechanic in a south London garage, and he came straight to the point.

'Here you are, have a look at these. This is the kind of stuff we buy: bearing shells, pistons, piston rings, valves, diesel injection equipment. Here is a list of the prices we pay; can your company improve on these? As an Englishman I show you this straight away; with a Greek I would have had to play all sorts of fucking games.

'Stock orders by sea freight are no problem; the paperwork is very simple. But air freight is only OK on Wednesdays. Air freight goes through Istanbul, you see, and it has to be unloaded and put on another aircraft for North Cyprus. Those thieving bastards at Istanbul steal half of it. Only on Wednesday the same aircraft is used for the whole trip and there is no unloading. So make sure you send air freight on Wednesday.

'Payment? We pay for each shipment on sight of documents. My account is with the Turkish Bank: the branch at the Elephant and Castle. If anyone asks for a letter of credit, I won't deal with them. I don't have time for all that fucking business. Either we trust each other or we don't.

'My son would be very interested to talk to you. He runs our branch in Nicosia. Here is the address, quite easy to find, and I'll telephone to say you will call. I am sure he would like to meet you.'

Finally, as if in contradiction of his earlier statement: 'Have you done business in Cyprus before? Well, you be careful. People will tell you all kinds of stories and you can't trust them. Greeks and Turks, we are all rogues alike!'

Uproarious laughter, and the Levantine pantomime of burnt fingers.

★   ★   ★   ★

On the outskirts of Famagusta, near a half-built hotel where a sentry stood out on the mezzanine watching over the plain, groups of men were drifting through the doors of the TMT social club. We took a wrong turn and found ourselves running past rotating windmills towards British territory – the Dhekelia Base. We thought there might be British soldiers at the end of the road, but the barriers were manned only by black-uniformed Turkish policemen. There was nothing else to see, so we turned around and returned to the fast, straight road from Famagusta to Nicosia.

I noticed that some of the shepherdesses watching flocks on the Mesaoria carried their babies slung on their backs like Red Indian papooses. Fingers of sunlight stretched through the banks of cloud which had drifted from the Troodos mountains, and descended to the ground among the ruined church towers and stranded villages of the plain. As we approached Nicosia, we could see distant smoke rising from an unseen fire in the Greek sector and the distinctive flat-topped hills towards Larnaca. Near the Line at Mia Milea, soldiers were exercising beside the road, crouching around machine guns set up in the fields.

We never tired of watching the craftsmen in the back streets of Nicosia, where one might see a brass samovar being beaten out by hand, a man with an ingenious machine for stuffing mattresses, or a blacksmith welding together an elaborate iron grille to cover a window. The furniture makers were truly wonderful, producing elegant sofas and chairs covered in pale satins, which were then left out in the street where the afternoon wind blew the dust of the city in little whirlpools. Best of all were the wood carvers and carpenters, and we found Mr Hikmet at one of these, across Haydar Pasha Street from his own shop.

'Hallo, my dears. How are you? I drove through Lapta on Sunday with my family. We called in to see you, but you were out.'

'I'm sorry, we were by the sea.'

'And we went to the mountains. We had a celebration to make, because we heard that our younger son passed his accountancy examinations. We went to a little restaurant I know, where they cook a whole lamb sealed up in a clay oven. Have you heard of lamb *klephtiko?* We arrived just as they were breaking the oven open and picked our favourite pieces.' He licked his lips at the memory. 'Really, my dears, you positively must come with us next time.'

He introduced us to the carpenter, who was engaged in carving a complicated pattern into the thick wood of a door.

'Have you ever seen carpenters like we have in Cyprus? People have cut the trees of this island since the beginning of history. The Phoenicians built their ships here. Now we use the pines for building houses, but not for furniture. There is too much resin. If you see an old house with really big heavy beams, and there are many in Nicosia, they will be made of oak. They used to tow whole trees across the sea from Turkey in the old days. Of course the forests of Cyprus are nothing to what they were once.'

I told of the mountain slopes of Crete, where giant cypress trees once grew before man's greed for timber removed them for ever and goats completed the denudation as the island's springs dried up little by little.

'I think, perhaps, that is what is happening here in Cyprus. It is a great shame . . . Ah, now I have an idea for you. I should have suggested this when you came before. If you are interested in Nicosia, you should go and have tea on the top floor of the Seray Palace Hotel. It is the highest building in the old city and from there you can see everything.'

And so, at sunset, we stood on the balcony, eight floors up, overlooking the city. The Kyrenia mountains to the north were shrouded in deep purple, while closer at hand the lights were beginning to come on in Omorphita and Ortakeuy. The great block of the Ledra Palace Hotel caught the last of the sun's rays and a *muezzin*'s cry floated from a minaret. Beyond the battered towers flying the UN flag along the Green Line, the high-rise office buildings of the modern part of the city were a mute testament to the commercial success of Greek Cyprus.

After retiring inside to drink our tea, we found ourselves eavesdropping on a government minister entertaining Arab businessmen, discussing orange shipments and politics in English over cigars and fruit juice.

'We value our connections with Arab markets very highly,' he was saying. 'If any problems arise at all, I would like you to contact me personally at the Ministry.'

The deal, it seemed, had been struck. More orange juice was brought to the table, together with a jug of iced water.

'We are very proud of our water supply here,' said the minister. 'In fact, you can drink it quite safely from the taps.' The Arabs seemed suitably impressed.

'How is the financial situation this year?' one of them ventured. 'What price are oranges at the moment in London?'

He had expressed the whole problem of the North in a nutshell.

★　★　★　★

Nicosia becomes a strange and magical place at dusk, when a cool wind from the mountains stirs through the streets, and the ancient buildings sink into shadow. In the Archduke Louis' day, a tattoo was sounded three hours after sunset, after which:

> . . . nobody is allowed to go out without a lantern. Any stranger infringing this regulation is shown home; if an inhabitant of the town, he is brought into the Serai, where he has to pass the night.

(Archduke Louis Salvator of Austria, *Levkosia*)

One evening, when the bats were flitting on silent wings around St Sophia and the Bedestan, and the sound of Christian bells could be heard from across the Line, I found Joan in conversation with an elderly gentleman on the corner of Haydar Pasha Street. He wore a beautiful tweed suit, his grey hair and moustache were cut short in military fashion and he stood holding a shiny black bicycle.

'Good evening, sir,' he said, shaking hands. 'My name is Turkut, Sergeant Turkut. I could not resist talking to your lady when I saw her here, for we do not often have the pleasure of English visitors.'

'Sergeant Turkut?'

'I was a policeman nearly all my life, except for a time as a soldier, and as a policeman under the British I learned to speak English. It was a very happy time for me.'

Sergeant Turkut, beautifully mannered, was afraid that he would bore us, talking on a cold street corner as the light faded. But in time we drew his whole life story out of him.

'In 1939, when the German War began, the British asked for volunteers. There would be no loss of pension or seniority for those who joined the British army, and many of us joined. We thought perhaps we would see the world. I was a young chap then, ready for anything, or so I thought. Because of my police experience, I was made a sergeant almost at once. We were three months training at a camp near Famagusta. There were shepherds, farmers, fishermen: all kinds of people learning to be soldiers. At first, there was nothing but confusion. You can imagine how difficult it was to train such a collection in three months. We were to work as drivers, labourers, loading parties and the like to take food and ammunition to the front.

'First we went to Egypt, then to Libya against the Italians. After three months, to my surprise, I was promoted to Sergeant Major.'

He must have noticed my involuntary stiffening, and he laughed.

'A powerful man, you think? Oh, it's a terrible job you know; you can never allow yourself to smile, always with your chin up. We went to Greece with the British Expeditionary Force. Crete? We never got so far; the Germans captured us in Salonika. You know they got 14,000 of us there. We were kept in Salonika waiting for transport, because the railway lines had been bombed. Sir, are you sure I am not boring you; will your lady not catch cold?'

'Please, we're very interested.'

'We were kept locked in carriages. No, not carriages, places for animals. Cattle trucks, yes, thank you. We waited for seven days, packed in tight, like sardines as you say. And strangely, that is what they fed us, just one time. Some hard bread and Italian tinned fish. It was very old, and after we ate it almost all of us became ill – and, excuse me, madam, but there were no lavatories, and the doors were kept barred. You can imagine how it was. We were not taken out until we reached Czechoslovakia. I was in prison camps for four years: one year in Czechoslovakia and three years in Germany, until we were liberated.

'We were freed by the Americans, by the famous General Patton, the one with the pistols. A marvellous man I thought, and I'll never forget him, although he was very cruel, very hard in war. He never cared how many died. I heard that he was killed six months later in a motor car accident. I still have his photograph though; I asked the American Consulate here, and they got it for me.

'We were flown to France in relays of planes. Then we had to wait there for twelve days because all the pilots were drunk. It's quite true; they had all been given leave to celebrate VE Day, and they got so drunk that we had to wait for them to sober up. And so we came home at last.

'Sir, madam, are you quite sure that I am not detaining you? You are very kind to be interested. Well, I was a policeman again and very happy until the troubles began, the time of EOKA. Then I saw things that I could not tell to you, madam, if you will excuse me. But I remember going to the cemetery with a British officer, Mr Peck, to mend – how do you say, tend? – the graves of British soldiers. Now these graves had been attacked, damaged. They were all young men, no more than boys. We had letters from their people at home; it would break your heart. But the extraordinary thing was how I remember Mr Peck. His face was not red, he was not angry or full of insults for the Greeks who had done this. I asked him, 'However can you be so calm? I could not bear this.'

'He only said sadly, "Sergeant Turkut, the soldiers died doing their duty, and the Greeks too believe that they are doing their duty." I could not understand it then, and I still find it difficult. There were many English like that.

'After the Republic came, I retired in 1962 and the Greeks behaved as we had expected. You know those bloody Greeks, if you will excuse me, are all dreamers, romantic people with their heads in the clouds. Turkey, they imagined, was no more than a fly they could brush from the face of the world. But in 1974 they got a bloody nose, you might say, a shock they won't ever forget. If they attack us, we will fight again, but I don't think they will trouble us for a long time.

'So now the politicians talk about settlements and agreements, but I don't think that anything will happen very soon. There is no one on the Greek side we can negotiate with. Papandreou? I don't trust Papandreou. One day he is talking with Arabs, then with the Russians. He even rejects NATO and threatens to throw out the Americans. Who can trust a crazy man like that, who doesn't even understand who his own friends are? Now Papandreou is asking for all the guaranteeing powers to withdraw: the Greeks, the British, the UN. If the Turkish army withdrew, the Greek Cypriot National Guard would be here within hours, and all the world knows it. Karamanlis, now he was a wily old fox. Karamanlis you could deal with. Given time, we might have done something with him.'

'If you had to make the decision the British made in 1960,' I asked him, 'what would you have done in our place? How could the peace have been preserved in Cyprus?'

'My dear sir, the answer to that question is so very simple. You had a written, constitutional right to Cyprus from the Treaty of Lausanne in 1923. You should have stayed here for a hundred, two hundred years. My dear sir and madam, the ground beneath your feet, these very paving stones, should belong to you today! We Turks never wanted the British to leave. Truly, we never believed that you would, not until the very end. How could you leave us with things as they were? Just look at us now. I once had a passport showing me as a citizen of the British Empire. Great Britain is the happiest and most fortunate country in the world, and now we have lost our rights there. I have no hope of living in Britain now.'

The miniature Chapel of Ayios Iakovas at Trikomo

CHAPTER SIXTEEN

BUFFAVENTO

The military roadblock at Koutsovendis, or Gungor, had now been moved below the village to the crossroads. We had come prepared to walk up to Buffavento Castle, but the new sentry refused to allow our passage. Tashkent and Kaynakkoy were accessible, he indicated, pointing along the foothills to the west, but Gungor and its environs were out of bounds.

A shepherd standing with his animals beside the road near Mia Milea was more encouraging. He wasn't sure about Buffavento, but he was almost certain that we could use the forest road as far as the monastery below. But which monastery, he wanted to know, for there were two in those hills. And a careful check of the map proved him correct; a mile or two to the east of Ayios Ioannis Chrysostomos lay the Monastery of Panayia Absinthiotissa, above the village of Vouno. Nevertheless, we were determined not to be baulked again. After a long drive around to Pentadactylos, we turned off the main road on to the forest track and – had our eyes deceived us before? – there was no minatory sign to be seen. For several miles we bumped along through the trees, occasionally glimpsing the open cast mines below. The path grew narrow with a precipitous drop on the left, and the trees gave way to bare rocks, until eventually we were travelling along a narrow gallery dynamited out of the cliff. We tried to avoid looking down, and I felt my palms growing damp on the steering wheel. There was an adequate width for the car, perhaps a couple of feet to spare for the outer wheels, but no question of turning around at any point. In one place a rockfall had spread over the track and we inched round it, carefully watching the crumbling lip as our wheels came close.

Suddenly, we rounded a corner to come upon a notice: 'Restricted Military Zone – No Photography'. The red and white striped barrier had been left swung up vertically, and after a moment's hesitation we continued on our way. It was not a difficult decision, for the road had been nerve-racking enough when travelling forwards, and the prospect of reversing along it for a mile or more was beyond contemplation. We moved forward slowly, and Joan in the front passenger seat

233

found herself looking down on the military camp a few hundred feet below. Lorries and jeeps were parked in long lines, while soldiers milled about on the parade ground. Amazingly, no one looked up.

Were we really supposed to be here? Having come so far, we felt committed and breathed a sigh of relief when we turned a corner and could no longer be seen from the camp. But within a mile, we found ourselves crawling like flies on a wall above the targets of a field firing range, where about 100 soldiers could be seen grouped around an instructor. I had been vacillating between two views of the situation: we were being either unnecessarily timid or else extremely foolhardy. I was coming to the conclusion that the latter was the case. But once again, not a face was raised in our direction and, at a junction where a dirt road from the camp came up to join ours, a rise in the ground hid our car from sight.

An ancient sign pointed up the hill to Buffavento Castle. The last few yards of the track and a tiny parking area were grown over with grass and moss. Obviously no one came here nowadays.

'No wonder,' said Joan, climbing our of the car with relief. 'Who would be insane enough to drive along that road for pleasure?'

We began to climb the steep slope towards the summit, following a narrow path which wound its way back and forth among the stones and dwarf cypress trees. Above us, we could see the uneven towers of the castle projecting like rotten teeth from the ridge. The firing range came into view again, and, as we watched, the soldiers fanned out from the instructor. Distant sounds rose up to us. They were actually singing: a stirring and martial-sounding chant. Then, in a line, they sprinted over the flat ground and suddenly flung themselves down. A couple of seconds later an appalling cacophony of detonations from the high-velocity weapons rang from one peak to the next, rolling and echoing between the crags. After about 30 seconds the firing ceased, and the sounds slowly died away. Once more, the tiny figures of the toy soldiers merged into a compact group.

We slowly made our way higher. We could see the monastery now, with its cypress trees, by the main camp. The road which led down the hill from our parked car passed its gate. All the villages of the western Mesaoria were spread before us, and Nicosia lay in its own haze of dust and smoke. After fifteen minutes, again the chanting and running before the deafening noise of the firing below made our eardrums ache. Shortly afterwards, the sun was blotted out for a moment, and there was an even louder roar as a large passenger jet startled us by thundering over the crest, apparently with only a few feet to spare, before banking steeply on its way down to Ercan airfield. A blackish haze of unburnt kerosene was left hanging in the air behind it.

We were still uncertain as to whether or not we were trespassing in a military area. If so, surely we would have been stopped while passing close above the camp or the firing range? But had we been seen at all? It is a common phenomenon that people in familiar surroundings very rarely look above their heads without cause. We decided to keep our heads down once the castle was reached, and to leave as quietly as possible when an opportunity arose. The camera had been left in the glove box of the car and we hoped that our binoculars would not be regarded as incriminating.

The first fortifications we reached, Lusignan stone over older Byzantine brickwork, distracted us from the modern warfare being rehearsed below. Suddenly the ground fell away in front of us; we could see the friendly roofs of Kyrenia basking in the sun by the sea, and knew that Bellapais was only a short glide for an eagle across the cliffs. Behind us, the guns still pounded. Then we passed from the exposed mountainside into the welcome shelter of the gatehouse.

Buffavento Castle (Blown by the Winds), variously called Butphens or Buffaventum by early writers, is the highest of the three fortresses of the Kyrenia mountains. Three thousand feet above the Mesaoria, it clings to spikes of rock overlooking great abysses to the north and west. The castle is visible for an immense distance over the plain, and Sir Samuel Baker could see it clearly from the governor's residence at Nicosia. Byzantine Greeks built the first watchtower here, and it was already a stronghold in the time of Richard the Lionheart. Sources differ as to whether it was the tyrant Isaac Comnenus or his daughter who sheltered here for a time in 1191, when hunted by the forces of the English King. Guy de Lusignan is generally credited with capturing Buffavento, as he did Kyrenia, although one account has the castle surrendering directly to Richard.

Legend associates this castle, as well as Kantara and St Hilarion, with the mysterious Queen, who may perhaps be a survival of the powerful goddess Aphrodite, who ruled unchallenged in Cyprus for so long. The country people still call the ruins *Spitia tis Reginas*, the Houses of the Queen. So it was that Ali Bey, in 1806, spied the 'Palace of the Queen' with glasses from the plain near Nicosia. He made his way to the Monastery of Ayios Ioannis Chrysostomas below, where but three monks were in residence. They confused him with their story that the ruins of Buffavento were those of another monastery, founded by the same queen who had built their own house, and showed him an icon, supposedly depicting the great lady. Ali Bey, hot on the trail of Aphrodite, was unconvinced and climbed alone to the prehistoric ruins, sure that he had found a 'Temple of Venus'. He was, he believed, the first modern European to have been here.

Another story concerns a Byzantine princess in the time of the Templars' short but oppressive reign. Afflicted by the dreadful medieval curse of leprosy, she was sent to live a remote and lonely life here at Buffavento. Her little dog had caught the disease from his royal mistress, but he took to wandering away for long periods every day on the mountainside, and, as time went on, his skin began to heal. One day, the princess followed him and saw him bathe in a spring, far below the castle. She followed suit and in time was cured herself. In gratitude, she founded the Monastery of Ayios Ioannis Chrysostomos beside the healing waters, which still flow into a pool. The princess is said to be buried here with two servants, and her crown and sceptre were kept in the monastery. This, substantially, was the story told by the monks to Van Bruyn in 1683, and they showed him the graves of the princess and her servants in the church. The Dutchman also scrambled up here to the ruins of Buffavento (describing the climb as extremely perilous), but he, altogether a more practical man than Ali Bey 123 years later, admitted that he had no idea what they were. Below the mountain, he had found the fossilised bones of pygmy hippopotamuses, venerated by the peasants in the belief that they had belonged to martyred saints (there are several instances of this, in various districts of Cyprus).

The Lusignans turned Buffavento into a grim prison. The nobleman Visconti, who had informed Peter I of his wife's adultery, was starved to death here for his trouble. Perot de Montolf, who was imprisoned here with his brother Wilmot for treason by James I, made a dramatic escape by jumping from his cell window over the northern precipice, using the trees to arrest his fall. But he was retaken shortly afterwards in Kyrenia and beheaded with his brother, to be buried at La Cava, near Nicosia. Towards the end of the Venetian period, the fortifications were slighted and the castle abandoned. Nevertheless, in 1570, when Lala Mustapha Pasha was besieging Nicosia, some of the population fled to this refuge, from which they would have been able to see their city taken and sacked.

We wandered through empty rooms, made cold by the mountain wind blowing through the open windows, past deep cisterns and the exposed arch of a chapel. Turkish soldiers had climbed up here since 1974, and scratched their names and those of their units on the walls. We were careful not to flash the binoculars in the direction of the firing range, from which volleys rang out regularly. Surely they would leave soon for lunch? The lorries in which they had driven up from the camp were parked behind them. There was a moment of anxiety when a jeep moved rapidly up from the walls of the monastery, the pennant on its radio aerial waving wildly as the vehicle lurched over the rough ground. In another 100 yards the occupants would be able

236

to see our parked car. Would they come up to investigate? But at the crossroads they turned down to join the group at the firing range. We sat down on a flight of steps, worn and smoothed by centuries of use, waiting for them to leave.

There is an alternative story of the origin of the monastery, later dedicated to Ayios Chrysostomos, the 'golden-tongued Father of the Church', who criticised the pagan tendencies of the Empress Eudoxia, for which he was exiled and eventually died in great hardship. This attributes the foundation to St Helena, mother of Constantine the Great and finder of the True Cross. Helena would seem to have wandered far and wide across Cyprus, laden with pieces of the True Cross for the endowment of religious houses, and also the entire cross of the Penitent Thief, which she left at Stavrovouni, the Mountain of the Cross.

The monastery, which belongs to the Church of the Holy Sepulchre in Jerusalem, has two churches standing today. The older, that of the Holy Trinity, is believed to have been built by Philocales Eumathius in 1110. In 1963 the frescos were restored by Americans of the Dumbarton Oaks Byzantine Institute, which carried out such valuable work at Istanbul, Trebizond and throughout the Orthodox world. The marble doorway was copied by the British for Government House in Nicosia. The other church, St Chrysostomos, was completely rebuilt in 1891, incorporating a few fragments of the original Byzantine basilica, a wooden door, remarkable for being secured without nails, and some icons. But we were unable to venture closer to the monastery and cannot vouch for its conditon. This was a military area even before 1974, and only one priest had been in residence. Somewhere nearby is the ruin of another Byzantine church, the Virgin of Koutsovendis, with a fresco showing Mary mourning over the body of Christ. But search as we might with our binoculars, we could not locate this.

The firing had ceased at last, and the soldiers were once more grouped around the instructor. Then they sat down on the ground, cross-legged in squares. Joan studied them closely with the glasses.

'They're eating a packed lunch,' she decided after a time.

We were not going to remain on our lofty perch all afternoon, and so we began to make our way down the path. In the unaccustomed quiet, we could hear the *muezzin*'s cry from the minaret of distant Tashkent. When we reached the car, we started the engine and crawled as quietly as possible along the track. The picnic was still in progress as we passed above the firing range: every man relaxed and talking to his neighbour. Again, no one looked up at us, although I would have thought that the sound of our engine was audible. No one challenged us at the camp either, and we decided, as we left the precipitous road and the military zone for the main road, that we had been unnecessarily worried after all. We have since been informed that access to Buffavento Castle is officially permitted.

★ ★ ★ ★

The guardian of the Kyrenia Folk Museum accompanied us along the water front, carrying an iron key almost a foot long: not a key to put in your pocket while shopping. At the door of one of the old houses overlooking the harbour, most of which have been converted into restaurants and flats, this cumbersome tool was inserted and rotated with considerable effort. The heavy door, carved with lions, birds and angels, was pushed open to reveal the dark cavernous recesses of the ground floor beneath massive roof beams. The house, like the others along the quay, had been both a family home and a merchant's ware-house. Here we were shown a wooden olive press, pestle and mortar, grinding quern and the heavy, flint-toothed sledge which was once pulled over the cobbled threshing floor by yoked oxen at harvest time. All these things were commonplace in the countryside not so long ago – they still are in other parts of the Middle East, but Cyprus achieved modernisations in advance of her neighbours. Twenty and thirty years ago, Cypriots had the highest living standards in the Eastern Mediterranean. Only in 1974 – at least in the North – reverse gear was in a sense engaged.

Upstairs, the traditional dress of the island was displayed, mostly that of the Greeks: the long boots and *vrakes*, the baggy breeches of the men, which were worn with a sash and short waistcoat; a wedding dress from the Karpas; the women's beautiful embroidery and the lace of Pano Lefkara. We saw a charcoal brazier, camel bells, old leather jugs and plates, and huge *pithoi*, the wine jars which are much as the ancient Greeks made them. There was a carved four-poster bed and one of the famous dowry chests from Akanthou.

I walked out on the gallery, high above the street, where once the merchant winched his sacks of goods to the upper storeys. People of all races were sitting at the tables of the English-owned Café Chimaera, which caters for yachtsmen. An ancient taxi, a black Mercedes diesel, rattled over the cobbles. A contrastingly smart saloon came round the corner and stopped in front of the café, a blue pennant fluttering from a flag mast. UN Commander, Area Six was inscribed on the door.

In the modern town, at the top of the hill, Joan and the boys selected souvenirs to take home: *kebab* skewers, including the ingenious double ones for cooking sausages, and tiny, delicate coffee cups. A pedlar with a van was selling oranges from Morphou, not the very best quality admittedly, for the equivalent of 25p an *oka*, or 9p a pound. Above the castle, I came to the police station, painted green, with a corrugated-iron roof and a balcony looking out towards Turkey. These back streets were always cool and quiet. I found a café with a terrace, and sat for a long time over a glass of wine, watching the waters of the Straits gradually darken as the shadows grew.

★   ★   ★   ★

The fig tree was now fully in leaf, the twigs, like thick fleshy fingers, becoming hidden by the new growth. I took a photograph of Salih, sitting with his coffee and the inevitable cigarette. His garden was now filled with riotous colour, for everything was growing and blossoming with bewildering speed before the onset of the summer drought. Always Salih talked of plants and herbs. He was amazed to hear that we cooked with mint, something never done in Cyprus apparently.

The swimming pool which Mr Kemal had tended with such care had become green with algal scum. This, together with Salih's garden, was to be dug up and completely remodelled, a new scheme of the Bey to which Salih seemed resigned.

The spring was advancing, but the knowledge that our time in Cyprus would now be short dampened our spirits a little. We gravitated towards the west, and walked at the mouth of the Paleomylos river among the tall reeds. Two soldiers were working on the engine of a recalcitrant bulldozer. Outside Morphou the orange pickers were eating an early lunch from reed baskets, seated on the grass by their wooden bus. And at Syrianokhori we passed once again the house painted so fiercely with the emblem of TMT.

Rauf Denktash's Volkan was officially prohibited by the British in November 1957. The Turk Mudafa Teskilati, which succeded it immediately afterwards, had all the patriotic fervour and narrow-mindedness of EOKA:

Oh Turkish Youth!
   The day is near when you will be called upon to sacrifice your life and blood in the PARTITION struggle – to the struggle for freedom.
   You are a brave Turk. You are faithful to your country and nation and are entrusted with the task of demonstrating Turkish might. Be ready to break the chains of slavery with your determination and willpower and with your love of freedom.
   All Turkdom, right and justice and God are with you.
   PARTITION or DEATH.

EOKA, the National Organisation of Cypriot Fighters founded by Grivas in 1955 to fight the British, used similar rhetoric in the famous oath of allegiance sworn by all its members:

> I swear in the name of the Holy Trinity that:
> 1. I shall work with all my power for the liberation of Cyprus from British rule, sacrificing for this even my life.
> 2. I shall perform without objection all the instructions which may be entrusted to me and I shall not raise any objection, however difficult and dangerous these may be.
> 3. I shall not abandon the struggle unless I receive instructions from the leader of the organisation or until our aim has been accomplished.
> 4. I shall never reveal to anyone any secret of our organisation, neither the names of my superiors nor those of the other members, even if I am caught and tortured.
> 5. I shall not reveal any instructions or orders which may be given to me, even to my fellow combatants.
> If I disobey my oath, I shall be worthy of every punishment as a traitor and may eternal contempt cover me.

Of course many were caught, and indeed tortured; some talked, but most, more afraid of EOKA than the pain, did not. The greatest misfortune was that the British security forces employed Turks as torturers. The British had always felt that they could rely upon the Turks. Even in 1879 Baker had written:

> There can be no better soldier than the Turk under British officers . . . There is nothing to fear from the Turkish population in Cyprus, and they would willingly enlist in our service, and could always be depended on in time of necessity . . . The extremely low cost of wines and spirits is terribly adverse to the sanitary condition of the English soldier. The staunch sobriety of the Turk, his extreme hardihood, which enables him to endure great fatigue upon the most simple fare, and his amenity to discipline, together with an instinctive knowledge of arms and a natural capacity for a military profession, render him a valuable material for our requirements in organising a defensive force in Cyprus.

> (Samuel Baker, *Cyprus as I Saw It in 1879*).

So, while British officers asked the questions, Turkish auxiliary policemen struck the blows, as many middle-aged Greeks will testify. The Turks themselves may have regarded it as no more than a little rough justice – although sometimes it was very rough indeed – a blow for law and order, or the chastisement of hooligans. Certainly the charge, occasionally made by Greeks, that the hostility between the communities originated in the British use of the Turks during the

EOKA campaign is unreasonable. But undoubtedly it drove the wedge a little deeper into the split.

Outside one of Syrianokhoris's little whitewashed cottages, surrounded by flowers planted in every shape and size of rusty tin, an old man, very short with a thick shock of grey hair, was squatting in the sun, constructing something like a cartwheel from split stems of reed. His wife, even smaller, her hair reddened with henna, came out of the house to greet us. Would we like to see some that they had finished, ready for the market in Nicosia?

The interior of the tiny house was a revelation, for almost everything had been made by hand. Turkish carpets covered the floor, while a portrait of Denktash on the wall was surrounded by embroidered tapestries. The bed was a huge, carved wooden four-poster, very high, almost filling the room and covered by a flamboyant counterpane. The stock of baskets was kept beneath this, and two large ones were brought out. How much did they want for these? But the old couple, for all their skill in handicrafts, could not write the figure down, and we could not understand the price in Turkish. So I offered my wallet, and the old man selected some notes and pronounced himself quite content. He wanted the equivalent of 65 pence for each basket, and these proved, in time, to be as robust as they appeared.

Our orange-farmer friend waved to us from the steps of the café as we drove on into the marshes towards the coast. We picnicked on the beach, although a strong wind was now whipping into Morphou Bay and the blue waters were discoloured by sand and seaweed churned up from the bottom. The wind was so strong that our fire would not light easily, and when it did the heat and smoke were carried rapidly away. Cyprus crows flapped raggedly above the reed stems which were bending and dancing in the gale. It was Saturday, but as usual everyone was busy in the orange groves, or ensconced in the café, and the coast was deserted.

★   ★   ★   ★

The war-like veterans of Ghaziveran kept bees now: rows and rows of hives near the road. Outside the gates of a factory, upon which a protest banner had been hung, two tents were pitched on the muddy ground, and a crowd had gathered in a carnival mood: the men eating and drinking, the women knitting. Many of them were still there, gathered around fires burning by the tents, when we passed back in the dark. It looked more like a festival than a strike.

★   ★   ★   ★

The tumbled hills below Vouni Palace must be one of the most beautiful corners of the island. Here, early in the EOKA campaign, three nervous young Greeks prepared an ambush, opened fire on a British army jeep and killed its driver. The surviving soldier, Major Brian Coombe, managed to reach cover and return the fire, killing one of the inexperienced terrorists and actually capturing the other two, Andreas Zakos and Charilaos Mikhail. These, the recipients of the emotional and feverish sympathies of the entire Greek population, were sentenced to death, together with Iakovos Patatsos, a religious and patriotic youth who had shot at a Turkish policeman.

EOKA took an English civilian named Cremer hostage, and threatened to execute this elderly man if the hangings were carried out. It was Zakos who, when given the opportunity, made a broadcast directly aimed at Grivas in order to defuse the situation: 'What I did, I did of my own free will, and I am willingly paying the forfeit. Cremer is innocent, and the innocent should not suffer.' EOKA released their hostage, and the three youths were hanged shortly afterwards in Nicosia.

★ ★ ★ ★

In the old part of Lefka, below the square, the guests from a wedding reception spilled out over the pavement. Everyone was dressed very formally: small boys in navy blue suits trimmed with gold braid, bow ties and ruffled dress shirts; little girls in frilly party dresses. But the mood of the adult guests was anything but formal, more like that in an East End pub towards closing time. Turkish dance music was playing from the loudspeakers, and the wine and *raki* had plainly flowed like water.

In a village shop, we queued to buy almonds and a loaf of bread. Every so often, an antique side-valve BSA motorcycle went thumping down the street: models which are all in the hands of collectors and museums in England. We walked on through the lanes and gardens which became increasingly wonderful. Every traveller remarks on the palm groves of Lefka, but there grew too, in profusion, figs, oranges and lemons, white poplars, pines, maples, elm, ash and cypress trees. There were cool, lush hedgerows grown with anemones and white convolvulus. Amazingly, there were the stinging nettles of northern Europe, and blackberries, still ripe on their briars, beneath blossoming almond trees, all shaded by the majestic sweep of the palms of Africa. Water, climate and the copper-red soil have combined here with extraordinary results.

There was a freshness and coolness in the air. Tumble-down houses of mud-brick were slipping down the hill towards the river. We passed a woman picking salad lettuces in a cottage garden; a rich smell of roasting *kebabs* came from within. Down by the water, the tall reed beds stirred in the breeze. An ancient woman, dressed in black with a white headscarf and yellow sash, and hunched over her stick, came walking slowly along a track through the palms. She looked at us, and then up at the mountains, mumbling something in which we caught only the word 'Troodos'. Did she imagine that we had walked across the Line?

The water ran along numberless concrete troughs by the roadside, and so through the groves, led from the river which had already dried up in parts of its lower course. Every garden had a little iron water gate in the irrigation channel, to be lifted according to requirement and entitlement. The dams and tanks along the river were already raucous with the croaking of frogs. One water channel was in the process of construction; a complicated shuttering of wooden slats was ready for the poured concrete.

We came to the nineteenth-century Mosque of Piri Osman Pasha, which stands alone beside the road, a trickling rivulet in front, and cypresses and palms surrounding open ground behind. The octagonal minaret was gilded by the afternoon sun, and in the graveyard, half buried in luxuriant geranium flowers and protected by an iron railing, we found the Pasha's tomb. A three-tiered turban and stone fez are supported on long marble columns, and the white sarcophagus is carved with crossed pistols, swords and pens. The porch of the mosque is painted green, and we entered to find the arched chamber shabby from long use. Among the threadbare carpets of traditional oriental pattern were two garish new ones, embroidered with peacocks, apparently in defiance of the Koran's strictures against the representation of living creatures in the decoration of holy places. Seated at one of the windows in the worn, green-painted wall, we could look out across the foothills at the Greek Troodos, apparently no more than a few minutes' walk away.

We left, disturbing friendly chickens pecking around the roots of huge cactus plants, and passing the *muezzin*, on his way to sing the evening prayer. As we took the narrow path by the river in the fast-falling darkness, we could hear the high, unearthly note of his voice from the minaret silhouetted on the skyline amid the palm heads. The river meandered through the trees of a steep valley, and we found our way with difficulty past reedy pools, concrete cisterns and basins of dried and cracked silt. After a time, we could hear nothing but the deafening noise of the frogs in the mud, and see very little more than the outlines of poplars and palms against the remaining light in the sky. It was with relief that we emerged, muddy and scratched, into the lit streets of the busy town.

* * * *

By the brook which runs into the gorge near Gecitkoy, the Village of
the Mountain Pass, we sat dangling our feet into deep limestone bath
tubs, reading, and drinking the beer we had cooled in the water.
These pools must hold water all through the year, for there were
miniscule creatures in them: corixae and caddis larvae. Baker reported that somewhere in this gorge he had found a seam of green and
rose-coloured marble, which might, he thought, be exploited com-
mercially. The shepherd who rode his mule along the road, herding
his sheep before him, waved to us like an old friend. We put on our
shoes and, walking through cypress, ilex and pine trees, followed the
course of the stream in its tiny valley through the hills. Our feet
bruised clumps of fragrant sage, white, yellow and blue anemones,
and occasional red poppies. We found the spring among the boles of
rotting pines and thick oleander bushes, before climbing out of the
steep place to find ourselves, surprisingly, among flat, cultivated
fields.

★   ★   ★   ★

The road to Nicosia led through rolling grasslands at first, then across
the flat plain of the Mesaoria. Every village – Asomatos, Kondemenos, Skylloura, Ayios Vasilios and Yerolakkos – had been occupied by the army. Turkish and Greek, these communities had
turned viciously upon each other during the 1950's, culminating in
the massacre at Geunyeli. Skylloura had been renamed Yilmazkoy,
the Village without Fear, while Yerolakkos was now, aptly enough,
the Village of the Regiment. Rows of lorries and jeeps were parked out
in the fields. Private soldiers worked in the gardens of the officers'
married quarters and, outside a canteen, kitchen orderlies peeled potatoes on long tables in the open air.

At Ayios Vasilios a memorial stood beside the road: a strange construction of cast concrete slabs, from which protruded aluminium
pipes like those of a church organ. A notice proclaimed that it marked
the 'Common graves of Turkish Cypriots massacred by Greeks at
Ayios Vasilios in December 1963'. The flags of Turkey and Turkish
Cyprus flew together. Protected under glass were the same photographs as were displayed in the Museum of Barbarism: the white-
coated, masked orderlies disinterring the rotting corpses, while the
press photographers of the world stood watching in a half-circle, cameras primed.

The Greek and Turkish maps disagreed as to the position of the
Attila Line here. The Turks, it transpired, were correct, for we were
able to drive into Ortakeuy, on the northern outskirts of Nicosia,
without encountering any obstruction. In this dusty suburb we even-

tully found a sleazy, flyblown little restaurant. The owner opened a smelly refrigerator to show us spits of *kebab* meat ready for grilling. We were hungry enough to take a chance, and he fanned up the charcoal on the hearth and set the skewers in place to cook while he prepared a salad, *pitta* bread and thick yoghurt, squeezed through muslin. A soldier came in and wandered about the kitchen in a proprietorial manner, organising his own meal. Meanwhile, we made use of the hole and two planks in the courtyard which served as a toilet. The food all tasted surprisingly good, though we drank a quantity of *raki* to kill the microbes.

Blocks of flats and factories are being built all over Ortakeuy, much of which is an ugly wasteland strewn with builders' rubble. The district must be indescribably unpleasant during the long summer. A single shepherd sat incongruously on his mule, watching his animals graze the sparse grass before a line of terraced, box-like apartments.

★   ★   ★   ★

One golden afternoon we walked up the valley of the Paleomylos into the White Hills between Myrtou and Mount Kornos. The river wound through broad grasslands enclosed by gorse-covered hillsides. Hawthorns and olives dipped their roots in the water and stands of giant reed grew in the low places. We came to a reddish cliff where the river had undercut the hill, the roosting place of crows which took to the air with a great commotion at our approach. Occasionally we saw a partridge. Thick, fleshy stalks of wild fennel hung over the path.

Once or twice, we took off our shoes and forded the stream where it ran shallow over a gravel bed. At the head of the valley, where the ruins of the Monastery of Panayia ton Katharon stand on a slope above the water, we could hear the tinkling of goatbells and the sound of a gun from far away towards Mount Kornos. In the sunset, a shepherd walked along the horizon, and raised his hand to us in greeting. The shepherds here carry plain staffs, not crooks as in Greece.

In the darkness of the gorge at Gecitkoy, two women were walking along the road near the houses occupied by people from the mainland. For a moment the headlamps caught exotic red and gold trousers, sequinned slippers and dark eyes above white veils.

★   ★   ★   ★

We dined late in Kyrenia, at a little restaurant on Attila Street kept by a man who was fascinated by the oriental martial arts. On the walls, apart from the polished casings of shells from the fighting in 1974, were karate and judo certificates, signed by Rauf Denktash himself, and ceremonial swords won in Stuttgart and Istanbul. We fell into conversation with a man who had emigrated to Australia in 1973 and had now returned for a long holiday. He had done well in his adopted country, and had just been to West Germany to buy a personal export Mercedes to be shipped home. He was very conscious of his good fortune in avoiding the invasion and the hard times which followed, although, like every Turk, he shuddered to recall the days of the Republic, when the communities lived under armed guard.

'You locked your door at night, never sure that they might not break in and murder you in your bed. All the time you lived in fear. The British should have done something for us after independence – if independence had to come. British soldiers were here, and they should have done something more to protect the minority.

'*Enosis* would have been disastrous for us. Already we were discriminated against, suffering violence and aggression from the Greeks, victimised in our own country. No, this situation now is the best we can expect – to be separate and protected by a strong army.'

CHAPTER SEVENTEEN

BENEATH THE TREE OF IDLENESS

'Jasmine,' said Salih, handing over a cut spray as he took his coffee cup.

'What do you call it in Turkish?'

'The same. Yasemin.'

Salih, as a native of the wine-growing district of Paphos, knew all about pruning vines. He shook his head when he looked at the small neglected vineyard across the fields nearby. Most of the grape varieties are native to Cyprus and it is important to know how to get the best from them.

'Never too much grapes from those vines now,' he said sadly.

We walked up to Salih's village of Karavas, past plane trees growing by the stream bed and stone aqueducts running down the valley. The last blossom was now falling from the almonds, scattered over the bonnet and seat of a tractor parked in the street. English roses twined in the hedge and cistus grew against the walls of ruined houses. Iron bars ran from one house to another to support the great vines which would shade the street in summer. From a deep gorge, where the giant reed grew nearly 30 feet high, the water was led to ancient stone cisterns. The sound of the water rushing through dark mossy channels could be heard everywhere. Outside the Church of Ayia Irini, on a patch of ground grown with cactus and palm, a group of women sat sewing lace on to the hems of garments.

We followed the stream above the village to a place where a wealthy colonial had built a great house in the pine woods. The path narrowed, and entered a cleft in the mountain where two sheepdogs, who had been left guarding a fold, came bounding towards us, snarling and barking. But, at a word from the shepherd a short distance up the hill, they halted with impressive obedience and trotted back to lie down in the shade of a tree. The man was hauling water from the stream in a bucket and emptying it into a trough for his flock. Higher up, the stream was dry, though concrete pipes and channels had been built. The UN had built a cistern at the *kephalovryson*: a circular concrete drum with a metal ladder leading to the top. An enormous lizard ran up the side and crammed itself into a pipe protruding from the lip, the long tail disappearing very slowly.

This was the place where the charcoal burner had been working, on our first day in Cyprus. He was long gone, leaving only a scorched circular patch where the mound of charcoal had stood, and the flat stones of his own cooking hearth. The boys climbed the dry stone chimney cut by the water, until they found themselves out on the open mountainside. As we descended, a large black snake came sliding very quickly across the road, giving us all a start. Drummond, I remembered, had written in the eighteenth century that the reapers fixed bells to their sickles 'to frighten away the asp'. It was said that Cleopatra's asp came from her island possession of Cyprus.

In a pleasant garden of flowers, two women were sitting and knitting: one young and slim, the other approaching middle age, with a handsome, open face. Between them was a bowl filled with lemon peel. The older of the two looked up on hearing our approaching footsteps.

'Won't you come and sit with us?' she said simply. Her companion slipped indoors and reappeared with more chairs.

'My friend does not speak English,' the older woman explained, as the younger smiled shyly, knowing that she was being talked about. 'My name is Rose.'

'That sounds like an English name.'

'I think it is. For a long time I worked for an English lady in Kyrenia, Mrs Brownlow. She always called me Rose, so . . . well, you call me Rose too.'

'Do you come from Karavas?'

'No, I came here from Istanbul in 1975. My friend here was born in the village.'

'And what happened to Mrs Brownlow?'

'Oh, she went back to England in the end. I was very sad when she left. I miss Mrs Brownlow; we had such fun together.'

She ruffled Steven's hair in absent-minded affection and went on with her knitting.

'You work differently to the way we do it in England,' said Joan, looking closely at the unfolding pattern. 'You go from the other side.'

'We do? Show me how you do it.'

'But it will spoil what you have done.'

'Oh I can unpick it. Come and show me.'

So Joan went behind her, leaned over her shoulder and showed her the different method amidst much girlish laughter. Mrs Brownlow, I supposed, had not knitted.

'What is the lemon rind for?' we asked.

248

'You don't know? Rose put down the knitting, picked up the rind of half a lemon, rolled it tightly and secured it with a strand of cotton.

'Then we boil them with sugar. Wait, I will get you some.'

She went indoors, and emerged after a minute with plates, long forks, glasses of water and a large jar of *glyko*, or in Turkish *tatli*, the candied peel which is traditionally offered to guests before coffee.

We stayed for some time. Mrs Brownlow still wrote, but Rose did not think that she would ever return to Cyprus.

★　★　★　★

On a remote beach near Troulli, we grilled slices of black pudding and cheese over a pile of driftwood, munched at wedges of bread and drank a bottle of straw-coloured wine. I swam out to deep water where great rocks showed clearly far below, for the sea was like crystal. In the sandy shallows, Malcolm and Steven were playing with an improvised raft: a wooden pallet washed from a freighter's deck and now growing a crop of barnacles.

The carefree mood ended abruptly when we realised that the soles of our feet had become clogged with a thick black sludge which underlay the sand. However idyllic, no shore of the Mediterranean is proof against the illegally discharging oil tanker, and the terminus of the Syrian pipeline is not far away. We sat disconsolately on a rock and attempted to clean ourselves with a rag dipped in *raki*. It was quite effective.

We crossed the mountains by the Halevga Forest Station and that wild landscape of trees and cliffs which separates the coast from the dry foothills above the Mesaoria. We stopped in Tashkent, the Stone City, merely because its new Turkish name intrigued us. The Greeks had called it Vouno, the Mountain, and there was a sixteenth-century monastery of St Romanos. The Turks had erected a flagstaff and monument, which stood surrounded by almonds near the road.

At Sykhari, or Kaynakkoy, the Village of the Spring, a mile or two further west, a gravel track led up into the mountains through a *phrygana* of thorn bushes and occasional scattered cypress trees. We were approaching the Absinthiotissa Monastery, which the Greeks had guarded from sentry boxes. We passed one beside the track; the double-headed Byzantine eagle had been beautifully reproduced in Hellenic blue. '*H Kypros einai Elleniki*' had been written beside it: 'Cyprus is Greek'.

The monastery nestled shyly in the trees, the domed church gradually revealing itself as we rounded a bend in the road. A clamour of crows took wing at our approach and circled over the hillside in a bewildering series of turns, like pigeons above a loft. The church is

Byzantine: rebuilt in the fifteenth century and restored again only a few years ago, it had been beautiful. Now, a flock of neglected sheep was penned inside, and the floor was littered with straw and droppings. Sheets of corrugated iron were drawn across the door, and the ancient frescos were peeling with the plaster from the walls. Outside were reminders of the monks' daily life, such as a military row of wash basins and lavatories in a cracked, concrete building with a collapsed roof. The monastery must once have been very extensive, for in the pine woods nearby were the walls and foundations of a whole village of subsidiary houses.

Before the church stood a crude sentry box, reached by six steps and giving a fine view over the Mesaoria in the sunset. '1973' had been scratched into the concrete while still wet. Lost in thought, we walked back to the village in the dusk through a silent landscape. Occasionally a hare hopped uncertainly across our path, and the lights of Nicosia flickered before us.

* * * *

From the winding, tortuous streets of upper Lapithos, where old people sat on wooden chairs against the walls of the houses, we set our car to attack the forest road. Somewhat to our surprise, it managed the climb with no more protest than a high temperature gauge reading on the last slope. The long drive along the ridge was more worrying, with deep gullies and fallen trees to be contended with, but at last, to our relief, we arrived at St Hilarion Castle from the west. It was a day of sun and high winds, puffs of cloud scudding along the line of the valley.

A United Nations coach was reversing in the little car park, full of Danes in blue berets with slung cameras, accompanied by wives and children. The driver backed over the precipice as far as his back wheels, so that 12 feet or more of his vehicle projected over the drop. I admired his nerve, and also sympathised with the panic-stricken passengers at the rear as they realised what he was about. St Hilarion has long been a popular excursion – in 1879 Sir Samuel Baker and his wife were invited to join Sir Garnet Wolsey, the High Commissioner, and his ladies on a picnic party to the castle, from where they would ride on to Kyrenia. This expedition apparently caused the Cypriots some amusement: 'The energy of English ladies rather astonishes the people of this country, where inertia is considered to be happiness.'

The guardian saw our reed basket from Yayla and asked how much we had paid; he looked mortified when he heard. He had paid twice as much for his; hardly an excessive price in Nicosia, but no Cypriot likes the idea of anyone else, let alone a foreigner, making a better deal.

His old dog came limping with us to the upper gatehouse. The restaurant was open, and a splendid cheese had been set on a plate in a stone window, in order that it might breathe, or perhaps enjoy the view. While the boys clambered all over the fortress, accompanied by the faithful dog, we read our books in the Queen's Window. I absolutely refused to stand on Prince John's Tower in this wind, but spent some time contemplating the appalling precipice where the Bulgarian mercenaries had been thrown to their destruction. According to Leontios Makhairas, the last man had somehow survived to tell the tale later.

As for Prince John himself, from that time he had behaved like a man who knew that he was doomed. When the vengeful Spanish Queen later invited him to dine in Nicosia, he had ignored all the warnings and entreaties of his friends not to attend. Even his charger had ominously stumbled and slipped on to its knees as he mounted. At dinner, he sat overwhelmed by foreboding, but as if powerless to avoid his fate: 'Oh my heart, my heart! I do not know why, but it is as bound; I do not know what is upon me.' And then Queen Eleanor had a dish served before him; when it was uncovered he was confronted by the blood-stained shirt of her husband, the murdered King Peter, and a moment later the assassins who had been concealed behind the hangings of the chamber were around him.

★ ★ ★ ★

We lunched on toasted sandwiches and beer, sitting outside the Café Chimaera on the quay of Kyrenia. Joan and the boys went up to the new town to look at the shops while I lazed through the long afternoon over a coffee. Faces in Kyrenia were becoming familiar, I realised. The Englishman who owned the café came out for a chat. The tourists would soon be coming, he thought, with summer approaching, and the political situation was gradually easing. People had become less nervous about visiting North Cyprus. The people from the yachts kept the business ticking over through the winter.

The yachts came from Ottawa, Amsterdam and Hamburg, and their owners were the lotus-eaters who can be found wintering in a hundred Mediterranean ports between Spain and Syria. A whole family were working on the rigging of one: two boys, two girls and a cat. A Canadian was involved in protracted negotiations with the boat chandler, while drinking coffee at the next table. Certainly the part could be ordered, but it might not be available in stainless steel. The Canadian insisted that nothing else but stainless steel would do for his boat, and the conversation went on and on. The waitresses were discussing what the kitchen would need from the market in the town, and drawing up a shopping list. The Turkish sailors from the gunboat were still playing football under the walls of the castle. The UN sightseers arrived, having left their coach by the Dome Hotel, and came strolling in groups along the wharf, taking photographs of the harbour. The owners of the expensive fish restaurants unlocked their doors and began to set out colourful displays of lobster and red mullet under glass, which would hopefully lure a few customers inside that evening.

On the wall of the harbourmaster's office were minatory notices. It had come to his attention that some yachtsmen had been accepting money from tourists to take them as 'guests' along the coast. Unless the boat concerned possessed a charter licence, this unauthorised hiring would be severely dealt with in future. There was to be no diving near the new harbour works. A map showed areas where fishing was restricted, especially around the Karpas peninsula.

It had been warm outside the café in the bright sun, but on the outer harbour wall the wind made itself felt. Periodically, a heavy sea sent spray slopping across the breakwater, and a frail old lady, obviously English, came walking along the wet stones, clutching a plastic headscarf around her chin. Two workmen were sitting smoking cigarettes at the foot of the crane being used to extend the outer end of the mole. The flags on the castle flickered like red and white flames in the breeze, standing out against the backdrop of mountains. A fishing caique rolled and tugged at its mooring against the Byzantine pillar in the middle of the harbour. The water was clear enough to reveal shoals of silvery fish sheltering beneath the boat hulls, old corroded cables lying tangled on the bottom, petrol tins, bottles and broken crockery.

Kyrenia was a cultural desert, said Joan on her return. There were shops everywhere selling pop records, cassettes and lurid video tapes, but no bookshop. There were countless shelves of cheap china souvenirs. Someone had tried to sell her gold earrings, weighing out pair after pair on the scales, before she made her escape.

Together, we watched the sun falling somewhere beyond Cape Kormakiti, turning the minaret of the mosque and the palm trees a rich, ruby red. That night we would say goodbye to Ibrahim at the soldiers' restaurant and pack our cases. Early next morning we would return our hired car and climb on to the bus for the airport. But here, under these mountains which had grown so familiar, we could linger for a while longer, before the inevitable turmoil of travel and deadlines swept us away. The *muezzin*'s prayer flew like a bird, thin and high, over a town whose usurped houses and quays had become transmuted into something more precious than stone, as if they had been recast in Cypriot copper and burnished until they shone.

⋆　⋆　⋆　⋆

Salih helped us with our cases on to the bus, and shook our hands: a stooped bow-legged figure, waving as we set off along the coast road. He was quite affected. I would have liked to do something nice for Salih.

We were late at Ercan Airport because the driver called at several villages off the route in order to give lifts to friends, not all of whom were ready as arranged. The security at the airport was as heavy as before, and armoured cars were drawn up at the main gate. Cheerful confusion reigned inside the terminal building as London-bound travellers climbed over each other and their luggage to check in first. The official at the desk was quite embarrassed.

'Why are you behaving like this?' he asked. 'Why cannot you queue quietly and await your turn like this English gentleman? What will he think of us?'

The Cypriots looked at each other in consternation. They had meant no harm, for it was not their custom to queue. One of them offered me an orange. I looked over my shoulder as I reached the top of the aircraft steps, to see two soldiers in red and white steel helmets, carbines at the slant, slowly pacing, looking left, looking right, like marionettes, in unison.

HISTORICAL CHRONOLOGY

c.6000 BC	First human settlement, probably from Syria or Palestine.
c.1600–1250 BC	Bronze Age Cypriots gradually establish trading connections in the eastern Mediterranean, and become wealthy through working copper.
c.1250 BC on	A number of independent city-states are established in Cyprus, first by Mycenaean refugees from warfare in the Aegean, and later by Phoenician traders.
708–663 BC	Cypriot cities are dominated by Assyria, although they retain local autonomy.
c.560–540 BC	Egyptian rule by the Pharaoh Amasis.
c.540–322 BC	A period of increasing Persian influence results in most of the Cypriot cities joining the Ionian Revolt against the Great King in 500 BC. The failure of the rebellion is followed by the installation of Persian puppets as rulers of the city-states.
332–294 BC	Alexander the Great frees Cyprus of Persian domination, and many Cypriots take part in his eastern campaigns. After Alexander's death, Cyprus is caught up in the civil war between Antigonus and Ptolemy over the division of his empire.
294–58 BC	Ptolemaic rule from Egypt, and the autonomy of the cities is finally abolished.
58 BC	Cyprus falls to Rome.
45–6 AD	Christianity is introduced.
115–16 AD	The great Jewish rebellion.
330–1191 AD	Cyprus is included in the Byzantine Empire of the East. The autocephaly of the Cypriot Orthodox Church is established. The early part of the Byzantine period is marked by destructive

255

earthquakes and droughts; from the seventh to the tenth centuries the raids of Arab pirates render the island almost uninhabitable.

1191 AD Cyprus is taken by Richard I of England, who sells the island first to the Order of Knights Templar, and secondly to his fellow crusader Guy de Lusignan, ex-King of Jerusalem.

1192–1489 AD A dynasty of Frankish Lusignan kings rules Cyprus on the feudal model of western Europe. The Orthodox Church is subordinated to the Catholic. The Black Death kills almost a third of the population in 1348–9, but the island grows extremely rich on the profits of the eastern trade. The Genoese control the important port of Famagusta between 1374 and 1464, and King Janus is ransomed following an Egyptian invasion in 1426.

1489 AD Venice obtains Cyprus by astute diplomacy and a dynastic marriage.

1571–1878 AD Cyprus is captured by Lala Mustapha Pasha for the Ottoman Empire. The Orthodox Church is restored to its primary position as the voice of the Christian population and the Greeks are freed from serfdom, though subject to ever-increasing taxation. The excesses of corrupt governors lead to a series of rebellions supported by both Christians and Muslims: notably those of Mehmed Agha Boyaji-Oghlu in 1680, and of Khalil Agha in 1765. In 1821 the Turkish Governor Kutchuk Mehmed massacres the leading clergymen of the Orthodox Church, in order to pre-empt a rising in sympathy with the rebellion in Greece.

1878 AD Following the Russo-Turkish War, Great Britain is granted the administration – though not the sovereignty – of Cyprus at the Congress of Berlin. The Greeks of the island almost immediately submit the first of many requests for *enosis*, union with Greece.

1914 AD After the opening of hostilities with Turkey, Britain ceases payment of the 'Cyprus tribute', and formally annexes the island.

1925 AD Cyprus becomes a Crown Colony. Greek Cypriots continue to strive for *enosis*.

1931 AD   During a period of severe economic depression, violent enosist riots break out, followed by deportations, press censorship and repressive legislation.

1939–45 AD   Both Greek and Turkish Cypriots are among the first to enlist in the colonial forces. Cypriot muleteers take part in the evacuation of Dunkirk, and 2,100 Cypriot soldiers are lost during the withdrawal from Greece and Crete.

1950 AD   A plebiscite taken among the Christians produces a 96% majority in favour of *enosis*. The young Michael Kykkotis is enthroned as Archbishop Makarios III, *ethnarch*, or leader, of the Greek Christians.

1955–60 AD   The underground organisation EOKA, led by George Grivas, commences an escalating campaign of terror, with *enosis* as its goal. British security forces fail to prevent sabotage and murder. Many Turks identify themselves with the British regime and the security operations; others form an underground organisation of their own – Volkan, or TMT – hoping to obtain partition of the island between Greece and Turkey, or 'double *enosis*'. The two communities become polarised; riots and sectarian murders are commonplace. Following protracted diplomatic negotiations, Makarios is persuaded to forgo *enosis* in favour of an independent republic, although Greek extremists regard this as a betrayal. The guarantors of the new Republic of Cyprus are Great Britain, Greece and Turkey, and the constitution includes built-in safeguards and privileges for the Turkish minority. Britain retains 'Sovereign Base Areas' on the island.

1963–74 AD   Widespread violence breaks out after Greek attempts to revise the constitution in order to remove the Turkish power of veto. British troops from the SBAs, and later a special United Nations force, undertake a policing role with great difficulty; a 'Green Line' is drawn to separate the Greek and Turkish quarters of Nicosia. The Turkish minority ceases to participate in the Republic of Cyprus, and withdraws to a series of enclaves where it sets up what amounts to a rival administration. In most parts of the island the two communities live uneasily in separate armed camps, watched by the UN peace-keeping force. Sporadic outbursts of violence continue.

1974 AD The Colonels' Junta in Greece engineer a coup, involving the assassination of Makarios and his replacement by the enosist EOKA–B activist Nikos Sampson. But Makarios escapes, and Turkey's response is to invade North Cyprus with the declared intention of protecting Turkish Cypriots by an enforced partition. The Junta in Greece and Sampson's satellite regime in Cyprus fall almost immediately. Turkish troops eventually occupy about one-third of the island, including northern Nicosia and the port of Famagusta. Within a year, the vast majority of Greeks remaining in the North have fled to the South, and Turks from the Greek sector have moved across the Line to the occupied zone.

1975 AD Turkish Cypriots under their leader Rauf Denktash declare a 'Turkish Federated State of Cyprus'.

1977 AD Death of Archbishop Makarios.

1983 AD Turkish Cypriots declare an independent 'Turkish Republic of North Cyprus', which the UN Security Council later condemns as illegal.

Situation in 1990

Very little has changed since the invasion of 1974. The island is still divided, and the Line is still policed by UNFICYP, which has now spent 26 years striving to keep the peace in Cyprus. A large Turkish army contingent is stationed in the North. Following severe problems caused by a massive influx of refugees and the loss of valuable assets in the occupied zone, the Greek Cypriot economy has made a remarkable recovery and is experiencing an unprecedented boom. The economy of Turkish Cyprus remains severely depressed and is largely underwritten by mainland Turkey. Periodic talks have taken place, with refugees' hopes raised accordingly, but neither party has been prepared to make any major concessions, and negotiations have always ended in stalemate.

GLOSSARY AND ABBREVIATIONS

In an island where Greek, Turkish and English are widely spoken, where minorities speak Armenian and an obscure dialect of Arabic, and where French and Italian influences have left their mark, an inevitable blurring and confusion of languages has occurred, particularly in the kitchen. Both Turkish and Greek words are given here, but they would be familiar to most Cypriots.

araba   motor car or carriage

ASIZ   *Askeri Inzibat*, or Turkish Military Police

Attila   Operation Attila was the code name used for the Turkish invasion of 1974. The partition line established by the invasion is generally known as the Attila Line, or sometimes the *Sahin*, or Falcon Line. The Green Line, strictly speaking, refers only to the section of the Line which divides Nicosia.

baklavas   pastry with nuts and honey

cadi   Turkish judge

chiftlik   large Turkish farm or estate

dolmades   vine leaves stuffed with rice and meat, usually flavoured with lemon; often spoken of in the Greek affectionate diminutive, i.e. *dolmadakia*.

donum   archaic Turkish measure of land, approximately 920 square metres

ekklisia   church

enosis   literally 'union', the joining of Cyprus to the Greek motherland, as happened in the case of the Ionian islands, Crete and many other parts of modern Greece (see also *Megali Idea*)

EOKA   *Ethniki Organosis Kyprion Agoniston* (National Organisation of Cypriot Fighters), the underground movement of Greek Cypriots led by George Grivas which fought for *enosis* between 1955 and 1960

EOKA-B   Formed in 1972, EOKA-B was the most aggressive of a series of right-wing groups set up by anti-Makarios elements to promote the cause of *enosis*, infiltrating the government and security

259

forces of the Republic. Working closely with the Colonels' Junta in Athens and George Grivas, who had returned clandestinely to Cyprus in 1971, EOKA-B gunmen carried out shooting attacks and bombings. In July 1974, EOKA-B, together with the Junta and the Greek contingent of the National Guard, were responsible for the coup and assassination attempt against Makarios.

glyko   candied fruit peel, traditionally offered to guests with a glass of water

gule-gule   literally 'smiling-smiling', Turkish farewell

gunaydin   good morning

hodja   Muslim village priest

hos geldiniz   welcome

houmous   purée of chickpeas with sesame oil, cayenne and lemon, popular all over the Levant

iconostasis   screen in an Orthodox church, usually of carved wood, which divides the sanctuary from the nave, and on which religious pictures, or icons, are hung

imam   Muslim priest and religious teacher

Janissaries (*Yenicheri* or 'New Soldiers'), an élite corps of the Ottoman army, originally made up of sons taken in their childhood as tribute from Christian families

kaimakan   Turkish district administrator

kalesi   castle

Kathara Deftera   'Clean Monday', the first day of Lent, traditionally celebrated by Greeks with picnics and kite-flying

keftedes   meatballs fried with fragrant herbs

kephalovryson   springhead or fountain

kharatch   the notorious poll tax of the Ottoman Empire, familiar to late twentieth-century Britain as the Community Charge

kilim   hand-woven rug

komboloyia   string of worry beads, like a rosary, habitually carried by Greek males

liman   harbour

Linobambakoi   literally 'linen-cottoners', Crypto-Christians who masqueraded as Muslims to avoid taxation under Ottoman rule

loukoumi   Turkish delight

Megali Idea   The 'Great Idea', much discussed in Greece during the late nineteenth and early twentieth centuries; the concept of expanding Greece's frontiers to include all the ethnically Greek communities once scattered about the Levant and the Black Sea. The irredentist dream is normally assumed to have ended with the disastrous Asia Minor War against Turkey in 1922, and the subsequent exchange of populations.

mesdjid   small Muslim chapel

mezethes snacks or hors-d'oeuvres, the great forte of Cypriot cuisine

muezzin chorister who calls Muslims to pray at the mosque

muktar word used throughout the Ottoman Empire for a mayor or village headman

muraglia Venetian walls of Nicosia

oka archaic Turkish measure of weight, 1.283 kg

phrygana low growth of thorny bushes on otherwise bare mountainsides

raki fiery spirit made by distilling the grape mash left after wine-making, usually flavoured with aniseed in Cyprus

rayah literally 'cattle', the subject peoples of the Ottoman Empire

SBA Sovereign Base Area, the bases at Akrotiri, Episkopi and Dhekelia retained by Britain in 1960

selam Turkish greetings

seray palace, or governor's residence

shalvar baggy trousers commonly worn in western Asia from Turkey to Pakistan

sheftalia grilled spicy sausages

soumada sweet drink made from almond juice, served either hot or cold

souvlakia Greek word for spit-roasted meat, or Turkish *kebabs*

strategos Greek general or governor of Ptolemaic Cyprus

tabayia basket suspended from the ceiling to preserve bread from vermin

taksim partition, the Turkish solution of dividing Cyprus into two independent states

taramosalata paté of smoked roes of cod or grey mullet, made up with lemon, breadcrumbs and olive oil; a dish which Christians could eat with a clear conscience during the fasting days of Lent

tekke monastery of dervishes

tespi Turkish rosary, usually consisting of 99 beads divided into three groups, to represent the sacred names of Allah

TMT *Turk Mudafaa Teskilati*, (Turkish Defence Organisation), the underground movement of Turkish Cypriots, superseding Volkan in 1957 and set up as a counter to the enosist aspirations of EOKA. The declared aims of TMT were to resist the possiblity of Greek rule, and to achieve *taksim*, or partition. Organised on similar lines to EOKA, TMT was also responsible for intimidation and sectarian murders.

UNFICYP United Nations Forces in Cyprus

Volkan 'Volcano', Rauf Denktash's Turkish nationalist organisation, outlawed by the British administration in November 1957 (see also *TMT*)

xerete Greek formal greeting (on arrival or departure)

BIBLIOGRAPHY

Alastos, Doros, *Cyprus Guerrilla: Grivas, Makarios and the British*, Heinemann, 1960.

——, *Cyprus in History: A Survey of 5,000 years*, Zeno, 1955.

Arnold, P., *The Cyprus Challenge*, Hogarth, 1956.

Baker, Samuel, *Cyprus as I Saw It in 1879*, Macmillan, 1879.

Balfour, Patrick, *The Orphaned Realm*, Marshall, 1951.

Barber, Noel, *The Lords of the Golden Horn*, Macmillan, 1973.

Birge, J.K., *The Bektashi Order of Dervishes*, London, 1937.

Bitsios, D.S., *Cyprus: the Vulnerable Republic*, Institute for Balkan Studies, Thessaloniki, 1975.

Brassey, Annie, *Sunshine and Storm in the East*, Longman, 1880.

Byford-Jones, H., *Grivas and the story of EOKA*, Robert Hale, 1959.

Casson, Stanley, *Ancient Cyprus: Its Art and Archaeology*, Methuen, 1937.

Cesnola, Louis Palma di, *Cyprus: Its Ancient Cities, Tombs and Temples*, 1877.

——, *Cypriot Antiquities in the Metropolitan Museum of Art*, New York, 1903.

Chapman, Olive Murray, *Across Cyprus*, The Bodley Head, 1937.

Clogg, Richard, *A Short History of Modern Greece*, Cambridge University Press, 1979.

Cobham, Claude Delaval, *Excerpta Cypria: Materials for a History of Cyprus*, Herbert E. Clarke, Nicosia, 1895.

——, *An Attempt at a Bibliography of Cyprus*, Nicosia, 1929.

——, 'The story of Umm Haram', *Journal of the Royal Asiatic Society*, 1897.

Cyprus: Commission of Enquiry into the Incidents at Geunyeli, 1958.

Cyprus Truce: Diary of Principal Internal Security Incidents 14.3.57 – 31.3.58.

Denktash, R., *The Cyprus Triangle*, Allen & Unwin, 1982.

Dikaios, P. and Stewart, J.R., *The Swedish Cyprus Expedition*, Lund, 1962.

Dixon, W. Hepworth, *British Cyprus*, Chapman & Hall, 1879.

Durrell, Lawrence, *Bitter Lemons of Cyprus*, Faber & Faber, 1957.

Eliades, G.S., *The Ethnographical Museum*, Paphos, 1987.

Engin, A., *The Voice of the Cypriot Turks*, Istanbul 1964.

Foglietta, U., *The Sieges of Nicosia and Famagusta in Cyprus*, Waterlow & Sons, London, 1903.

Foley, Charles, *Island in Revolt*, Longman, 1962.

———, *Legacy of Strife: Cyprus from Rebellion to Civil War*, Penguin, 1964.

Foley, Charles and Scobie, W.I., *The Struggle for Cyprus*, Hoover Institution Press, Stanford, California, 1975.

Foot, F.L., *Emergency Exit*, Chatto & Windus, 1960.

Forwood, William, *Cyprus Invitation*, Garnstone, 1971.

Gjerstad, Einar, Lindros, John, Sjoqvist, Eric and Westholm, Alfred, *Swedish Cyprus Expedition, 1927–1931*.

———, *Swedish Cyprus Expedition, 1934–1956*.

Grivas, G., *Guerrilla Warfare and EOKA's Struggle*, Longman, 1964.

Gunnis, Rupert, *Historic Cyprus*, London 1936.

Hackett, John, *A History of the Orthodox Church of Cyprus*, Methuen, 1901.

Hadjicosta, Ismene, *Cyprus and its Life*, Nicosia, 1943.

Haggard, Henry Rider, *A Winter Pilgrimage in Palestine, Italy and Cyprus*, Longman, 1901.

Hamilton-Lang, R., *Cyprus: Its Present Resources and Future Prospects*, Macmillan, 1878.

Harbottle, Michael, *The Impartial Soldier*, Oxford University Press, 1970.

Hasselquist, Frederick, *Voyages and Travels in the Levant*, Davis & Reymers, 1766.

Herodotus, *Histories*, (trs. G. Rawlinson), J.M. Dent & Sons, 1910.

Hill, George, *A History of Cyprus*, Cambridge University Press, 1940–52.

Hogarth, D.G., *A Wandering Scholar in the Levant*, John Murray, 1896.

———, *The Nearer East*, London 1902.

———, *Devia Cypria: Notes of an Archaeological Journey in Cyprus in 1888*, Henry Frowde, 1889.

Holmboe, Jens, *Studies on the Vegetation of Cyprus*, Bergen, 1914.

Home, Gordon, *Cyprus Then and Now*, J.M. Dent, 1960.

Hunt, D., *On the Spot: An Ambassador Remembers*, Peter Davis, 1975.

Inalcok, Halil, *The Ottoman Empire: The Classical Age 1300–1600*, 1975.

Jeffrey, George, E., *Cyprus under an English King*, W.J. Archer, Nicosia, 1926.

————, *A Description of the Historic Monuments of Cyprus*, W.J. Archer, Nicosia, 1918.

Karageorghis, Vassos, *Salamis in Cyprus*, Thames & Hudson, 1969.

————, *Mycenaean Art from Cyprus*, Department of Antiquities, Cyprus, 1968.

————, *The Ancient Civilisation of Cyprus*, Barrie & Jenkins, 1970.

————, *Cyprus: From the Stone Age to the Romans*, Thames & Hudson, 1982.

Lancaster, Osbert, *Sailing to Byzantium*, John Murray, 1969.

Lewis, Mrs, *A Lady's Impression of Cyprus in 1893*, Remington, 1894.

Luke, Harry, *Cyprus under the Turks 1571–1878*, Oxford University Press, 1921.

————, *Cyprus, a Portrait and an Appreciation*, Harrap, 1957.

————, *Cypriote Shrines*, Faith Press, 1920.

Lymbourides, Achilles, *Cyprus, the Island of Aphrodite*, Nicosia, 1962.

Maier, F.G., *Cyprus from the Earliest Times to the Present Day*, Elek, London, 1968.

Makhairas, Leontios, *Recital Concerning the Sweet Land of Cyprus* (trs. and ed. by R.M. Dawkins), Clarendon, 1932.

Mariti, Giovanni, *Travels in the Island of Cyprus in 1769* (trs. C.D. Cobham), Herbert E. Clarke, Nicosia, 1895.

Mogabgab, Theophilus A.H., *Supplementary Excerpts on Cyprus*, Pusey Press/Zavalli Press, Nicosia, 1941–5.

Morton, H.V., *In the Steps of St Paul*, Rich & Cowan, 1936.

Newman, Philip, *A Short History of Cyprus*, London, 1940.

Orr, C.W.J., *Cyprus under British Rule*, Robert Scott, 1918.

Panteli, Stavros, *A New History of Cyprus*, East–West Publications, 1984.

Papandreou, Andreas, *Democracy at Gunpoint: The Greek Front*, Penguin, 1973.

Pausanias, *Guide to Greece* (trs. Peter Levi), Penguin, 1971.

Peto, Gladys, *Malta and Cyprus*, Dent, 1928.

Pococke, Richard, *A Description of the East and Some Other Countries*, W. Bowyer, 1745.

Purcell, M.D., *Cyprus*, Ernest Benn, 1969.

Rice, D. Talbot, Gunnis, Rupert, Rice, Tamara Talbot, *The Icons of Cyprus*, Allen & Unwin, 1937.

Riley-Smith, Jonathan, *The Knights of St John in Jerusalem and Cyprus 1050–1310*, Macmillan, 1967.

Ross, Ludwig, *A Journey to Cyprus* (trs. C.D. Cobham), Nicosia, 1910.

Salvator, Archduke Louis of Austria, *Levkosia: The Capital of Cyprus*, C. Kegan Paul & Co, 1881.

Sitas, Aramanth, *Kopiaste: Cyprus Customs and Cuisine*, Zeno, Limassol, 1968.

Spencer, Edmund, *Travels in European Turkey*, London, 1851.

Spyridakis, K., *A Brief History of Cyprus*, Nicosia, 1974.

——, *Studies, Lectures, Speeches, Articles*, Nicosia, 1972–4.

Stephens, R., *Cyprus, a Place of Arms*, Pall Mall, London, 1966.

Storrs, Ronald, *A Chronology of Cyprus*, 1930.

——, *Orientations*, Nicholson & Watson, 1937.

Storrs, Ronald and O'Brien, B.J., *The Handbook of Cyprus*, London, 1930.

Stylianou, Andreas and Judith, *The Painted Churches of Cyprus*, The Research Centre, Cyprus, 1964.

——, *Byzantine Cyprus as Reflected in Art*, Nicosia, 1948.

Thubron, Colin, *Journey into Cyprus*, William Heinemann, 1975.

Toy, Barbara, *Rendezvous in Cyprus*, 1946.

Vanezis, P.N., *Makarios: Life and Leadership*, Abelard-Schuman Ltd, 1979.

Westholm, Alfred, *The Temples of Soli*, Swedish Cyprus Expedition, Stockholm, 1936.

Woodhouse, C.M., *The Rise and Fall of the Greek Colonels*, Granada, 1985.

——, *Karamanlis: The Restorer of Greek Democracy*, Clarendon Press, 1982.

——, *British Foreign Policy since the Second World War*, Hutchinson, 1961.

——, *The Struggle for Greece 1941–1949*, Hart-Davis MacGibbon, 1976.

INDEX

Abdemon, King of Salamis, 108
Abdul Hamid I, 171
Abdul Hamid II, 3, 170
Abu'l Awar, 16
Achaeans, 36, 105, 106, 112
Acre, 37, 38, 85
Adon, 2
Aepia, see Soli
Aghirda, 181
Agridhaki, 136
Aimée, Sultana, 171
Ajax, 106
Akanthou, 120, 143–5, 149, 150, 238
Akcicek, see Sisklipos
Akhenaten, Pharaoh, 105
Akhiropiitos Monastery, 13–15, 27
Akova, see Gypsos
Alakati, 199, 142
Albanians, 22, 84, 89, 165
l'Aleman, Joanna, 39, 40
Alemdag, see Agridhaki
Alexander the Great, 17, 61, 108
Alexandria, 17, 38, 41, 111, 114
Algiers, 17
Ali Bey, 80, 81, 235, 236
Alice of Champagne, 163
Alsancak, see Karavas
Altiparnak, 120
Amathus, 107, 109
Ambelikou, 205
Anamur, Cape, 22
Anemouri, 38
Angastina, 84
Antalya, 38, 123
Anthemios, Bishop of Salamis, 113
Antioch, 113, 114
Antiphonitis Monastery, 220, 221
Apati Monastery, 220, 221
Aphendrika, 131

Aphrodision, 150
Aphrodite, 45, 56, 61, 80, 81, 84,
    133, 235
Apostolos Andreas, Cape, 124, 126,
    127
Apostolos Andreas Monastery, 100,
    124, 127, 132, 133
Apostolos Varnavas Monastery, 113
Arapkoy, see Klepini
Armenia and the Armenians, 38, 89,
    100, 101, 155, 156, 163, 219,
    220
Arodaphnoussa, 38
Artaxerxes, 108
ASIZ, 9, 20, 26, 59, 64
Asomatos, 137, 244
Assyrians, 107
Astarte, 2
Athens and the Athenians, 106–8
Attila Line, 13, 31, 59, 63–5, 67, 103,
    128, 139, 202, 204–7, 227, 244
Attila, Operation, 4, 34, 129, 185,
    191, 203, 204
Augustinians, 73
Augustus, Emperor, 61, 85
Ayia Irini, 200, 201
Ayios Amvrosios, 119, 194, 198,
    220–2
Ayios Andronikos, 123
Ayios Auxentios, 121
Ayios Chrysostomos, 237
Ayios Epiktitos, 187
Ayios Ermolaos, 140
Ayios Ioannis Chrysostomos
    Monastery, 77, 233, 235, 236
Ayios Mamas Monastery, 55–8
Ayios Photios tis Selinas, Church of,
    133, 134
Ayios Simeon, 124

Ayios Theodoros, Church of, 124
Ayios Theodoros (Karpas), 121
Ayios Theodoros (Tillyria), 128
Ayios Thyrsos, Church of, 124
Ayios Vasilios, 244
Ayios Yeoryios (Kormakiti), 20
Ayios Yeoryios (Kyrenia), 33

Baf, *see* Paphos
Baghdad, 23
Baker, Sir Samuel, 34, 44, 52, 78, 80,
    96, 99, 105, 122, 124, 133, 160,
    181, 206, 210, 222, 225, 235,
    240, 244, 250
Balfour, Patrick (Lord Kinross), 45
Balkan Wars, 170
Barbarossa, 164
Bar-Jesus, 109
Barlais, Sir Aimery, 148
Bayraktar family, 190–3, 210–16
Belgrade, 164
Bellapais, 72–6
Berengaria of Navarre, 37
Besparmak, *see* Pentadactylos
Bessim Pasha, 159
Bey Keuy, 223
Black Death, 38, 49
Black Prince, 38
Bogaz, 82, 134, 225
Bragadino, Marco Antonio, 89–92,
    102
Britain and the British, 2, 74, 79,
    126, 147, 152, 159–61, 202,
    203, 237, 239–42, 246
Buffavento Castle, 39, 46, 49, 75–8,
    233–8
Bulgarians, 40, 49, 251
Bulla Cypria, 41
buses, 27, 173
Buyukkonuk, *see* Komi Kebir
Byzantium and Byzantine period, 2,
    16, 17, 22, 32, 35–7, 41, 45–7,
    57, 110, 163, 198, 220, 235–7,
    250

Café Chimaera, 238, 251
Cairo, 38, 41
Calepio, Angelo, 91, 167, 205
Callaghan, James, 203
camels and camel drivers, 24, 25,
    55
Camlibel, *see* Myrtou

Caramanian Straits, 22, 45, 208, 209,
    219, 239
Catholic Church, 41, 62, 74
Cayirova, *see* Ayios Theodoros
Chalcutzes, Nikitas, 17
Chamberlain, Colonial Secretary, 74
charcoal burning, 19
Charles IV, Emperor, 38
Charlotte, Queen, 41
Chaucer, 38, 40
Chelebi Mehmet Effendi, 96
Chrysanthos, Archbishop, 120
Chrysostomos, Archbishop, 114
Church of Cyprus, 16, 41, 74, 95,
    113, 114
Churchill, Winston, 161
Chytri, 79
Cilicia, 108, 132
Circassians, 122, 123
Cleopatra, 108, 248
Communist party, 55
Comnenus, Isaac, 37, 46, 133, 147,
    235
Congress of Berlin, 3
Constantia, *see* Salamis
Constantine I, Emperor, 237
Constantine II, Emperor, 110
Constantinople, 2, 36, 37, 41, 92, 96,
    111, 113, 123, 158, 162, 164,
    165, 170, 171
Constantius, Archbishop of Sinai,
    122
Coombe, Major Brian, 242
copper, 58, 59, 61, 206, 207
Cornaro, Catherine, Queen, 41, 102
Cornaro, George
Cortese, Andrea, 166
Cotovicus, Ioannis, 144, 145, 210
Cremer, 242
Crusaders, 2, 37, 40, 41, 44, 122,
    147
Cyprus Mines Corporation, 55, 61,
    206

Dardanelles, 92
Darius, 108
Degirmenlik, *see* Kythrea
Demetrios Poliorcetes, 108, 122, 131,
    132
Demophoon of Athens, 60
Denktash, Rauf, 7, 24, 100, 153, 213,
    214, 239, 246

Dhavlos, 121, 146
Dhekelia, 85, 227
Dhirios Forest, 54, 200
Diedo, Giacomo, 166
Dighenis Akritas, 76
Dipkarpaz, *see* Rizokarpaso
Disraeli, 160
Djamboulat Bey, 86, 90
Dome Hotel, 35
Dortyol, *see* Prastio
Dracos, Marcos, 43, 154
Drummond, Alexander, 57, 124, 248
Dumbarton Oaks Byzantine Institute, 237
Dunkirk, 25
Durrell, Lawrence, 73, 75, 76, 141, 142, 213

Edremit, 50
Edward III of England, 38
Egypt, 17, 34, 40, 61, 107, 108, 110, 112, 126
El Amarna, 105
Eleanor of Aragon, 39, 40, 49, 251
Enkomi, 105, 112
Enkomi-Alassia, 105, 106
Enver Bey, 170
EOKA & EOKA campaign, 42, 76, 202, 239, 240
Epikho, 223
Ercan Airport, 8, 253
Eudoxia, Empress, 237
Eumathius, Philocales, 237
Euripides, 106
Eurymedon, 107
Evagoras, King of Salamis, 108
Evelthon, King of Salamis, 107
Exometokhi, 223
Ezousas, river, 11

Famagusta, 29, 31, 40–2, 55, 85–103, 105, 110, 123, 148, 163, 225–7
    Church of Ayios Yeoryios Xorinos (Nestorian or 'millionaire's church'), 93, 94
    Lala Mustapha Pasha Mosque, 87, 92, 97, 102, 103
    Martinengo Bastion, 94, 101
    Monastery of the Caller, 95
    Othello's Tower, 94, 98–102
    St George of the Latins, 96

Varosha, 29, 85, 100, 103
Five Mile Beach, 33
forestry, 45, 126, 127
Foscarini, Nicolo, 99
France, 38
Franks, 2, 37, 41, 42, 85
Frederick II, Emperor of Germany, 46, 47

Gaidhouras, 84
Galilee, Prince of, 38
Galounia, 121
Gazi Magusa, *see* Famagusta
Gecitkale, *see* Lefkoniko
Gecitkoy, *see* Panagra
Gemayel, Sadiq, 182
Gemikonagi, *see* Karavostasi
Genoa and the Genoese, 40, 41, 49, 74, 85, 86, 148, 163
George, King of the Hellenes, 25
Geunyeli, 20, 153, 244
Ghaziveran, 58, 205, 241
Giourgiou, Maria, 132
Girne, *see* Kyrenia
Gladstone, 160
Gorgos, King of Salamis, 107
Green Line, 19, 154, 168–70, 172, 174, 179, 228
Grivas, George, 76, 128, 180, 224, 225, 242
Gudum, Hasan Yusuf, 178
Gungor, *see* Koutsovendis
Guzelyali, *see* Vavilas
Guzelyurt, *see* Morphou
Gyani, Lieutenant-General, 180
Gypsos, 224

Halevga Forest Station, 218
Harun-ar-Rashid, 17
Haspolat, *see* Mia Milea
Hasselquist, 96
Hay, Vice-Admiral Lord John, 159
Hazireti Omer Tekke, 142
Hedjaz, 92
Henry I, 46
Henry II, 85
Heraclius, Emperor, 23
Herod the Great, 61
Hikmet, Hizber, 172–4, 227, 228
Hittites, 60, 105, 150
Holy Land, 17, 23, 38, 40, 46
Hugh III, 73

Hugh IV, 38, 49

d'Ibelin, Echive, 17
d'Ibelin, John, 46, 47
Ibrahim, 28–30, 32, 150, 151, 182, 183
Ibrahim, Grand Vizier, 164
Ilhan, Major Nihat and family, 177–9
Ioannikos, 84
Iskele, *see* Trikomo
Isocrates, 108
Issus, 108
Italy and the Italians, 39, 165
Izmir, 1, 6

James I, 236
James II, 41
Janus, King, 40, 41, 155
Jennaz, 137
Jerusalem, 37, 38, 40, 48, 73, 102, 114, 155, 163, 237
Jewish revolt, 109
John, Prince of Antioch, 49, 148, 251
Judea, 47
Justinian II, Emperor, 16

Kantara castle, 46, 49, 110, 147–9, 223
Kantara Forest, 120, 147, 149
Kaplica, *see* Dhavlos
Karaman, *see* Karmi
Karaouglanoglu, *see* Ayios Yeoryios (Kyrenia)
Karavas, 10, 13, 17, 18, 67, 208, 247
Karavostasi, 59, 202–5
Karmi, 13, 50
Karpas peninsula, 7, 10, 38, 84, 100, 108, 121–34, 148, 238
Karpasha, 26, 137
Karpasha Forest, 26, 54, 137
Karpasia, *see* Karpas peninsula
Karpasia, ancient city, 131, 140
Karpasia Forest, 124, 130
Karsiyaka, *see* Vasilia
Kayalar, *see* Orga
Kaynakkoy, 77, 249, 250
Kazaphani, 72, 210
Kemal Ataturk, 4, 6, 18, 19, 43, 149, 156, 158, 206, 215
Kemal, Mr, 12, 25, 32, 54, 199, 239
Kemal, Naimik, 96
Keumurju, 181

Khalil Agha, 42
Kharcha, 218
Kimon of Athens, 66, 107
Kinneir, John MacDonald, 34, 159
Kirpasa, *see* Karpas peninsula
Kitchener, Herbert Horatio, 80, 171, 172
Kition, 107, 109, 133
Klepini, 187, 188
Klidhes, 133
Knights Hospitallers (Knights of St John), 97, 102
Knights Templar, 37, 84, 97, 155
to Koinon ton Kyprion, 108
Kokkina, 59, 64, 65, 123, 127–9, 180, 196
Kollis, Konstantinos, 72, 73
Koloni, 11
Kolota, 148
Koma tou Yialou, 123
Komi Kebir, 121
Kondemenos, 137, 244
Konya, 156
Kormakiti, Cape, 20–2, 36, 49, 186
Kormakiti village, 22–4, 138, 139, 185, 186
Kornesios, Hadjigeorghakis, 119, 120
Kornos, Mount, 20, 71, 72, 135, 183–5, 245
Koronia Forest, 123
Korphi Forest, 72, 135, 141
Korucan, *see* Kormakiti
Kourion, 107, 109
Koutsovendis, 78, 233
Kozan, *see* Larnaca tis Lapithou
Krini, 181
Kumyali, *see* Koma tou Yialou
Kutchuk, Dr Fazil, 177
Kutup Osman, 96
Kyrenia, 8, 9, 13, 19, 20, 33–44, 46, 73, 97, 99, 107, 150, 186, 187, 210, 235, 236, 238, 239, 245, 246, 251, 252
  Castle, 35–43, 46, 49, 75
  Ship, 43
Kyrenia mountains, 9, 20, 22, 26, 44, 45, 49, 54, 64, 71, 78, 135–7, 219–22
Kythrea, 79–82, 111, 187, 223

La Cava castle, 236
Lachas family, 93

Lachas, Sir Francis, 86
Lambousa, 13, 15, 17, 32
Lala Mustapha Pasha, 89, 91, 92, 96,
    101, 165, 236
Langlais, Jean, 102
Lapithos, 9, 13, 15, 17, 19, 27, 31,
    53, 67, 69, 70, 79, 107, 139,
    185, 208–10
Lapta, *see* Lapithos
Larnaca, 40, 55, 80, 97, 133, 177,
    227
Larnaca tis Lapithou, 19, 136, 141,
    185
Latakia, 122, 123
Lausanne, Treaty of, 161
Lebanon, 23, 133, 138
Ledra, 155
Lefka, 58, 128, 205–7, 242, 243
    Piri Osman Pasha Mosque, 243
Lefkoniko, 134, 224
Lefkosa, *see* Nicosia
Lefkosia, *see* Nicosia
Leonarisso, 123
Leontius, Emperor, 16
Levkosia, *see* Nicosia
Limassol, 31, 34, 37, 40, 107, 165,
    191, 192, 203
Limnitis, 66
Linobambakoi, 65, 66
Liveras, 21, 22
Livia, Empress, 111
locusts, 224
Lombards, 47
Lusignan, Aimery de, 73
Lusignan dynasty, 17, 24, 37–41, 44,
    46, 102, 155, 156, 163, 236
Lusignan, Guy de, 37, 46, 48, 155,
    235
Lythrangomi, 123

Mahemet Sokolli, 164
Mahmud II, 171
Makarios III, Archbishop, 11, 95,
    177, 180, 225
Makhairas, Leontios, 2, 39, 148, 251
Makheras Monastery, 154
Mamelukes, 38, 40, 41, 155, 163
Mansoura, 128
Marathasa, 59
Margi, *see* Myrtou
Maria, Queen of Romania, 225
Marion, 66, 107

Mark Anthony, 108
Maronites, 7, 22–5, 78, 79, 86, 100,
    137–9, 201
Martoni, Nicholas, 93, 168
Mavrovouni, 206
Meggen, Jodicus de, 88, 154
Mehemed Veiss Pasha, 159
Mehmed Kiamil, 170
Mehmet IV, 96
Mendesia, Gracia de, 165
Mersin, 29, 99, 151
Mersinlik, *see* Phlamoudi
Mesaoria plain, 19, 54, 79, 80, 83,
    84, 106, 112–16, 134, 136, 137,
    148, 153, 223–5, 244
Mevlana Jalal-ad-din-Rumi, 157, 158
Mia Milea, 79, 83, 227, 233
Midas, bandit, 181
Mikhail, Charilaos, 242
Mogabgab, Theophilus, 100
Mohammad, 16
Monophysites, 22
Montolf, Perot and Wilmot de, 236
Morphou, 54–8, 62, 201, 202, 238,
    239
Morphou Bay, 38, 57–66, 202, 241
Morphou, John de, 39
Morton, H.V., 66, 113
Mu'awiyah, 16, 110
mules, 25
Mycenaeans, 61, 105, 106
Myrtou, 26, 27, 54, 137, 185, 186

Nasi, Joseph (Joao Miques), 165
National Guard, 26, 128, 177, 180
Naves, Sor de, 18
Nazim, 195–8
Nea Justinianopolis, 16
Nereides, 150
Nestorians, 86, 93
Neta, 124
New People's Democracy Party, 213,
    214
Nicocreon, King of Salamis, 112
Nicosia, 7, 19, 20, 40, 42, 47, 54,
    55, 73, 74, 79, 80, 88, 89, 119,
    153–79, 205, 227–31, 235, 236,
    251
    Abbey of St Dominic, 156
    Arab Ahmed Mosque, 170
    bazaars, 169
    Bedestan, 168, 229

Beuyuk Hamam, 163
Beuyuk Khan, 162, 163
Haydar Pasha Mosque, 171
Kumarjilar Khan, 162
Kyrenia Gate, 154
Mevlevi Tekke, 156–8
Mosque of the Standard-Bearer,
  166
'Museum of Barbarism', 179–80
Selimye Mosque, 163, 168, 229
Yeni Jami Mosque, 175, 176
Novare, Philip de, 47, 148

Olympus, Mount, 120, 143
Omar, Caliph, 16
Onesilos, 107
Orga, 20
Ortakeuy, 20, 152, 244
Oscar, 192, 193
Osman Pasha, 3
Ottoman Turks and Empire, 2, 3, 42,
  65, 157
Ozankoy, *see* Kazaphani
Ozhan, *see* Asomatos

Palaeologa, Helena, 41
Palekythro, 84
Paleomylos river, 20, 200, 239, 245
Palestine, 11, 37, 93
Pamphylia, 107, 109
Pamukla, *see* Tavros
Panagra, 200, 244, 245
Panayia Absinthiotissa Monastery,
  233, 249, 250
Panayia ton Katharon Monastery,
  245
Panayia Melandryna Monastery, 194
Panayia Pergaminiotissa, Church of,
  145, 146
Pano Lefkara, 238
Paphos, 11, 31, 46, 59, 71, 107–9,
  153
Paphos Forest, 64, 66, 127
Paruta, Paolo, 88–92, 166
Patatsos, Iakovos, 242
Patriki, 121
Pedhieos river, 105, 152, 153, 156
Pendayia, 38
Pentadactylos Forest, 79
Pentadactylos, Mount, 8, 76, 79, 119,
  187, 233
Pergamon, 145

Peristeria, 149
Persia and the Persians, 2, 60, 61, 66,
  102, 107, 108, 122
Peter I, 38, 49, 86, 155, 236
Peter II, 40, 49, 86, 155
Petra tou Dhigeni, 223
Pheretima of Cyrene, 107
Philocyprus, 60
Phlamoudi, 149
Phoenicians, 107, 108
Phokas, Nicephoros, Emperor, 17
Piccolomini, Eneo Silvio de (Pope
  Pius II), 46
Pileri, 181
Pirhan, *see* Pyrga
Plataniotissa Forest, 218
Plevna, 3
Pnytagoras, King of Salamis, 108
Pococke, Richard, 34, 61, 62, 70, 96,
  132, 133, 149, 156
Podocatoro, Captain, 166
Polis, 59, 66, 128
Polis tis Khrysokhous, 74
Prastio, 115
Prison of St Catherine, 111, 112
Profitis Elias, Mount, 181
Psilatos, 224
Ptolemy, 17, 108, 112
Pyrga, 84

Queen, Legend of the, 49, 124, 149,
  235

Raqqa, 17
Ras-Shamra, 105
Rhodes, 38, 102, 164
Richard the Lionheart, 37, 38, 46,
  133, 147, 155
Rieter of Sebaldt, 86
Rizokarpaso, 124–31
Rome and the Romans, 2, 57, 59, 61,
  79, 108–10
Rose, 248, 249
Roxelana, Sultana, 164
Russia and the Russians, 3, 57, 128,
  160, 161, 180

Sadiq Pasha, 42
Sadrazamkoy, *see* Liveras
St Andrew, 132
St Barnabas, 108, 109, 113, 114
St Bridget of Sweden, 102

St Catherine's Grove, 111, 112
St Demetrianos of Kythrea, 80
St Epiphanius, 111
St Helena, 237
St Hilarion Castle, 20, 44–50, 52, 72, 180, 185, 250, 251
St Mark, 109, 113
St Maron Monastery, 23
St Neophytos, 46
St Norbet, Canons of, 73
St Pantaleimon Monastery, 26, 140
St Paul, 108, 109
Saladin, 37
Salamis, 16, 79, 80, 85, 88, 100, 102, 105–11, 113, 114, 155, 162, 168
Salih, 10, 13, 32, 83, 117, 118, 199, 200, 239, 247, 253
Salisbury, Lord, 160
Salvator, Archduke Louis of Austria, 11, 18, 65, 97, 156, 159, 162, 163, 229
Sami Pasha, 159
Samson, Nikos, 225
Sandys, Duncan, 180
Sandys, George, 61
Sanmichelli, Giovanni Girolamo, 94
Saracen Arabs, 2, 15–17, 35, 36, 80, 110, 114, 118, 122, 131, 147, 153, 155
Scotland, 38
Selim II, 163–5, 168
Selim Debe, Sheik, 156
Seljuk Turks, 36, 37, 156
Septimius Severus, Emperor, 80
Sergius Paulus, 109
Serrakhis river, 201
Sevres, Treaty of, 161
Sibthorp, Dr, 28, 29, 96, 133, 221
silk, 18, 40
Sillu, *see* Soli
Simeon, hermit, 147
Sinai Monastery, 71, 72
Sinai, Mount, 147
Sinclitiki, Maria, 168
Sirinevle, *see* Ayios Ermolaos
Sisklipos, 140, 141
Skalifourda Forest, 123
Skouriotissa, 59, 202, 206
Skylloura, 140, 244
slavery and the slave trade, 17, 50, 97, 122
Smyrna, 6

Sofronios II, Archbishop, 25
Soli, 59, 60–2, 66, 107
Solon of Athens, 60
Sourp Magar Monastery, 219, 220
Speglio, Andrea, 166
Spencer, Edmund, 3
Stavrovouni, 237
Storrs, Sir Ronald, 170
Strongylos, 115
Subh-i-Ezel, 96
Suez Canal, 62, 92, 96, 160
Suleiman the Magnificent, 164, 165
Sutluce, *see* Psilatos
Sykhari, 249
Syngrasis, 224
Syria, 7, 16, 23, 34, 47, 85, 88, 92, 121, 132, 133, 138, 162, 224
Syriac, 24
Syrianokhori, 13, 201, 202, 239, 241

Tamassos, 107, 108
Tashkent, *see* Vouno
Tatlisu, *see* Akanthou
Taurus mountains, 22, 45
Tavros, 123
Telamon, 106
Temblos, 50
Tepebasi, 26
Teucer, 106, 108
Thierry, Archbishop, 163
Thomas, Peter de, 95
Thubron, Colin, 124
Tillyria, 13, 64, 201, 205
TMT, 20, 82, 128, 129, 153, 173, 201, 203, 204, 239
Torunculo, *see* Strongylos
Toumba tou Skouru, 56
Trakhoni, 84
Trapeza, 188, 189
Tree of Idleness, 73, 75
Trikomo, 134, 224, 225
Trimithi, 50
Trojan War, 106
Troodos mountains, 25, 54, 59, 64, 67, 143, 153, 181, 205, 218, 243
Troulli, 142, 249
True Cross, 74
Turkut, Sergeant, 229–31
Tuzla, *see* Enkomi
Tuzluca, *see* Patriki
Tymbou airfield, 8
Tyre, 108

Ucok, Hamit, 51, 52, 82
United Nations Commission for
    Refugees, 14
UNFICYP, 60, 62, 63, 67, 78, 105,
    128, 129, 180, 205
Urania, 132
Uslucan, Mahmut, 135
USA, 128, 180

Van Bruyn, Cornelis, 96, 181, 236
Vasilia, 19, 51, 71
Vavilas, 19, 141
Venice and the Venetians, 2, 40–2,
    74, 85–92, 94, 95, 98, 99, 101,
    102, 122, 147, 152, 155, 156,
    162, 165–8, 236
Venizelos, Eleftherios, 6
Vienna, 164
Villani, 224
Visconti, John, 39, 236
Volkan, 153, 239
Von Baumgarten, 88
Von Suchen, 85, 86, 155
Vouni Palace, 60, 64–6, 205, 241
Vouno, 13, 77, 233, 249
Vourkaris, 188

Vrysin, 119

Willibald, 16, 17
wines, 31, 69, 70, 93, 129, 130
Wolseley, Sir Garnet, 160, 250

Xeros, 59, 206
Xerxes, 107

Yayla, *see* Syrianokhori
Yeni Erenkoy, *see* Yialousa
Yenice Koy, *see* Petra tou Dhigeni
Yerolakkos, 244
Yesilirmak, *see* Limnitis
Yesilkoy, *see* Ayios Andronikos
Yialias river, 105
Yialousa, 123, 131
Yilmazkoy, *see* Skylloura
Yolustu, *see* Koloni
Young Turks, 4, 170

Zakos, Andreas, 242
Zeno the Isaurian, 113
Zeytinlik, *see* Temblos
Zigamet, *see* Leonarisso

·UNDER·
·MOUNT IDA·
A JOURNEY INTO CRETE

OLIVER BURCH

Under Mount Ida is armchair travel
in the finest tradition: an affectionate celebration of the
landscape, people and culture of Crete from an exciting and
original new talent. Oliver Burch skilfully evokes the full
character of this most popular and historic of Mediterranean
islands, from the windswept villages of the mountainous
interior to the sun-drenched tourist beaches. Tales from
Crete's turbulent past combine with sometimes sad,
sometimes hilarious encounters with the less-noble
present to produce a fascinating portrait
of this beautiful island under siege.

Available from bookshops or direct from:
Ashford, Buchan & Enright, 1 Church Rd, Shedfield, Hants SO3 2HW
ISBN: 1 85253 202 5   £13.95 plus £1.50 postage and packing.